# the **game** cookbook

clarissa dickson wright and johnny scott

# the game
## cookbook

clarissa dickson wright and johnny scott

with food photography by gus filgate

kyle cathie limited

First published in Great Britain 2004 by
Kyle Cathie Limited
23 Howland Street
London W1T 4AY
general.enquiries@kyle-cathie.com
www.kylecathie.com

15 14 13 12 11 10

ISBN 978 1 85626 749 6

**Senior Editor** Kyle Cathie
**Design and art direction** Geoff Hayes
**Photography** Gus Filgate
**Home Economist** David Morgan
**Food Stylist** Penny Markham
**Copy editor** Sophie Allen
**Indexer** Alex Corrin
**Production** Sha Huxtable and Alice Holloway

A Cataloguing In Publication record for this title is available from
the British Library.

Colour reproduction by Sang Choy, Singapore
Printed and bound by Tien Wah Press, Singapore

*Dedication:*
To Sam Scott in the hope that he and all his generation may enjoy the
fruits of the chase for his life and for the centuries to come.

*Acknowledgments:*
CDW: Thanks go to my butcher and friend Colin Peat of Haddington for
supplying most of the game for these recipes. To Kyle Cathie for having
the foresight to publish this book. To gamekeepers, stalkers, ghillies and
waterbalifs everywhere and to all who keep faith with the Countryside.

JS: British Association of Shooting and Conservation
Countryside Alliance
Federation of Fieldsports Associations of the European Union.
The Game Conservancy Trust
Colin McElvie
Colin Woolf

**Most recipes serve 4. Game birds, with the exception of
pheasant, serve 1 per head, pheasant serves 2–3 people.
A 450g (1lb) pie serves 2 people.**

**The bold line in the text indicates the division between
Johnny Scott's text and Clarissa Dickson Wright's.**

# contents

# introduction

Game, the very word evokes an incredible memory range of sights, sounds and scents. It is midges and the honey perfume of purple heather flower. It is birch trees, running water and a raven croaking high above a highland corrie; darkness and the iodine smell of the sea; dawn, and skeins of geese honking overhead; the russet plumage of a woodcock blending with the gold of dead bracken; numb feet and thin wintry sunlight glinting on a high pheasant. It is the scraping 'cheep' of a snipe jinxing away above the rushes of an Irish bog; the earthy smell of wet dog, the exquisite sensation of hot water on frozen limbs, log fires and in all its forms, the most delicious food.

The preservation and possession of game is entwined in the antiquity and history of Europe. As a vital winter food source, its value influenced our constitutions and the laws of land ownership. Our manners are directly attributable to the glorification of game during the Age of Chivalry. It was the subject of the earliest picture

form and continued to be the inspiration for a major part of the heritage of our art and literature. Game was responsible for the most dramatic improvement in firearm manufacture in four hundred years. Percussion detonation, invented by a wildfowling Minister of the Kirk, is the exploding mechanism that propels every shell, bullet or shot anywhere in the world.

Perhaps the most significant role that game has filled is in the conservation of other wildlife species. As the population grew, cultivation and the ever increasing demand for timber gradually destroyed huge areas of natural wildlife habitat. Between 1700 and 1800, over two million acres of heath and common land were enclosed and miles of hedging planted. The Napoleonic Wars created an enormous demand for corn and much of the enclosed land was arable, providing ideal conditions for partridges. Most of these were walked-up and shot over pointers, but the invention of the percussion cap early in the nineteenth century saw the end

of flintlocks and enabled sportsmen to shoot driven game.

The agricultural depression that followed the end of hostilities with France, better transport, rapid improvements in shotgun manufacture, an increasingly wealthy middle class and the rationalisation of ancient and repressive game laws combined to bring a great change to rural scenery. Prior to 1831, the sale of game had been forbidden, now landlords had a saleable commodity and a ready demand from the expanding urban population. Hedges were allowed to grow thicker and taller to provide the challenge of driven partridges and this habitat encouraged an increase in pheasant numbers. Shooting rentals, a concept hitherto unheard of, became an attractive addition to falling agricultural incomes.

Woodland replanting specifically for game cover became an essential part of land management and it is these conservation practices, continued with increasing importance in the modern day, that provide habitats for our song bird population, nesting sights for migratory visitors and a whole biodiversity of animal and insect life. An ethos that was best described by King George VI when he remarked, 'the wildlife of today is not ours to dispose of as we please. We have it in trust. We must account for it to those who come after."

What actually constitutes game? In Britain and Northern Ireland, game has come to be interpreted by sportsmen as anything that can be legally shot within their various seasons. Traditionally, game is only those species that were classified under the 1831 Game Act: pheasants, partridges, red grouse, black game and ptarmigan. There were others which have either become extinct like bustards or are on the protected birds list. However, snipe, woodcock, golden plover and curlew in Northern Ireland, and certain ducks and geese categorised under the Wildlife and Countryside Acts as permissible to be shot in season, are also considered game. Deer are regarded as game but come under the Deer Act. Hares are game but do not have a closed season, although sportsmen always ensure that hares are only shot or hunted from October to the beginning of March. Each country has its own game laws and is subject to international wildlife legislation. Some countries have very much more restrictive game laws than others. In the Netherlands for example, it is restricted to: wood pigeon, pheasant and hare from 15th October to 31st January and for rabbit and mallard from 15th August to 31st January. All other species are protected and can only be killed with special licences from the provincial government.

Game in Britain generates in excess of four hundred million pounds by direct expenditure from shooting and stalking alone, to say nothing of fishing, plus a further two hundred and fifty million from the ancillary businesses connected with the industry. These figures and their significance to wildlife conservation are an impressive part of our own economy, but tiny when compared internationally. The Federation of Fieldsports Associations of the Europian Union represents seven million sportsmen from the fifteen member countries plus those of Switzerland, Malta, Slovenia, Hungary, Poland, The Czech Republic and Slovakia. The most recent study by the Institut National Agronomique in Paris calculated that the expenditure on fieldsports in Europe, including money spent on habitat preservation, ran to well over ten billion euros and generated a hundred thousand jobs. Leaving aside the industries in South America, Canada and Africa, a similar

survey in the USA, by the Teddy Roosevelt Conservation Alliance, produced figures in tens of billions of dollars.

There is a historical precedent of farming certain species of game, particularly deer. The Chinese were at it two thousand years ago, primarily for medicinal purposes. The Romans brought us a culture of living larders – hares, pheasant and possibly fallow deer and rabbits, which they had inherited from earlier civilisations. The Normans did the same, bringing with them the ancient practice of fish farming. The purpose of living larders was to provide a readily available supply of food and the practice has persisted in one form or another into the modern age.

Game farming becomes a diversity from normal agriculture when the consumer demand for a particular species exceeds the supply of wild animals. Deer farming is by far the biggest industry with well over four million red deer, reindeer, wapiti, sika, elk, fallow, rusa and musk deer being farmed in the USA, Russia ,China, Korea, Australia, New Zealand and across Europe. In Britain and Ireland 165,000 deer are raised for meat on over 5000 farms.

Fish farming is another industry with a long history and the controversial intensive farming of salmon was created by consumer demand. Quail, partridges and more recently, mallard are also farmed to a greater or lesser degree depending on the requirements of different countries. Some species, like grouse and migratory wildfowl and waders can never be domesticated. Farmed game, because of the nature of modern farming will never have the wonderful flavour of its wild counterpart. Domesticated animals do not run free or eat the natural herbage that makes wild game so sought after. It does, however, provide those

without access to wild game a chance to experience the next best thing.

Game is healthy, low in fat, high in protein and, if you like the good things in life, it holds its head among the best. Game is also inexpensive and easy to cook. At one time, game was in every butcher's window in Britain during the season and hung outside the stalls of markets like London's Leadenhall. Sadly, urban dominated society has largely forgotten that the finest food flies, runs or swims free, as it has done since the dawn of time and much of our game is exported.

I hope our book will remind those who have forgotten, and inspire those who have yet to experience it, the pleasure of eating the world's most wonderful produce.

game birds

# partridge

The chubby gray partridge (*Perdix perdix*) with his orange face and tail, brown coat and distinctive dark inverted horseshoe mark on his light grey breast, is native to Britain and to a greater or lesser degree, from Cape Finisterre to central Asia. Grays, or Hungarians as they are sometimes known, are ground nesters and running birds, only breaking into flight on their short whirring wings when forced to do so. These shy, secretive birds originated from the southern steppes and their ideal habitat is open spaces with good ground cover to nest in and rear their broods, safe from hawks and corvids.

Early European farmers created perfect conditions for partridges and their numbers continually increased with agricultural expansion. For centuries they were the principal game bird here and in Europe, becoming so much part of the diet that '*toujours perdix*', indicating a monotony in food, is still a common expression in France.

Under the rigid Norman Forest laws, which applied to both Britain and France, partridges, rabbits, hares and the few pheasants that existed, were classified as beasts and fowls of Free Warren. All game belonged to the King, but the right to hunt game in either forest, chase or warren was handed out as a reward or bribe to the nobles and clergy. The right of Free Warren was a fairly minor, if potentially lucrative, perk that was often granted to monastic houses. During the early Middle Ages, partridges became synonymous with a privileged and increasingly decadent priesthood. The connection between partridges and excess among the clergy persisted to the extent that, when Henry IV of France condemned the wretched Bishop of Dijon to life imprisonment, an added twist to the sentence was that he should be fed on nothing but partridges.

Not only were partridges prolific, but their behavioural pattern made them obligingly easy to catch. Until they separate to mate in late winter, partridges stick together in family groups known as coveys and their harsh, rasping call is a familiar sound in the countryside. At the first sign of danger they scuttle together, crouching immobile until it passes or they are forced into the air. If partridges were required in any quantity, a setting dog was used that had been trained to locate coveys and approach the birds stealthily,

holding their attention whilst a net was drawn over them. A kite shaped like a hawk was equally effective and, as techniques in falconry improved with knowledge acquired in the Middle East during the crusades, peregrine falcons were used to take partridges on the wing.

Gun powder was first used in European warfare in the thirteenth century. By the 1500s primitive military matchlocks and delicate wheellocks, firing a solid lump of lead, were being used to bag the occasional deer and unsuspecting bustard. The shotgun came into being with the invention of small shot in the second half of the century. History does not relate who had the idea of cutting a sheet of lead into small squares and rattling the pieces around in a metal box until they became vaguely spherical, but the potential was instantly recognised and immediately condemned.

Despite the difficulties involved in actually getting a shot at game – most matchlocks and wheel-locks had barrels 1.8m (6ft) long and had to be fired from a gun stand – shooting with hail shot grew in popularity, infuriating the hawking fraternity. Realistically, for the next hundred and fifty years, the majority of partridges continued to be netted across Europe. Shooting was more advanced on the continent. The best sporting guns were made in Italy and France, and shooting partridges on the wing, as coveys took to the air, had been in vogue for some time. Cavaliers returning from Europe after the Restoration introduced this innovation in shooting, but it was many decades before 'shooting flying' became common practice in Britain. During the same period, Charles II brought over several pairs of French or red-legged partridge (Alectoris rufa) from Chambord, which were put down in Windsor Great Park in 1673. These natives of southern France are slightly bigger than grays and have white faces ribbed with a black stripe, red beaks, red legs and boldly barred silver and black flanks. The original birds did not survive but later importations were to outnumber the native species in some areas.

The partridge population expanded rapidly during the agricultural revolution of the eighteenth and early nineteenth centuries. Miles of quick set hedging was planted as thousands of acres of poor quality land became enclosed and improved. Lord Townsend of Raynham Hall in Norfolk, one of the great agricultural improvers of the day, introduced turnips as winter feed for sheep, rotating turnips, cereals and grass leys to maximise land use. These practices were adopted by farmers as more and more land went under the plough to meet demands for grain. The hedges, ditches and wide grassy headlands enabled the partridge to flourish in these conditions. Tall, hand scythed corn stubbles and the broad leafed root crops were all perfect habitat for partridges, providing deep cover and a plentiful food source.

By the middle of the eighteenth century partridges were being shot 'walked-up', and on the wing, a change in fashion that had much to do with the popularity of the Grand Tour. Those embarking on this adventure saw that continental gentry regularly shot game flying, with guns which were infinitely superior to anything made in Britain. 'Shooting flying' rapidly became the vogue and inspired the gun trade to make quality guns along continental lines. Partridges were now shot immediately after harvest, with the aid of pointers originally imported from Spain. These large, heavy, slow working dogs had phenomenal noses ideal for the deep scythed stubbles and, later on, the turnip fields. Trained to quarter the ground searching for coveys, they stood 'on point' as soon as one was scented. This enabled sportsmen, usually no more than two of them, to cock their flintlocks, check their powder and creep forward, ready to fire the moment the covey took to the air.

Red-legged partridges became established at the end of the eighteenth century. The Marquess of Hertford brought over several pairs and thousands of eggs from France, which were hatched under broody chickens. From a shooting point of view, French partridges looked like being something of a failure, as it soon became apparent that, instead of obligingly keeping still when marked by pointers and taking to the wing only when guns were cocked and ready to fire, these irritating foreign birds continually crept away from the dogs, only deigning to fly when they were well out of range.

However the red-legged patridge's true potential was soon to be realised. Gun making improved during the nineteenth century. Percussion caps had largely replaced the weather-sensitive open flintlock firing mechanism by the late 1820s, allowing sportsmen to shoot in all weather, at any angle without the risk of powder getting damp or falling out of the pan, for the first time in four hundred years. Barrels were lighter, shorter and, in many cases, double rather than single. Powder was becoming dependable and shot round and regular, thanks to a Bristol plumber who had discovered that molten lead poured from a height into water solidified into pellets that were almost perfectly spherical.

The old game laws that restricted shooting to those who could show a certain level of income, and a more recent amendment restricting it to landowners and their eldest sons, had been repealed. Now landlords could invite whom they liked and even let their land for shooting. Hundreds of acres of poor, unproductive land had been planted during the long agricultural depression after Waterloo, creating further habitat for partridges and encouraging the spread of pheasants. Into this sporting utopia, made accessible by ever improving roads and railways, stepped parties of 'guns' shooting together for the first time. The solitary man or at the most two, working their pointers across the stubbles was now replaced by a group of guns walking abreast.

Gray partridges were still shot going forward, and red-legged Frenchmen continued to induce apoplexy and xenophobic explosions by creeping forward ahead of guns and only flying when confronted by an obstacle like a hedge. Someone, presumably out of sheer frustration, had the idea of positioning himself behind such a barrier and firing as partridges flew over him. The novelty caught on and the concept of driving coveys over forward-standing guns concealed behind high hedges, was experimented with widely. The value of red-legged Frenchmen was now appreciated. Unlike gray partridges that flew in coveys and were soon over the guns, they came forward in ones and twos, providing a continuity of sporting shots. The first organised driven partridge shoot, involving an army of beaters and some of the crack shots of the day, took place in 1845 at Heveningham Hall in Suffolk, the seat of Lord Huntingfield. The day was considered to be a huge success. The bag was impressive and his Lordship, who is reputed to have practised for weeks on potatoes lobbed over the high walled kitchen gardens, shot well. There was one obvious drawback. Guns were still loaded at the muzzle, and keeping pace with driven partridge necessitated as many as four double-barrelled shot guns per person and as many loaders. The whole performance of trying to pour powder and shot into a muzzle loader in the heat of the moment, with birds whizzing over and an impatient employer yelling for a fresh gun was, as one loader put it succinctly in the Huntingfield Arms that night, 'bloody dangerous'.

Two major items at the Great Exhibition in 1851 revolutionised shooting and partridge shooting in particular – a mechanical reaper, invented by Robert and Cyrus McCormick, and a sporting gun by Casimir Lefaucheux. The McCormick

reaper reduced stubble cover to the level where both gray and red partridges now ran ahead of guns, making walking up over pointers hopelessly unproductive, but driven birds much more manageable. Lefaucheux's gun hinged open at the breech to be loaded by a cartridge containing powder, shot and its own ignition. By 1860, gun makers had improved Lefaucheux's breech loader to the extent that sportsmen were able to shoot as fast as they could load Eley's new composite cartridge. Driven partridges were now all the rage.

The next fifty years, up until the First World War, was the era of the great shooting house parties. Landowners all over Europe went to enormous trouble to create habitats for game cover which not only shaped the landscape, but provided us with a conservation legacy that benefits all wildlife species. As in Scotland, royalty led the way with Queen Victoria developing the shoot at Windsor. Not to be outdone, the future King Edward VII bought Sandringham in 1860, and his pioneering example in game management was followed on many other estates. Names like Merton, Elveden, Quidenham, Crichel, Chatsworth, Blenheim, Castle Rising, Welbeck and in particular Holkham, are only a few of those that resound through the history of shooting and conservation.

There was equal enthusiasm for shooting in Europe with exchanges of invitations and ideas among British and European landowners. Bohemia and Hungary were the main attractions, with the estates of Baron Hirsch at St Johann, Count Karolyi at Totmagyar and Count Trautmansdorf in Bohemia being the best invitations, where partridges swarmed in an open landscape of maize strips and arable stubbles. Baron Hirsch advised the future Edward VII on partridge rearing and, after a

series of disastrous wet springs towards the end of the 1870s, sent over stock from Hungary to replace the losses at Sandringham. Ever helpful, Baron Hirsch also supplied plans of the enormous game larders at St Johann on which the ones at Sandringham are based.

There was some decent partridge shooting to be had in Germany, but elsewhere driven shooting did not catch on and game continued to be walked-up over pointers on the Continent as it is today, with the exception of Spain. Among the European crowned heads invited to shoot in England, was King Alfonso XIII of Spain, who astonished everyone by proving to be a surprisingly good shot. So impressed was the King with the driven partridges he shot at Windsor, and grouse as the guest of the Duke of Sutherland, that he determined to create something similar on his estate at Casa de Campo. He engaged a keeper named Watts who arrived in Spain with several thousand pheasant eggs and a quantity of red-legged partridges. The pheasants were not a success, but driven partridges in Spain have since become one of the most sought after shooting experiences.

Many great estates, particularly in middle Europe, ceased to exist after the First World War, but partridge conservation and their popularity as game birds continued. In the 1920s, the forerunner of the Game Conservancy Trust, a pioneer research organisation in wildlife habitat conservation, started work on the causes of disease among wild gray partridge. At the same time, thousands of grays from Hungary were imported into North America to augment a small population that had become established in 1790. These new birds, and further importations of two sub species of red-legged – the Chukar and Barbary in 1937 – have made partridges one of North America's principal game birds.

The 1960s were a desperate period for all wildlife in Europe, especially the wild British partridge. The extensive use of agricultural herbicides and pesticides destroyed both habitat and feed sources. Prairie farming removed miles of hedge cover and small field nesting, and brood rearing sights. The Game Conservancy Trust and other conservation bodies here and in Europe were largely responsible for persuading their respective governments to ban the use of Dieldrin, Aldron and Heptachlor. The Game Conservancy Trust, and similar organisations in Europe and America, continue to be world leaders in environmental research, working closely with their respective agricultural ministries persuaded their governments to ban the most dangerous herbicides and to help farmers create environments which benefit all wildlife species and encourage gray partridge to breed.

I yearn for partridge during the intervening months, gray partridge that is, although the red-legged described by the poet, Robert Browning as 'plump as bishops' repays the attention you may lavish on it. I feel partridge should feature in the meal I eat before they hang me. If you have a young gray partridge roast it, otherwise here, on the following pages, are some ideas for you.

## Ageing

It is easy to age a young gray partridge at the beginning of the season as the legs will be yellowish, the beak dark and the bones soft, whilst adults are grey beaked, grey legged and hard boned. As winter starts, I use the flight feather test as the two primaries will be pointed; if these feathers are pointed but bedraggled and faded they denote a bird born later in the previous season which has not yet moulted, but it will be obvious. In the Bursa test (see page 24)

a toothpick will go up 1cm ($^1$/2in) in a young bird. With red-legged partridges, the primaries are tipped with cream coloured plumage in a young bird.

## Hanging

Young grays have such a delicate flavour that they shouldn't be hung for more than 3–5 days according to temperature; older birds should be given 5–7 days to tenderise. If you are lucky enough to have young grays, promise me you will simply roast them, all the complicated recipes are for the more tasteless and now common red-legged Frenchman as they are often called.

## Plucking and drawing

As for pheasant (see page 24–25).

## Roasting

Insert a piece of seasoned butter in the bird's cavity and cover the breast with barding fat, rather than bacon, to keep the delicate flavour. Cook in a very hot oven at 220ºC/425ºF/gas 7 for 30 minutes, removing the fat for the last 10 minutes to brown. Baste frequently but, if you don't have time for this, cook the birds on their breasts and turn upright to brown at the end. Serve with thin gravy, bread sauce, and fried breadcrumbs.

Allow one roasted partridge per person. Serve the birds whole (unless you are casseroling of course).

## partridge with lentils and pickled lemons

I think I could eat partridge every day. I invented this dish having received some red-legged partridges whilst reading Freya Stark and dreaming of Araby. I think it's rather good.

*350g (12oz) green or brown lentils*
*50ml (2oz) olive oil*
*2 cloves garlic, chopped*
*2 partridges, halved*
*2 large Swiss chard leaves (remove the stems and cut them into*
*  small pieces, then slice the leaves diagonally into narrow strips)*
*300ml (1/2 pint) water*
*2 pickled lemons, cut into pieces, or 1 tablespoon fresh*
*  lemon juice*
*salt and pepper*

Cook the lentils in lightly salted, boiling water for 20 minutes, drain them and keep the liquid. Heat the oil in a heavy frying pan with a lid. Fry the garlic for a few minutes, then remove and discard it. Brown the partridges all over in the oil and then set them aside.

Wilt the chard strips in the hot oil for 2 minutes, remove, drain on kitchen paper and set aside. Return the partridges to the pan together with the lentils, chard stalks, pickled lemon pieces or juice, and a little of the lentil water; cover and simmer for 20 minutes or until the partridges are tender. Add the chard strips, heat through and serve with a fresh crisp green salad.

## grilled partridge with garlic, oil, lemon and cayenne

This is a very simple way of cooking tender young red-legs that don't have a great deal of flavour of their own, but respond very well to grilling. It makes a quick dish for hungry shots. You need to cut the partridge through the back and flatten them out. It is also a dish that can be cooked over the embers of an open fire out of doors.

*4 tablespoons olive oil*
*4 cloves garlic, crushed*
*juice of 1 lemon*
*4 partridges, spatchcocked*
*1 tablespoon cayenne*
*salt and pepper*

Mix the oil, garlic and lemon juice together and marinate the partridges in it for 1–3 hours.

Take them from the marinade, season and sprinkle on the cayenne. Grill, turning from time to time for about 15–20 minutes. Be careful not to overcook and baste them with the marinade from time to time.

## partridge in a pilaff

*6 partridges*

*1 medium onion, peeled*

*3 cloves*

*1 cinnamon stick*

*600ml (1 pint) stock made from pheasant, chicken or partridge*

*2 tablespoons olive oil*

*110g (4oz) blanched almonds*

*110g (4oz) pinenuts*

*2 tablespoons clarified butter*

*450g (1lb) long grain rice (if it's not quick cook, soak the rice for*
*  30 minutes and drain well)*

*1/2 teaspoon ground cinnamon*

*1/2 teaspoon ground allspice*

*salt and pepper*

Season the partridges and put them in a large pan with the onion (into which you have stuck the cloves), the cinnamon stick and the stock; add water to cover. Bring to the boil and simmer gently for 15–20 minutes. Drain, saving the stock and cut the birds into halves down the back. Keep warm.

Heat the oil in a frying pan and cook the almonds until golden, then set aside; do the same with the pinenuts.

In a pan with a tight-fitting lid melt the clarified butter, add the rice and stir until it is all coated with the butter. Add 425ml (15fl oz) of the reserved stock, bring to the boil and cook until the rice is tender – about 15–20 minutes; add the ground cinnamon and allspice and more stock if necessary.

Turn the rice onto a dish and mix in the nuts. Lay the partridge pieces on top, and serve with Arab flatbread and yoghurt.

## partridges stuffed with chestnuts

**Chestnuts always remind me of partridges; they have the same appealing shape and smallness. I tend to buy mine ready peeled but, if you have a tree and children, the fresh ones will repay the extra effort.**

*50g (2oz) butter*

*2 shallots, chopped*

*4 partridges (livers reserved if possible, otherwise use other game*
*  bird livers or chicken livers)*

*450g (1lb) peeled chestnuts*

*150ml (5fl oz) whole milk*

*barding bacon*

*a little stock*

*salt and pepper*

Heat the butter in a frying pan and soften the shallots in the butter. Cut the livers in half, add them and cook a little longer. Add the chestnuts and cook gently for about 5 minutes. Remove to a bowl and pour over the milk; leave to stand and infuse for 30 minutes.

Preheat the oven to 220°C/425°F/gas 7.

Either by hand or in a processor mash the chesnut mixture, leaving the nuts quite textured – so not puréed but a bit lumpy! Stuff the partridges with this mixture, truss and season them and then bard them with bacon and cook for about 20 minutes. Remove the bacon and return the partridges to brown the breasts for another 10 minutes. There will be some stuffing left over, so purée it finely and add to the pan juices, stir it in and add a little stock to make a sauce.

## la mancha

## partridges with peppers and tomato

The plains of La Mancha are home to thousands of Spanish partridge. I like to think of Don Quixote sitting by his fire eating partridge done in the same manner. The earthenware dish of water causes the jucies inside the dish to rise and fall back, moistening the braise to give a good flavour. The method of cooking, and the fried bread accompaniment gives the recipe a date of four hundred years, and it has survived the test of time.

4 partridges

225ml (8fl oz) strong red wine (Spanish of course)

1 tablespoon oil

25g (1oz) green streaky bacon, chopped

1 head garlic, cloves peeled

100g (3½oz) raw Spanish ham, sliced

1 bouquet garni or 2 cloves

8 peppercorns, crushed

½ cinnamon stick

thyme

2 slices bread, fried in olive oil

salt

Marinate the partridges in the red wine for 1 hour. Heat the oil and sauté the bacon and garlic cloves. When they begin to colour, drain the partridges, pat them dry with kitchen paper, add them to the pan and brown all over. Add the ham, bouquet garni, peppercorns, cinnamon stick and a sprig or two of thyme and 2 tablespoons of the marinade wine. Cook for 5 minutes, season with salt, and reduce the heat. Cover with tinfoil and place on top of an earthenware dish of warm water. Cook over a very low heat for 1½ hours, turning the partridges a couple of times during cooking. When the birds are tender remove to a dish and arrange the ham around them. Discard the bouquet garni, strain the sauce and pour it over. Serve with sippets of fried bread.

This is a dish that came about because I had made some *Marmouma*, a Tunisian dish from Claudia Roden's brilliant *Book of Jewish Food*. I was called away so didn't have it for lunch and fancied something meatier for my dinner, so I threw in the partridge and some lemon juice. I hope you enjoy it.

4 tablespoons olive oil

4 partridges

4 red peppers

3 cloves garlic, mashed with salt

700g (1½lb) tomatoes, peeled and roughly chopped

pinch of sugar

juice of ½ lemon

salt and pepper

Heat the oil in a heavy pan, season the partridges and brown them all over. Remove them from the pan and set aside.

Core and deseed the peppers and cut them into strips. Cook them in the oil, slowly turning as you go, for about 10 minutes. Add the garlic and cook until the peppers are beginning to soften. Add the tomatoes, sugar and lemon juice, season, and simmer uncovered for about 25–30 minutes, until the partridges are done and the sauce is jammy.

## partridges for lady lucy

Gerry Bramley asked me to cook a dinner for the Prince of Wales Trust once, and he chose as the venue James Percy's stylish Lodge at Linhope, in the middle of the Northumbrian Hills. James joined us in the kitchen for scraps and told me that this is how his wife treats partridge breasts, and an excellent idea it is too. The sauce I offer here is my own.

*4 partridge breasts*
*1 egg, beaten*
*4 tablespoons breadcrumbs, made with stale bread*

Cut the breasts from the partridges, trim and press them flat. Place each flattened breast between 2 pieces of cling film and gently beat flatter until they are as thin as you think they will go. Dip them in egg and breadcrumbs and fry quickly in butter.

For the sauce:
*A quantity of ratatouille (good tin will do)*
*400g (14oz) tin of chopped tomatoes*
*dash of Tabasco sauce*
*basil or coriander*
*salt and pepper*

Put all the ingredients in a blender and pulverise for a few seconds. Heat in a small saucepan and season to taste and serve with the partridges.

## partridges with cockles in a cataplana

This is a Portuguese recipe which Johnny gave me. It's an unusual dish but surprisingly good. A *cataplana* for those of you who don't know is a Portuguese double saucepan which locks closed, and which you can turn over to apply heat to either side. It is reputed to be the precursor to the pressure-cooker and is particular to the Algarve coast, so you may have picked one up on holiday; otherwise use a casserole. *Piri piri* is a Portuguese hot sauce readily available in supermarkets.

*50g (2oz) cockles, without their shells*
*50g (2oz) butter*
*3 cloves garlic, crushed*
*2 partridges, cut in half*
*piri piri to taste*
*200ml (7fl oz) dry port wine*
*300ml (1/2 pint) dry white wine*
*1 bay leaf*
*1 bunch of parsley, chopped*
*salt*

Wash the cockles well in salted water to remove any grit – unsalted water will kill them. Put the *cataplana* or casserole on the heat, and put in the butter and the garlic cloves.

Brown the partridges in the melted butter. Season with some salt and *piri piri*, and then add the wines and bay leaf. Close the *cataplana* and cook until the partridges are done – about 15–20 minutes. Add the cockles and continue to cook for a further 5 minutes to just cook them through. Don't overcook the cockles or they will be tough. Sprinkle with parsley.

## hungarian **bartash** with aubergine

The original Hungarian recipe was, I thought, rather bland. At the Bodega Toston in Fuengerola (arguably the best tapas restaurant in Spain), I had red peppers stuffed with partridge which were very good but lacked a dimension, so I have combined the two. It is an excellent dish for a buffet or a supper table and also makes a very nice starter. It can also be made with cold pheasant. The technique of putting your hot grilled peppers into a plastic bag makes them so much easier to peel – the skin just flakes off. Rinse them under a tap to remove any lingering black specks.

*the meat from 4 roast partridges or 1 pheasant, finely chopped*
*3 large aubergines*
*5 small red peppers*
*2 cloves garlic*
*1/2 teaspoon salt*
*300ml (10fl oz) full fat plain yoghurt*
*fresh mint*

Grill the aubergines, turning as you go, until they are well blackened and the pulp is soft. This will take about 15 minutes. Take the aubergines from the grill and put in the peppers on a tray to catch any oil that may run. Grill the peppers, turning as is necessary until they too are well blackened; place each in a plastic bag and allow to cool, when they will be easy to peel.

Scrape the pulp from the aubergines and leave to drain. Mash the garlic cloves with the salt, stir in the yoghurt and fresh chopped mint, and fold in the aubergine pulp. Add the meat. Peel the red peppers and remove the core carefully so as not to break them. Stuff them with the partridge–aubergine mixture and serve at room temperature.

## partridge with chicory

I love the bitterness of chicory and the fact that it sprouts happily in your garage in mid-winter and I have always cooked it like this. One day having a handy partridge I decided to add it, and was most pleased with the result, as I hope you will be. If you look at the base of the chicory head you will see a little round core, excise it with a knife and the plant loses its unacceptable bitterness.

*110g (4oz) butter*
*2 partridges*
*2 slices streaky bacon*
*3 heads chicory*
*juice of 1/2 lemon*
*salt and pepper*

Heat half the butter in a pan and brown the birds evenly, and then season them. If the birds are not young, continue cooking them gently in the butter for another 5 minutes.

Chop the bacon and carefully slice the chicory heads in half, removing the little core at the base of the heads that causes the bitterness. Melt the rest of the butter in a heavy pan and sauté the bacon for a few minutes, then toss in the chicory. Add the partridges with any remaining butter, and the lemon juice. Cover tightly and cook for 10–15 minutes over a low heat or until the partridges are tender.

# pheasant

No other bird is quite as synonymous with the countryside than a cock pheasant and yet, he is a complete stranger to these islands. The species we know today as the Old English black-neck originated, according to the Greek historian Aeschylus, from the marshy, rush-covered banks of the sluggish river Phasis, the modern Rioni in Georgia. Legend has it that these were brought back to Greece by the Argonauts and were received with as much rapture as the Golden Fleece itself.

Mythology aside, the Greeks certainly adorned their stockyards with these wondrous creatures and subsequently so did the Romans. Roman chefs loved anything exotic, and so pheasants were soon appearing, dressed for the table in all their plumage, at patrician banquets. Phalladius left records of the elaborate fattening process: chicks were fed for the first fortnight after hatching on a diet of boiled grain sprinkled with wine; then on a more robust diet of locusts and ants' eggs mixed with flour and olive oil, rolled into bite-sized balls, recommended to achieve the ultimate in desirable plumpness.

The Romans, who liked to travel with life's little luxuries, brought them across the Channel during their colonisation of Britain, and for the next five hundred years, the ancestors of our modern pheasant lived in pampered domesticity. The collapse of the Empire must have been a shock for those that were left behind but somehow, enough survived among the ruins of their former homes to breed the nucleus of a feral population.

The Saxons and Danes were hopeless historians and the earliest evidence of the naturalisation of pheasants appears in documents belonging to Waltham Abbey in Essex, where a regulation of King Harold in 1059 allows the canons the choice of exchanging a brace of partridges for one pheasant. The Normans imported more pheasants of Roman origin as part of their living larders, and the name appears regularly in historical records thereafter, either in the statistics of the nobility and clergy permitted to kill them, or as highly prized delicacies in the records of elaborate medieval feasting.

Vain, supercilious and quarrelsome, these immaculate creatures strut across the centuries, insouciantly rubbing shoulders with the great and the good. Under the Forest Laws, they were classified as Fowls of Warren and in the King's gift. The right to kill pheasants was doled out as a privilege to clergy and nobility, partly because it made them feel loved but also, I suspect, because it guaranteed pheasant would be on the menu if the King chose to stay in one of the religious houses. Even as semi-domesticated warren-bred birds, their rarity and value as a delicacy, ensured what must be a documentation unique to pheasants. Thus we know that Henry I granted the Abbot of Amesbury a licence to kill pheasants in 1100 and that Thomas à Becket had just dined off one on the 29th December 1179, when Henry II's heavies dropped in for a little chat. Prices were scrupulously recorded – 4d in 1299 had risen to 12d by 1512 with a massive leap in the middle of the century, to sixteen shillings. To ensure a regular supply, Henry VIII had his own pheasant breeder, a French monk, whom Henry considered so essential he paid the monk out of his privy purse.

In France, pheasants were even more revered. Knights embarking on a crusade took vows of chivalry over a pheasant, cooked and dressed in all its plumage. In 1453, after a particularly emotional party, Phillip Duke of Burgundy, who was obsessed with pheasants, swore a solemn oath over the carcase of a roast bird that, on the following day, he would lead all who cared to follow him to liberate Greece from the Turks. This outburst was enormously well received. It was a big party and the flower of France were all there. To a man they agreed to follow him and to a man, failed to turn up at the departure point. Undeterred by what a lesser man might have felt a humiliating set back, Phillip founded the Order of the Pheasant in 1455. The nobility, who were expected to become initiates, invoked the name of God, the Virgin and the Pheasant before making some Knightly vow.

The volume of literature on how to catch them in the wild is a further indication of their esteem. In most areas, pheasants were relatively scarce. From a falconer's point of view, their habitat of young woodland on the edge of cultivated land made them difficult to get at, but those surprised, scratching for seeds in the open, made an exciting alternative to partridges with their tremendous turn of speed and habit of rapidly gaining height between cover. They were flown at with peregrines and sparrow hawks or sometimes driven out of woodland by little beagley brachets for the fast, savage, goshawks.

I am extremely fortunate to have an original copy of *The Gentleman's Recreation* of 1676 by the great Nicholas Cox. This was the field sports bible of the time and Cox covers pheasant in great detail. Of the options available – snaring, liming and netting – netting ensured the biggest bag but required enormous skill. In all cases, an Eye (cock, hen and poults) had to be located first in some secluded copse. The netter had then to conceal himself for several days where he could listen and memorise the different calls used by adult birds as they warned the young of danger, summoned them to new feeding areas or chided

them when they straggled too far. Then came the painstaking business of softly imitating the different notes, to draw pheasants into an open area where a net could be thrown over them.

Snaring and liming required the same period of careful observation, before horse hair snares attached to bent withy rods were set along the paths used when the birds went to drink. Liming was widely used to catch a variety of birds and to catch pheasants, two bundles rods smeared with lime were used. One, the bushy top of a willow tree with a long stem, was pushed into the ground beside a tree in which pheasants were known to roost. Individual twigs were then set at intervals, covering an open space in front of the roosting sight. When both were in place, pheasants were called into the area. Some would panic when the lime covered twigs became stuck to their wings, frightening the others into the lime bush.

The odd pheasant was taken for the pot by a variety of means still used by poachers today:

soaking grain in alcohol and picking them up as they tottered drunkenly about unable to fly, or threading a horse hair through a raisin; prevented from swallowing but totally preoccupied in trying to, pheasants were easily caught. Very few were shot at this time but there was a fad in Italy of shooting them on their roosts, with crossbows by moonlight.

*Phasianus colchicus* was the only pheasant in England and parts of southern Scotland until the introduction of Chinese Ring-neck pheasants, brought back by tea clippers in the late seventeenth century. By the nineteenth century, as trade developed with the East, more exotic species were being introduced. T.B. Johnson, in his 1831 edition of *The Sportsman's Cyclopedia*, describes white, crested, spotted, pile, dark Argus and spectacular golden pheasants. The lovely Reeves pheasant, with its white head, black and gold banded body and 1.5m (4 1/2 ft) long tail, was imported at around the same time. These exotics were aviary or park birds but some escaped to breed with the

indigenous population and add their glorious plumage to the golds and reds of wild birds.

The agricultural improvements of the eighteenth and nineteenth centuries, which favoured the spread of partridges, also led to an expansion in the wild pheasant population. For hedgerow shooting a new type of gun dog evolved, the springer spaniel, bred small enough to put pheasants up from their cover and retrieve them when shot. Pheasants had all the food they could eat, thanks to the growth in arable farming, but they needed proper roosting cover. This was obligingly provided for them in the agricultural depression that followed Waterloo. Landowners were already beginning to sense the potential in planting cover for game. Shotguns were improving all the time and the interest in sporting recreation was growing as the road system improved. Lefaucheux's breech loader and the railways were still a long way off, but Forsyth's percussion cap was revolutionary, and the toll roads made the country accessible in a way that had been unthinkable to the previous generation.

With grain prices sliding, landlords started planting trees on pockets of poor quality land. Hedges grew taller and thicker with existing woodland replanted or enlarged. A new form of shooting evolved, with guns and beaters walking in line through woodland, shooting forward, with the line halting after each shot as the muzzle loaders of the day were re-loaded. In some areas woods were deliberately shaped or planted circular, so that pheasants curled back towards guns, giving a new experience of shooting a bird coming towards them. At some point, in about 1840, it occurred to someone that struggling through the undergrowth with a load of beaters was pretty daft when the most exciting shots were at birds flying away from beaters from one woodland to the next. Lord Leicester is generally recognised as starting driven shooting on his estates at Holkham in Norfolk, with guns standing in line to shoot pheasants driven over them. As with driven partridges, the limitations were the number of loaders required to keep up with the flow of birds.

Landlords were devoting time and money to conservation practices that were to benefit all wildlife and provide rural employment, with keepering a much sought after career opportunity. Shooting was increasingly popular among the wealthy middle classes and the railways made it available to them. The situation begged for an improved shotgun and Lefaucheux provided it in 1851. Joseph Lang was the first to improve Lefaucheux's action, but soon the major gun makers of the time were busy employing all the versatility and creative genius in precision engineering that were to make British gun making world famous. By 1860 the percussion cap muzzle loader was obsolete and pheasants had usurped partridges as the principal game bird. Covert planting took off again in earnest, to encourage pheasants to fly high and fast between woods. This woodland planting to provide habitat for pheasants, created the landscape and the biodiversity that encourages all wildlife species, and makes our British countryside so attractive.

The Japanese green pheasant began appearing in the coverts of the Gurney family on their estate in Norfolk around 1845, and by 1860 this hardy little bird was well established among the existing pheasant population across Europe. Further importations concentrated on developing a species that would provide a challenge to meet improvements in shotgun and cartridge manufacture. Towards the end of the century,

pheasants were introduced as game birds to America, Canada, New Zealand and, with varied success, parts of Australia. Today's pheasant is a hybrid of many different species, and is constantly being improved with infusions of new blood, either from Far Eastern stock or from Europe and America.

---

Until you have been around pheasant shoots you will not comprehend quite how many pheasants you have to deal with, and what a variety of ages and conditions you will find them in. I once worked on a large family shoot at Danehill in Sussex, and quite understood the story of the small boy arriving late at his boarding school and on being offered something to eat, replying 'Oh nothing that's any trouble, just some cold pheasant will do.' In my grandmother's day your social standing was determined by how many brace you were given for Christmas, curiously a Doctor only received one pheasant.

There is nothing lovelier at the start of the season than a young roast pheasant with all the trimmings: game chips, bread sauce, thin gravy, redcurrant jelly, and nothing nastier than a dried out old pheasant (unless you take care to prepare the old pheasant properly).

### Ageing
The first thing is to age your pheasant, which if you have seen a lot of pheasant becomes a matter of common sense. Julia Drysdale in her excellent book in association with the Game Conservancy in 1975, waxes eloquently on the Bursa Test. The Bursa is a blind vent above the anus, the purpose of which is still really unknown; it closes completely when the bird reaches sexual maturity, so a toothpick inserted

will tell all. I have to say in heaven knows how many years of ageing pheasants I have never tried this. For me the main test is the foot; as with humans old pheasant have old feet, long spurs and horny beaks and feet. Although some young pheasants have long spurs they are still much more pliable than the old ones. The plumage of the younger birds is brighter and the beaks less horny. If in doubt ask a keeper or your butcher for advice.

When buying pheasant don't let the butcher chop the feet off, ask him to pull them as this will take the tendons out of the legs and making them easier to eat.

### Hanging
This is a matter of personal taste and weather conditions. A lot of people are put off the thought of game by stories of pheasants crawling with maggots, as relished by our Victorian and Edwardian forebears. In the days before refridge-ration people were much more used to strong flavours and even today the Swedes yearn for Surstumming (rotten herring) and the Japanese and Finns for fermented fish; the Icelanders still eat shark rotted in the permafrost and there are gentlemen who like their stilton just short of the maggot stage. How ripe you eat your pheasant is a matter for you, but hang it you must, even if only for as little as three days, for all meat must be allowed to rest and mature.

The game larder should be well aired and protected from flies and other insects. People will hang pheasant in pairs, but ideally they should be hung singly so the air can circulate. Hang them by the neck, in feather with the innards intact. I don't like mine very high so I usually hang them until I can easily pull out the longest tail feather – about a week to ten days in cold weather.

## Plucking

Start at the neck, pulling against the way the feathers grow and taking particular care over the breast, so as not to tear the skin. Once you have plucked 2–3 birds you will find it comes easily to you. If the weather is fine pluck out of doors. I have it to such an art I tend to sit down and pluck into a dustbin bag, but then I've had years of practice.

Break the leg at the knee joint and twist it to loosen the tendons, then put the foot over a suitable hook and pull gently twisting as you pull. All the tendons will pull out with the foot and the meat on the legs will be totally edible. Singe a hairy bird by lighting a taper and running it over the skin.

## Drawing

Cut off the head just where the neck starts and discard. Pull out the crop which will reveal the pheasant's last meal and discard. Cut off the neck where it joins the pheasant's body and keep for stock. Make a slight slit at the vent and insert your first two fingers – the entrails will pull out quite easily. Retain the liver, the heart and the gizzards which you will need to cut open and clean out, and discard the rest. If the liver is discoloured cut out the damaged part.

## Roasting

*1 young pheasant*
*1/2 apple or 1/2 small onion*
*2 tablespoons butter*
*4 slices streaky bacon or barding fat*
*salt and pepper*

Season the bird inside and out. Place a piece of apple, cored and skinned, or half a small onion inside the bird together with half the butter. Rub the outside of the bird with the remaining butter and cover the breast with bacon or barding fat. Alternatively, omit the pork and wrap in tinfoil.

Roast at 190°C/375°F/gas 5 for 45 minutes, if it's not wrapped in tinfoil baste from time to time. Remove the bacon or peel back the tinfoil for the final 10 minutes to brown the breast. Make a thin gravy with the roasting juices and serve on a warm dish.

## Carving

Basically, follow the same procedure as for carving a chicken. Remove any trussing, and position the pheasant with the drumsticks pointing away from you. Insert your carving fork into the thick upper part of the left hand drumstick with the prongs straddling the bone, and lever away from the body. Cut down between body and thigh until the joint is exposed. Lever again and separate joint by probing with the knife's point.

Cut round the curvature of the body on either side of the joint and, if the thigh has still not separated, twist free by hand. Remove the wing by cutting through the joint where it is attached to the body, without touching the breast meat.

Now turn the bird so the pheasant's equivalent of the parson's nose is facing you. Insert the fork to the left of the breastbone and carve the first slice from the breast where the body curves round to the point of the wing joint. Continue carving slices in towards the breastbone 5mm (1/6in) thick. If the slices are too thin the delicate flavour will be lost. When one side is finished, repeat process. Serve the thigh and a drumstick as one portion.

One pheasant is enough for 2–3 people, and the cock bird is more generous than the hen.

## pheasant terrine with pickled walnuts

When I worked for Rebeka Hardy (the best boss I ever had) at Danehill, she also ran a successful family shoot so I had a great deal of pheasant to work with. I bitterly resented buying forcemeat for terrines and so I made this. Press down well when making it or it may crumble, but I am delighted with it.

2 pheasants
225ml (8fl oz) red vermouth
900g (2lb) fat or streaky bacon
225g (8oz) pickled walnuts, cut into slices (about 3 per walnut)
salt and pepper

Cut both the light and dark meat from the pheasants and then cut it into strips the thickness and half the length of your little finger. Soak overnight in the vermouth in the fridge. Line a greased terrine or loaf tin with bacon rashers making sure there are no gaps.

Preheat oven to 180°C/350°F/gas 4.

Remove the pheasant from the marinade, shake dry and season. Half fill the dish with pheasant strips and press down well. Slice as many walnuts as you need to make a single layer along the top of the pheasant. Fill the top half of the dish with pheasant, again pressing down well. Cover with the rest of the bacon. Bake in the oven with the dish in a pan of hot water, for 45 minutes. Leave to cool slightly and turn out.

## pheasant wth saffron and bread soup

This is a Middle Eastern dish and very good for using up badly shot birds. It is very heartening on a winter's night and a little different from ordinary game soup.

1 pheasant, quartered
50g (2oz) cooked chickpeas, drained
50g (2oz) butter
1 celery stalk and 6 sprigs parsley, tied together
1.2 litres (2 pints) water
pinch of cinnamon
pinch of saffron
2 eggs
juice of 1 lemon
2 tablespoons olive oil
1/2 stale white country loaf
salt and pepper

Put the pheasant, chickpeas, butter, celery and parsley, salt and pepper into a large pot, and add the water. Bring to the boil and simmer for 1 hour. Remove the celery and parsley. Take the pheasant out and either remove the meat from the bones, or carve. Sprinkle the cinnamon over the meat and set aside. Soften the saffron in a little of the hot broth. Beat the eggs in the bowl with 1 tablespoon of lemon juice, add 3–4 tablespoons of broth (which must have cooled slightly), and then beat the eggs back into the main pot of soup. Do not allow to boil.

Heat the olive oil in a separate pan, toss the pheasant in it to brown, and pour over the rest of the lemon juice. Put chunks of the stale bread into bowls, pour over the broth and divide the pheasant between each portion, or put the whole lot in a terrine. Alternatively if you have no stale bread, fry some bread croûtons and add them to the soup.

# **pheasant** with peanut butter, tomatoes and flageolet beans

**Thinking about how the Africans cook guinea fowl with peanuts, I came up with this way for pheasants. Trust me, it's very good.**

2 pheasants, cut into quarters

50g (2oz) butter

2 onions, chopped

450g (1lb) tomatoes, skinned and coarsely chopped,
  or 400ml (14fl oz) tin of chopped tomatoes

125ml (4fl oz) game stock

2 tablespoons peanut butter

1/2 teaspoon chilli powder

400ml (14fl oz) tin of flageolet beans or 450g (1lb) borlotti beans

salt and pepper

Season the pheasant with salt and pepper. In a heavy casserole heat the butter and brown the pheasant all over. Remove from the pan, and fry the onions until coloured slightly. Return the pheasant pieces to the pan and add the tomatoes (if using tinned include the juice), the stock and peanut butter. Bring to the boil, stirring well to mix in the peanut butter. Add salt, pepper and chilli powder, cover and simmer for 15 minutes. If you are using fresh beans, bring them to the boil in lightly salted water and cook for 10 minutes; drain and add the beans to the pan, cover again, and cook for a further 30 minutes, or until the pheasant is cooked. If you are using tinned beans, just tip them in and cook for 30 minutes. Transfer to a dish and, if there is too much juice, boil to reduce, then pour the sauce over the pheasant and serve with potatoes.

# pheasant chitarnee

My grandmother's second husband, who had the wonderful name of Ezekial Manasseh, came from the Sephardic Community in Calcutta. When he came to Singapore his mother sent a cook with him who used to prepare this dish with chicken; as my father shot quite well we had endless pheasants so my mother translated it to pheasant.

6 onions, finely chopped

3 tablespoons olive oil

3 cloves garlic, crushed

2.5cm (1in) ginger, finely chopped

1 teaspoon turmeric

1 tablespoon fresh coriander, chopped or 1 teaspoon, ground

6 green cardamom pods or 1 teaspoon, ground

1–2 red chillies, finely chopped

2 pheasants

400g (14oz) tin of chopped tomatoes

2 tablespoons wine vinegar

salt and pepper

Cook the onions gently in the oil until they are golden. Add the garlic, ginger, tumeric, coriander, cardomom and chillies and cook a little longer.

Cut the pheasants into serving portions and add to the pan to sauté, turning occasionally for about 20 minutes. Add the tomatoes and the vinegar and cook for 30 minutes until the pheasant is well coated with sauce, and the sauce is not too runny. If the dish is too sharp you may add a pinch of sugar. Serve with rice.

# pheasant with cremona mustard

Cremona mustard is that splendid Italian confection of glacée fruits in clear mustard liquid. Bizarre to us, if we receive it as presents from avant garde friends we recycle it as a present or open it, wonder at it, then throw it away. However it is very good to stuff a pheasant with, as the Futurist Fascist poet Marinetti tells us. I owe this translation to dear Robin Weir from his book *The Compleat Mustard*.

2 tablespoons Mostardo di Cremona *and a little extra syrup*

1 brace of pheasant with giblets

125g (4oz) butter

4 rashers back bacon

150ml (5fl oz) sweetish white wine

1 tablespoon flour

2 shallots, finely chopped

3 strips lemon peel

1 sprig of thyme

lemon juice

salt and pepper

Chop the mostardo fruits quite small. Chop the pheasant livers and add them to the fruits. Mix with the butter and chill until firm. Preheat the oven to 220°C/425°F/gas 7. Smear extra butter under the pheasant breasts and paint them with syrup. Cut the fruited butter in two and place half in the cavity of each bird. Season and lard with bacon. Put the pheasants in a roasting tin and pour over the wine. Roast for 45 minutes to 1 hour, depending on the birds. Baste frequently and add a little more wine if the bottom of the pan is getting dry. 10 minutes before they are done remove the bacon and reserve; dust the pheasants with flour and return to the oven to brown. Whilst the birds are cooking, make the stock with the giblets, shallots, lemon peel and thyme. Transfer the birds to a serving dish and keep warm. Add the pan juices to the strained stock, sharpen with lemon juice and serve.

## claypot pheasant

I remember my mother's excitement when she bought a claypot which had just come onto the market. For some reason they never took off in Britain, but they are still around and can be easily picked up in charity shops. In fact they are a simple way of cooking, and if the marketers had not tried to promote them as 'healthy', they would probably have done rather well. They are very similar to the old French daube pots which are also made of terracotta clay. In any event they are good for cooking pheasants. If you don't have one use a heavy casserole dish. If you don't have or want anchovies, replace them with 1/2 teaspoon of salt and, for the capers, you can replace them with a squeeze of lemon juice.

6 potatoes
1 leek
110g (4oz) celeriac
2 parsnips
275g (10 oz) Jerusalem artichokes
pepper
3 anchovies
1 tablespoon capers
1 pheasant
2 glasses dry white wine
salt

Preheat the oven to 220°C/425°F/gas 7.

Clean the vegetables and cut them into pieces. Place them in the pot and sprinkle with pepper and a layer of anchovy fillets and capers. Rub the pheasant well with salt and pepper and place on the vegetables. Pour over the wine and cook for 1 1/2 hours.

## pheasant with sauerkraut

This Alsation recipe is a very good way of using up old birds. It is also useful for supper parties because you can do all the simmering early, and then just put it in the oven before dinner. I happily use 2 pheasants to this amount of sauerkraut.

25g (1oz) goose fat
1 pheasant, barded
1 large onion, finely chopped
900g (2lb) sauerkraut, rinsed and squeezed
225ml (8fl oz) white wine
225ml (8fl oz) Madeira
225ml (8fl oz) game or chicken stock
150g (5oz) streaky bacon, cut into strips
salt and pepper

Melt half the goose fat in a pan and lightly brown the pheasant all over. Remove the pheasant to a plate. Add the onions to the pan and brown them lightly. Add the sauerkraut, both wines, stock and a pinch of salt and pepper. Return the pheasant to the pan and simmer gently, covered, for 1 hour. Preheat the oven to 190°C/375°F/gas 5. Transfer to a greased casserole, add the bacon, cover and cook for 30–40 minutes. Season and serve.

# circassian **pheasant**

The Circassians are from the Caucasus which is the birthplace of the pheasant. Although this dish is usually made with chicken, it struck me that they had pheasant before they had chicken, and it works very well. Don't tell me you don't have access to walnuts – try your health food shop –  and if all else fails the baking section of your supermarket! This is a good dish for using up old cock birds; as I have been heard to say there is a lot of good in an old cock. If you prefer you can poach the pheasant for less time, carve it and pour the sauce over the slices.

*2 pheasants*
*1 onion, roughly sliced*
*1 leek, chopped*
*6 allspice berries*
*10 black peppercorns*
*3 bay leaves*

For the sauce:
*110g (4oz) white bread, crusts off*
*125ml (4fl oz) milk*
*6 cloves garlic*
*175g (6oz) chopped walnuts*
*small bunch of parsley, chopped*
*1 tablespoon walnut oil (olive will do)*
*salt and pepper*

Put the pheasants in a large saucepan with the onion, leek, allspice, peppercorns and bay leaves and enough water to cover it all. Bring to the boil and simmer very gently for 1 hour or until the meat falls off the bones. Take the birds from the pot and remove the meat, discarding the skin and bones. Cut the meat into strips. Turn up the heat under the broth and boil for 15–20 minutes to reduce. Check the seasoning and strain.

Soak the bread in the milk for 30 minutes. Squeeze out well. In a mortar, pound the garlic and walnuts to a paste (alternatively you can do this in a food processor), add the parsley and the oil and pound a bit more. Add the bread, season and mix until it is all blended together. Transfer to a bowl and mix in spoonfuls of broth until the mixture is the consistency of mayonnaise.

Put the  pheasant on a dish and pour over the sauce.

## calabrian **pheasant** with macaroni

If you have pheasant, you often have it until it's coming out your ears, so this is an excellent way of using it up for a jolly supper.

3 tablespoons oil

1 large onion, chopped

450g (1lb) uncooked pheasant meat, cut into bite-size pieces

900g (2lb) tomatoes, peeled, seeded and chopped

225ml (8fl oz) dry white wine

1 packet macaroni

parmesan or hard cheese to grate

salt and pepper

In a heavy casserole heat the oil and brown the onion and the pheasant meat for about 10 minutes. Season, add the tomatoes and the wine and simmer for 45 minutes. Cook the pasta *al dente,* toss with the sauce and serve with the grated cheese.

## **pheasant** with noodles and horseradish cream

This is a recipe invented by my friend Marianne More-Gordon, a most frugal but excellent cook whose collection of recipes, *Scraping from a Scottish Kitchen,* is eagerly awaited by the cognoscenti. Don't overcook the pheasant breasts – they should be slightly pink – they aren't chicken so you won't have any problems with bugs!

75g (3oz) butter

4 pheasant breasts

4 shallots, chopped

1 clove garlic

2 tablespoons creamed horseradish, or 1 tablespoon strong horseradish, grated

juice of $^1/_2$ lemon

150ml (5fl oz) double cream

1 packet black or green Italian noodles or make your own chestnut noodles

small bunch of parsley, chopped

salt and pepper

Heat the butter in a heavy frying pan and sauté the pheasant breasts until they are sealed. Remove them and sauté the shallots and the garlic until the shallots are pale gold; remove and discard the garlic clove.

Stir the horseradish into the shallots and add a tablespoon or so of water and the lemon juice. Season. Return the pheasant breasts to the pan, add the cream and cover and cook gently for 15–20 minutes or until the breasts are just cooked. If the sauce is too wet, remove the breasts and zap up the heat to reduce; if it's too dry, add a little more cream or some dry white wine. Cook the noodles according to the instructions and drain. Serve the noodles with the pheasant and sprinkle chopped parsley on top.

# roast **pheasant** with truffled cheese

# issy's **pheasants**

It is not that unusual to insert soft cheese beneath the skin and over the breast of a pheasant as a medium for containing herbs and flavourings and for keeping the bird moist. I love the combination of truffles and pheasants, but nowadays they are horribly expensive so I often buy those little Italian cheeses flavoured with truffle scrapings (*ceasa di truffata*), and eventually realised that if I used one of these I would get less expensive truffled pheasant.

*1 pheasant*
*1 large shallot or small onion*
*1 ceasa di truffata*
*110g (4oz) butter*
*flour*
*white wine*
*salt and pepper*

Carefully insert your hand under the skin covering the breast of the bird and loosen it. Peel the shallot or onion and make a couple of deep incisions. Insert into the cavity of the pheasant. Carefully spread the cheese under the skin and over the breast of the pheasant. Season the pheasant, rub with softened butter and wrap in tinfoil. Leave to stand for 1 hour to allow the truffles to spread their flavour.

Preheat the oven to 220°C/425°F/gas 7. Roast the birds for 40 minutes. Fold back the tinfoil and allow to brown for a further 10 minutes. Remove the pheasant to a dish and thicken the juices with a little flour. Then add some white wine to make a gravy; if you have any champagne hanging about that is even better.

My friend and colleague Isabel Rutherford is a splendid cook, and various of her recipes adorn my earlier works. This is her pheasant dish and, like all her recipes, it is deceptively easy and very delicious. She cooks every year for A. A. Gill – what higher recommendation do you need!

*175g (6oz) butter*
*4 young pheasants*
*600ml (1 pint) double cream*
*450g (1lb) frozen peas*
*salt and pepper*

In a large pan with a closely fitting lid melt the butter. Season the birds and place breast down in the butter and cook for 15 minutes. Turn onto the other side and cook for another 15 minutes. Turn onto their backs and pour over the double cream. Cover tightly, and cook gently for 30 minutes.

Cook the peas, and arrange them on a carving dish. Remove the birds from the pan and whisk the liquid vigorously to mix the cream into the pan juices; allow to thicken slightly and check the seasoning. Carve the birds, arrange them on the peas and pour over the sauce.

# quail

These comic little birds, which look like miniature partridges, are summer migrants from North Africa and the few that breed here are rarely seen further than half way up the country. Quail are now protected in Britain and virtually all quail and quail eggs eaten in this country will have been reared domestically. Quail farming has become big business in Europe with France alone consuming thirty thousand tonnes of quail meat. There is also a vibrant quail farming industry in India supplying the Far East. British consumers are more cautious and the market is pretty well-saturated at seventy tonnes. Quail are very shy, secretive creatures, whose habitat is long grass, young cereal crops or tussocky heathland, preferably on chalky soil. Their dapple-brown plumage and striped, black and white head is such perfect camouflage that quail are generally heard rather than seen. The cock bird makes a very distinctive liquid three syllable call, which sounds not unlike 'wet my lip,' their Norfolk nickname, and the hen answers with a seductive, cooing 'bru bru'. Quail visitors fluctuate from year to year depending on weather conditions and a loss of their food source on the continent. These infrequent 'quail years' used to be an unexpected bonus for those who made their living trapping birds for the market, as quail were a delicacy very much in demand. Netters used to call quail by using a quail pipe, which resembled a miniature set of bagpipes, with the chanter made from a cat's thigh bone. The male call was answered by copying the female and vice versa until, according to Nicholas Cox, writing in the seventeenth century, both sexes would 'pursue the call with such greediness that they will play and skip about you, nay run over you... and will gaze and listen till the net is cast over them.' Netting quail has been banned here since 1937, although quail pipes are still used in parts of Italy.

Quail (*Coturnix coturnix*) have a distribution that extends across Europe, Eurasia, Australasia, Africa and North America (where the species are slightly larger and non-migratory). Quail migrat-ions in spring from North Africa remain one of nature's phenomena, with clouds of these little creatures, normally so reluctant to fly, crossing the Mediterranean at night on their short, stubby wings. Along the whole coastline, quail catchers would arrive weeks in advance of the migration and stake out claims to individual areas of shore. Exhausted quail were scooped up in their thousands, cleaned, salted and sent in barrels to Russia, the Lebanon and Syria. In 1900, the Bishop of Capri enjoyed an income of over one thousand pounds from quail caught on the tiny island. Others were packed live in specially designed crates to be taken inland, and hund-reds were sent like this from France, by relays of coaches, to Leadenhall market. On their return migration, in August and September, North African quail catchers were waiting to reap the harvest, as they had done since biblical times. Possibly the earliest written record of quail is in the book of Exodus; twice the Israelites were saved from starvation by the arrival of clouds of quail which 'covered the camp'.

Depending on their migration density, quail are a popular game bird across Europe, particularly in the old Eastern Bloc countries of Slovenia, Croatia and Hungary where quail, walked-up over pointers, are among the quarry species that have enabled these countries to develop lucrative sporting tourist industries. America has six quail species – mountain, scaled or blue quail, Gambels, California, Montezumas and bobwhite, that have adapted to climatic conditions ranging from semi-desert to densely wooden mountain country, with bobwhite being the most populous game bird of the south and east. Various attempts have been made to establish bobwhite quail in this country as an alternative game bird since the 1800s, but apart from a tiny population in East Anglia, none has survived our wet springs. Quail are arguably the most cherished and important American game bird whose numbers have declined in the last twenty five years due to habitat losses, as a result of agricultural expansion. Quails Unlimited, a conservation body formed in 1981, has work-ed tirelessly to ensure that habitat preservation is a central issue in protecting quail numbers.

'As fat as a quail' is an old fashioned expression referring to the thick subcutaneous layer of fat (so prized by cooks) that they store for their twice yearly migrations. Quail also retain body heat to the extent that in China, we are told by the great ornithologist, the Rev. C. A. Johns, 'they are said to be carried about in winter by the natives, to keep their hands warm'. I find the idea of a pet quail hand warmer absolutely enchanting and can only assume the Reverend's almost palpable note of disapproval had much to do with writing *British Birds in their Haunts*, at the same time as the Boxer Rebellion of 1905.

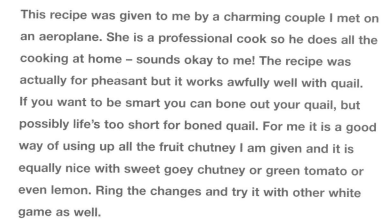

**To cook quail's eggs**

Bring to the boil in cold water and cook for 4 minutes. Plunge into cold water and peel. Eat with celery salt.

**Ageing**

Quail in this country are mostly imported and ageing isn't required.

**Hanging**

No need.

**Plucking**

The feathers are very small and it is a tiresome job but not difficult.

**Drawing**

As for pheasant (see pages 24-25).

**Roasting**

Quails are so small that they tend to dry out if roasted. Far better is to cook them over coals, when they take 15-20 minutes and are much juicier.

Allow 1–2 quails per person.

This recipe was given to me by a charming couple I met on an aeroplane. She is a professional cook so he does all the cooking at home – sounds okay to me! The recipe was actually for pheasant but it works awfully well with quail. If you want to be smart you can bone out your quail, but possibly life's too short for boned quail. For me it is a good way of using up all the fruit chutney I am given and it is equally nice with sweet goey chutney or green tomato or even lemon. Ring the changes and try it with other white game as well.

*1 or possibly 2 quail per person*
*25g (1oz) butter per quail*
*1 tablespoon fruit chutney per quail*
*salt and pepper*

Preheat the oven to 170ºC/325ºF/ gas 3.

Rub the quail all over with butter and salt and pepper and put a small piece of butter in each bird. Fill the cavity with half a tablespoon of chutney. Lay each quail on a piece of parchment or tinfoil and smear the remaining half tablespoon of chutney over the top. Wrap up the package and roast for 30 minutes. Either turn out or let people unwrap their own.

# thessalian **quail**

The lemons from this part of Greece are particularly highly scented and the dish becomes infused with their scent. We can't quite hope for that with supermarket lemons but this is still a delicious recipe. You can also cook wild duck in this fashion.

*6 quails*
*juice of 1 lemon*
*4 tablespoons olive oil*
*2 bay leaves*
*1–2 sprigs of thyme*
*4 juniper berries, crushed*
*3 cloves*
*rind of 1/2 orange, cut into julienne strips*
*50g (2oz) fresh breadcrumbs*
*1 onion, chopped*
*3 tablespoons flat parsley*
*50g (2oz) pinenuts, toasted*
*12 Greek olives*
*1 glass red wine*
*salt and pepper*

Rub the birds inside and out with half the lemon juice, olive oil and salt and pepper. Crumble the bay leaves together with the thyme, juniper berries, cloves and orange rind.

Preheat the oven to 190°C/375°F/gas 5. Heat the remaining olive oil in a pan and gently fry the breadcrumbs. Add all the other ingredients except the olives and wine to the breadcrumbs. Cook gently for a little longer and use to stuff the quails. There will be mixture left over; arrange this in an ovenproof dish and put the stuffed quails on top. Sprinkle the olives and the wine on top and cook in the oven until the quails are cooked – about 15–20 minutes.

## quail stuffed with feta and fenugreek

Here is a Cypriot recipe which uses fenugreek; it grows wild on the Trodos mountains of Cyprus. The Indians use fenugreek extensively, calling it *methi*. Feta is made from local ewes' milk. Try and buy mature feta or another similar ewes' milk cheese.

*bunch of fenugreek*
*225g (8oz) feta cheese*
*6 quails*
*oil from cheese or olive oil*
*salt and pepper*

Chop the fenugreek and the cheese together and season. Rub the quails inside and out with salt and pepper. Heat some oil in a heavy pan and brown the quails all over. Remove and leave to cool a little. When the birds are cool enough to handle, stuff with the feta mixture.

Preheat the oven to 180°C/350°F/gas 4. Return the quails to the pan, which should still have some oil remaining, otherwise add a little more. Cover and cook in the oven for 30 minutes, or until the birds are cooked right through.

## quail cooked in clay

This method of cooking, still found in the hills of Cyprus and remoter parts of Greece, is a perfect way of cooking quails and great fun to serve. You can buy clay in an art shop or builder's yard. Each bird will need about 50g (2oz) of clay. Don't roll it, but flatten it out with the heel of your hand, and remember to keep it under a damp cloth or it will dry out. Alternatively you can use parchment instead of clay.

*large bunch of mint, chopped*
*6 shallots, chopped*
*6 quails*
*olive oil*
*sufficient amount of modelling clay*
*salt and pepper*

Preheat the oven to 220°C/425°F/gas 7.

Mix the mint and shallots, season well and stuff the quails with the mixture. Rub the outside of the quails with salt and pepper and olive oil and wrap each quail carefully in a lump of clay. Seal each parcel carefully.

Put the quails in the oven and bake until the clay is hard – about 20 minutes.

Serve with a little tack hammer. When the mould is broken, out will come your perfectly-cooked quail.

# grouse

There are eighteen species of grouse, ten of them in North America: ruffed and spruce grouse in the east, Franklin's in the west and sage grouse across the prairie belt. There are sharp-tailed and pinnated grouse, otherwise known as prairie chicken, blue grouse of the Rocky mountain forests and Pacific coast, and rock, willow and white-tailed ptarmigan that change their plumage from mottled brown in summer, to white in winter. All, except the resinous tasting Franklin's, are pursued by connoisseurs of dark, gamey meat, from the gulf of Mexico to sub-arctic Canada. The remaining eight species are found in Eurasia. Capercaillie, the big turkey-like 'cock of the woods', black grouse, willow and rock ptarmigan, can be found throughout northern Europe, from Scandinavia to western Siberia. Hazel grouse have a dristribution that extends

right across the central land mass, wherever there is suitable forest habitat, from the coast of Sweden to Japan.

In Britain and southern Ireland we have capercaillie, black grouse, rock ptarmigan and red grouse. Capercaillie became extinct in Britain and Ireland at the end of the eighteenth century, but were reintroduced from Sweden to the eastern Highlands in 1837. Considered practically inedible, their numbers are diminishing due to habitat loss and they are now a protected species. Black grouse, with their beautiful lyre-shaped tail feathers are extinct in Ireland and relatively scarce in Scotland, northern England and Wales. They are delicious eating but most sportsmen now avoid shooting them. Ptarmigan are restricted to the highest and most inhospitable areas of the Scottish

highlands, rarely seen below 610m (2000ft); they are the same species found in Alaska, Canada and northern Russia. Their eating value has as much to do with the extreme physical labour involved in bagging them as their meat, flavoured by the alpine plants they eat. Our other grouse species and one that is unique to Britain and Ireland, is the red grouse (*Lagopus scoticus*) which is both internationally famous, and a vitally important element of our upland rural economy.

Cock grouse, in dappled russet plumage, explode out of the heather in spring, barking a challenge as they mark out mating territories with swooping, wing beating displays of aggression. Lighter coloured hens feign injury by trailing a wing to draw predators away from their chicks in early summer. Family coveys whistle overhead with a rush of wings in late summer, packing together in the autumn and splitting up again into pairs in the middle of winter. For nearly thirty years the annual cycle of these delightfully bellicose little birds were as much a part of my farming life as the hardy Black Face sheep with whom they shared the bleak heather moorland. The farm carried two hundred breeding pairs and their welfare, during extreme weather, was as much a concern to me as the hefted sheep.

The natural habitat of red grouse is heather, and this is also their food, the young shoots, flowers and seed heads, giving them their unique flavour. Primarily it is ling heather, but bell and cross-leave heather, if around, make up a diet which is varied at certain times of year with blueberry, cranberry, bog myrtle and other seasonal hill herbage. Grouse are completely wild, and attempts to rear them artificially have never been successful. Any increase in population can only be achieved by careful heather management and predator control.

There are red grouse in Ireland, on Dartmoor and Exmoor and some in Wales, where unfortunately the moors have been ruined by massive conifer plantations, but the main distribution is in the north of England and Scotland. Here, on the manicured carpet of heather, which tourists find so attractive when it blooms purple in late summer, we have a classic example of farming, field sports and conservation, each playing their part in preserving a wild bird population. Before the Industrial Revolution of the late eighteenth and nineteenth century, much of the uplands of northern England and Scotland were barren heaths covered in hawthorn, scrub birch and conifer, with gorse, thistles and bracken, giving way to old, coarse heather of little nutritional value on higher ground, and peaty soil. Comparatively few grouse survived these harsh surroundings. There was never enough food to support large numbers and, as ground nesters, they were vulnerable to a largely, uncontrolled predator population. Occasionally grouse made their way to the table either through hawking or netting, in much the same way that ptarmigan are still netted in Siberia today.

A rapidly-expanding urban population, the growth of colonies and an interminable period of

warfare led to increased demands for raw materials, particularly grain and wool. Much traditional pasture came under the plough and flockmasters pushed north in search of new grazings, reclaiming vast areas of newly enclosed heathland using the oldest form of agriculture – burning on a rotational basis to create new growth. That these fresh grazings were also benefiting the grouse population went largely unnoticed except by resident landowners and sporting eccentrics like Colonel Thornton, whose charming *Sporting Tour through the Northern Parts of England and Great Part of the Highlands of Scotland* of 1784, no doubt inspired that great sportsman, Peter Hawker, who went north and over the Border out of curiosity in 1812, complaining bitterly all the way. His description of execrable roads, verminous inns, Herculean struggles through deep heather and largely unsuccessful attempts to walk up Muir Game makes hugely

entertaining reading. Later enthusiasts were advised, in Thomas's *Shooters' Guide* of 1816, to copy the locals and 'to take this diversion on horseback, which of course, very much lessens the fatigue; and for this purpose Galloways or ponies are used, so trained that they will stand still with the bridle on their necks, while the sportsman takes aim and shoots'.

A western rail route to Edinburgh via Carlisle opened in 1848, and the eastern via Newcastle and York, two years later. There were connecting routes to Perth, Aberdeen, Inverness and Fort William. The north of England and Scotland, which had hitherto taken days of discomfort to reach, were now accessible within hours. Rumours that Scotland was a sporting paradise proved true. There was breathtaking scenery. The rivers heaved with salmon and the estuaries with wildfowl. There were partridges, hares and pheasants on the low ground. Where

graziers had burnt there were grouse on the heather moors and, with the collapse of the wool price, many sheep flocks had been taken off the high ground and red deer were coming back. Best of all, Queen Victoria had given Scotland a social cachet by buying the Balmoral Estate on Deeside in 1850.

With the rationalisation of the restrictive, archaic game laws in 1831 and improvements in gun technology over the next two decades, shooting had become enormously popular and now wealthy Victorians poured north. Scottish landowners, facing ruin with the collapse of sheep rents, were only too happy to let or sell their estates. The Twelfth of August became a great day in the social calendar and recognised as the official date that Queen Victoria and her court were in residence at Balmoral. From the beginning of the month, the nine hour Expresses that, by 1862 were leaving King's Cross daily at 10am, were crammed with people.

This scene was recorded in two magnificent paintings by George Earl (see page 42–43). The first, Going North, captures all the bustle, excitement and sense of imminent departure of early rail travel in a group of passengers waiting for the Express at King's Cross to take them north for the Glorious Twelfth. There are the piles of leather trunks, gun cases and fly rods. The gun dogs, pointers, setters and spaniels have their own straw strewn carriage. A little girl, daughter of the lady cloaked in red and gentleman in London clothes, is being watched by her Indian *ayah* and, wearing a fore-and-aft hat; a Highland game keeper is looking noble and dignified. In the second, the same party wait on Perth station for the return journey. Amongst the luggage are grouse, black cock and red deer antlers. A railway guard carries a hare and a wicker basket of salmon. The gun dogs are now looked after by

grooms. Our keeper has come to see the gentry off and the significance of his presence in both pictures is clearer to us. Without his knowledge of the landscape and its wildlife Scotland's sporting tourist industry, which saved the Highlands from bankruptcy, would never have been possible.

The new shooting tenants had much to learn. Far too little heather was burnt and grouse numbers began to dwindle. It took several years of trial and error before a policy of burning moors on a fifteen year rotation – in other words one fifteenth of the total area each year – became established. A properly managed moor should have an evenly distributed mosaic pattern of different ages and lengths of heather. This ensures that sheep graze evenly, and grouse and other ground-nesting moorland birds have the depth of cover required to nest in safety from aerial predators. Space between patches of longer heather is needed for their chicks to learn to fly and there has to be a plentiful supply of essential plant food. Muirburn is strictly governed by legislation. Below 550m (1500ft) it may only be carried out between 1st October and 15th April. There is an extension of a further fifteen days on ground above that altitude, and for both cases in a particularly wet spring, an extension of another fifteen days may be granted by the Secretary of State. The most important factor is to stop burning before ground nesting birds start laying their eggs. Driven grouse, hugging the contours of the landscape and travelling at 100kmph (60mph) with the wind under their tails towards a line of butts, has been described as the 'Sport of Kings'. Sportsmen come from all over the world to experience the ultimate shooting challenge. Carefully controlled shooting plays as large a part in maintaining a vigorous grouse population as heather burning and predator control.

The health of any quantity of animals is the balance between stocking rates and available food. It is the same with the sheep and grouse on heather moorland. At home, we calculated one ewe to two acres and one breeding pair of grouse to ten acres. Leaving aside natural disasters, like a blizzard in early May, a hen will rear an average of six young and, allowing for a percentage of losses to foxes, stoats, weasels and that black devil, the hooded crow, we need to reduce the grouse stock by five hundred brace during the season to leave a breeding nucleus of two hundred pairs. There is a further aspect which is equally important. Grouse, like all animals that survive in a harsh environment, are extremely territorial. As they get old, cock grouse become increasingly aggressive, ever extending their mating territory as they drive younger cock birds away. Grouse are monogamous and, unless the old birds are culled, the breeding stock will diminish. At the beginning of the season, grouse fly in family coveys led by old birds which tend to be the first ones shot. The same principle applies to grouse walked up over pointers. A rule of thumb is to shoot the first and last pair of a covey. That way, the old birds get taken out, leaving healthy stock.

There is something magic about grouse, they are such strange birds and resist any attempt at domestication thereby preserving the heather moorlands. My mother had a great tradition of eating grouse at the start of the season and, whilst her friends went to the Savoy, she would cart us all off to the Hilton where she said they cooked grouse beautifully. They did, but I suspect they only cooked them for her, and as she was known to double the bill by way of a tip if she couldn't work out 15%, they did so with great care and attention. A lot of old grouse is

discarded because people don't know what to do with it so I have tried to include a number of recipes for old and middle-aged grouse. The flavour of older birds is wonderful.

### Ageing

The Bursa Test to the rescue again, if the toothpick goes in 1cm ($^1$/$_2$in), it is a young bird and you should do nothing with it but roast it in my opinion. Another test is to look at the primaries; if these are rounded and similar to the other feathers, it is an old bird. If it is a bird of the previous year, the primaries will still be pointed, but they will look tattered and faded. Adult grouse shed their toenails between July and September, so if the nail is becoming detached it is an old bird; also look for a transverse scar across the top of the nail where the shed nail was attached; if it is there it is an old bird. Another test is to break the lower beak or crush the skull if the bird is young, but this is not always as reliable, as diet is a variant here.

### Hanging

If the bird is young and the weather is warm it will not need more than 2 days. Birds shot on the 12th are eaten right away and are perfectly good. No more than 4 days for young birds, and as long as you choose for older ones.

### Plucking and Drawing

As for pheasant (see page 24–25).

### Roasting

Put a piece of seasoned butter in each bird and cover the breasts with fat bacon or barding fat. Sauté the liver of the bird in butter, mash it and spread the mixture onto a piece of white toast. Roast at 190°C/375°F/gas 5 for 30–40 minutes, depending on how rare you like it. Serve with bread sauce, gravy, game chips and watercress salad. Allow one bird per person.

## buttered grouse

This cold grouse dish is very good for a shooting picnic. It is a Yorkshire dish which always endears it to me. All grouse moors are beautiful (on a fine day) but it was in Yorkshire that a group of antis was trying to disrupt a grouse shoot and got lost when the mist came down. They rang the local constabulary for help on their mobile phones to be told, 'It's quite warm and we're very busy, ring us again in the morning.' They spent a bedraggled, hungry night on the moors and straggled home at daybreak!

4 blades of mace
2 brace of grouse
110g (4oz) fat pork or bacon
cayenne
225g (8oz) butter
salt and pepper

Preheat the oven to 200°C/400°F/gas 6.

Place a blade of mace on the breast of each bird and tie a piece of pork or bacon fat over it. Place the grouse in a greased roasting tin, season and roast them for 10 minutes. Reduce the heat to 180°C/350°F/gas 4 and roast for a further 20–30 minutes depending on the age of the birds.

When the grouse are cool enough to handle, cut them into portions (half a grouse) and place in a pie dish. Add the butter to the drippings in the roasting pan, season with salt, pepper and cayenne, and pour over the birds. Serve cold with crusty bread.

## potted grouse

This is not only a way of using up old grouse, but provides a delicious starter and is equally effective with any other game bird. Serve it on hot buttered toast or thin oatcakes; it also makes an excellent sandwich filler. It should last for up to three weeks in a fridge or cold larder.

4 grouse, with giblets
Seasoning: 1 tablespoon of salt, pepper, cayenne mixed together
300ml (1/2 pint) game stock
150g (5oz) softened butter
110g (4oz) melted clarified butter
1 tablespoon port

Preheat the oven to 170°C/325°F/gas 3.

Cut the birds in half and rub the fleshy side with the seasoning. Put the giblets in a heavy casserole and lay the birds on top. Add the stock, cover and cook in the oven for 2 hours, or until the flesh falls from the bones.

When it's cool enough to handle, remove the meat. I shred it into small pieces but you can do the next step in a blender. Mix the butter, grouse meat, port and some of the strained cooking liquid. Press into small pots or one large one.

Chill, then pour on the clarified butter and leave to set. Serve at room temperature.

## casseroled grouse with marmalade

For this recipe you need a dark rich marmalade. If you are making your own, make sure you include black treacle or brown sugar. This is another method for using old grouse. I was aiming for a grouse and kumquat recipe, but it tasted of very little so I bunged in the marmalade. Nowadays I omit the kumquats.

4 onions
2 old grouse
175g (6oz) smoked bacon, cut into cubes
sprig of thyme
300ml (1/2 pint) stout or dark beer
3 tablespoons marmalade
1 small glass dry sherry
1 tablespoon butter
small bunch of young turnips, well scrubbed
salt and pepper

Preheat the oven to 180°C/350°F/gas 4.

Chop the onions into quarters and put them into a heavy based casserole. Cut the grouse in half and add to the pot. Put in the bacon and thyme, and season. Pour on the beer, bring to the boil on top of the stove, cover, and put into the oven for 1 hour. Mix together the marmalade, sherry and butter, and add to the casserole. Then add the turnips – if they are truly young they will not need peeling; if not, peel them.

Return the casserole to the oven and cook for another hour. If the dish is drying out, add a bit more beer.

## grouse pie

This is a good pie for using up old grouse. The addition of steak to such pies stems from the Georgian age and enriches the gravy. It doesn't do much for the steak, which I tend to discard, but then I do like my steak so a good vet can bring it back to life!

brace of old grouse
450g (1lb) rump or topside
600ml (1 pint) game stock
50g (2oz) bacon, diced
2 hard-boiled eggs, halved
pinch of mace
pinch of nutmeg
6 juniper berries, crushed
1 tablespoon sherry
50g (2oz) rough puff or shortcrust pastry
beaten egg to glaze
salt and pepper

Preheat the oven to 170°C/325°F/gas 3.

Divide the grouse into quarters, and cut the steak into 2.5cm (1in) cubes. Arrange the grouse and the steak in a 1.8 litre (3 pint) pie dish, add the stock, and scatter the bacon and hard-boiled eggs on top. Add the spices, juniper berries and season.

Cover the dish with tinfoil and cook in the oven for 1 hour. Allow the dish to cool slightly and then add the sherry. Roll out the pastry and cover the pie. Zap the oven up to 220°C/425°F/gas 7. Make a slit in the pastry to allow the steam to escape, and brush with egg.

Cook for a further 30 minutes or so until the pastry is golden. Serve with greens and mashed potato.

# carpaccio of **grouse**

I was shooting at Copstall in Wiltshire, the lovely estate that Paul van Gilsengen and his partner Caroline Tisdale have returned to wonderful organic conditions with wild bison, boar and hens that see off the deer hounds. After a splendid day's shooting Max Hastings remarked that he loved raw grouse, so Michel Roux and I leapt at this and Andy the young chef prepared some carpaccio. It is truly excellent.

*1 grouse breast per person*
*olive oil*
*lemon juice*
*cream of horseradish or freshly grated horseradish or wasabi*
*salt and ground pepper*

Remove the breasts from the grouse, wrap in cling film and freeze for 40 minutes to 1 hour.

Remove from the freezer, unwrap the grouse and slice as thinly as possible with a very sharp knife. Arrange the slices on a dish and scatter with salt and ground pepper, pour over some good olive oil and some lemon juice and leave to stand for 10 minutes. Dot with your chosen variant of horseradish.

Serve as a starter with a little rocket salad or on thin oatcakes as a canapé.

# hazel **grouse** in a russian style

This recipe comes from Elana Molokhovet's *A Gift for Young Housewives*, a sort of Mrs Beeton for Russia, but the truffles and caviar have been omitted. You can now buy crayfish from China and whilst you may well ask what are they fed on remember they, like all crustacea, are carrion eaters.

*4 hazel grouse*
*50g (2oz) flour*
*50g (2oz) butter*
*stock*
*1 glass Madeira or medium sherry*
*6 fresh field mushrooms, roughly chopped*
*1 egg, lightly beaten*
*breadcrumbs made with stale bread, not bought!*
*oil*
*salt and pepper*

For the ragoût:
*12 field mushrooms*
*2 tablespoons butter*
*12 crayfish tails, cooked and cleaned*
*truffle oil*
*lemon juice*

Remove the breasts from the birds as supremes – that is, including some of the wings by cutting them off at the first joint. Make a slit in the underside of the breasts for the stuffing. Mix a roux with the flour and butter, and add enough stock to make a thick sauce. Season and cook a little longer. Add the Madeira and mushrooms; bring to the boil and cook for 5 minutes. Stuff the breasts with this mixture and sew up. Dip them in egg and breadcrumbs and fry them, or dip them in egg white and deep-fry them. Arrange on a platter and fill the centre with crayfish tails and field mushrooms cooked in butter, season with truffle oil and lemon juice.

# grouse pudding

The flavour of old grouse is fantastic but tough as old boots so here is a recipe to reap the benefits without the shoe leather. The original recipe cooks for 4–6 hours, adding more stock after 2 hours but unless your grouse died of arthritis or you have lost all your teeth and can't afford false ones, I think this is *de trop*.

For the suet pastry:
*450g (1lb) plain flour*
*pinch of salt*
*450g (1lb) finely chopped suet*
*600ml (1 pint) water*

*2 old grouse*
*450g (1lb) beef or venison skirt*
*25g (1oz) seasoned flour*
*900g (2lb) suet pastry*
*1 onion, chopped*
*2 field mushrooms, chopped*
*2 tablespoons port, Madeira or medium sherry*
*300ml (1/2 pint) stock*
*salt and pepper*

For the suet pastry rub the flour, salt and suet together and add enough water to form a dough – this can be done in a magimix.

Strip the meat from the grouse and chop it, together with the skirt into cubes and dust with the seasoned flour. Line a 425ml (15fl oz) pudding basin with two-thirds of the pastry. Fill with the meats, the onion and the mushrooms. Add the alcohol and enough stock to cover the meat. Season. Put on a lid of the remaining pastry and tie in a muslin cloth. Steam for 4 hours, or 2 in a pressure cooker. Untie the cloth and flash the top under the grill, or with a salamander for a more attractive presentation, and serve.

# grouse duntreath

If you buy birds later in the season, they are often not in the first flush of youth. This is a really excellent way of cooking such birds, and in fact I know very good shots who prefer this to any other method of roasting grouse. The water has the effect of partially steaming the grouse, and helps break down the fibres.

*1 grouse per person*
*2–3 pieces of apple per person*
*2 streaky bacon rashers per person*
*salt and pepper*

Preheat the oven to 150°C/300°F/gas 2. Season the grouse inside and out. Put a couple of pieces of apple in each bird and wrap well in bacon. Stand the birds in 1cm (1/2in) water and cover with a lid of tinfoil. Roast in the oven for 45 minutes.

Remove the tinfoil lid, pour off the liquid and zap up the oven to 230°C/450°F/gas 8 and roast for 10 minutes more to brown the birds. Serve with the usual trimmings.

# grouse in a rye crust

This came about after I had cooked with Richard Blades at Simpsons for a programme on Samuel Pepys. Richard had the idea of cooking a lamprey pie using a hot water crust made with rye flour, as this is more malleable than the wheaten variety. My friend and butcher Colin Peat of Haddington found me a grouse so old I think it had died of arthritic shock. The end result has a most intense and extraordinary flavour, and is even good for those without teeth! The crust is not for eating but merely a cooking vessel. The word *coffyn*, despite its lugubrious modern connotations, simply means a box in Medieval English; in culinary terms it refers to a thick pastry box, with or without a lid, in which things were cooked and served direct to the table. In this recipe I suggest you bring the pie to the table and slice the top off and dish out the filling. This is a perfect dish for an Aga.

For the crust:

*450g (1lb) rye flour*

*1 level teaspoon salt*

*110g (4oz) lard*

*200ml (7fl oz) water*

*2 very old grouse*

*1 large strong onion*

*1/2 teaspoon nutmeg*

*1/2 teaspoon mace*

*1/2 teaspoon ground cloves*

*110g (4oz) clarified butter*

Sift the flour and salt into a bowl and make a well in the centre. Put the lard and water in a saucepan, heat until the lard melts, and then bring to the boil. Pour the liquid into the flour and mix in quickly to form a pliable dough. Turn onto a floured board and knead until smooth, and use quickly as it hardens up. If you must keep it, do so in a bowl covered with a warm cloth. Raise the pastry by hand to make a large container.

Preheat the oven to 200°C/400°F/gas 6.

Cut the grouse into manageable pieces that will fit in your pie crust. Peel the onion and cut in half widthways. Put one half of the onion, cut side down, in the raised coffyn and place the other half on top. Arrange the pieces of grouse around the onion and add all the seasonings. Pour in the clarified butter and put the lid on the pie. Put into the oven for 30 minutes to set the crust.

Reduce to 150°C/300°F/gas 2 and cook for 4 hours.

# wood pigeon

This remarkable and underrated bird provides meat that competes with any game and a shooting challenge to test the most experienced shot. In fact, a really good shot becomes one because he has wood pigeon to practise on out of season. And what practice it is. A wood pigeon's phenomenal eye sight, speed of reaction and ability to fly at speeds of 80kmph (50mph) enable it to provide opportunities, which to prove successful, require immense concentration and lightning fast eye and hand co-ordination. Whether coming in low towards a field of turnips like fast driven grouse, dropping in to decoys, or skimming the tree tops towards their roosting grounds, pigeons are extremely difficult to shoot.

Wood pigeons or ring doves (*Columba palumbus*) are one of the five species of dove that either live here or migrate from further north: collared doves, turtle doves, rock doves, stock doves and the miserable feral pigeon of our cities. The pretty little collared doves that are often seen round farm buildings, may be shot and make very good eating – more of a starter than a main course. Turtle doves are protected, as are stock doves and rock doves. The poor old feral pigeon is not protected and generally loathed by farmers and city dwellers alike; a sad end to a bird whose ancestors, the rock pigeon, were domesticated over a thousand years ago and were once Europe's mail service.

The 'cushy doo', as we call them in Scotland, with its throbbing soporific song, is one of our more beautiful woodland birds. Their plumage is a wonderful blend of pastel greys, with a semicircular white bar on either wing and at the base of the neck. They have a pink bib, that turns a light purple as the bird matures, dark red legs and beady yellow eyes. They breed three times a year and the squeakers are fed by both parents, on a cheesy smelling, milky curd and later, a goo of macerated vegetable matter. Unlike other birds, the young help themselves to these delicacies from their parents' mouths, rather than being fed by them. It is this high protein feeding, a characteristic of all pigeon species, and the rapid growth rate of their young (squabs) – they are fledged in about a month – that made them such a valuable food source when every manor had its own dovecote.

The problem with wood pigeons is their sheer quantity. In the last two hundred and fifty years we have created the perfect environment for a bird that had previously been present in numbers that were part of an acceptable balance. The European landscape, with its patchwork of woods and farmland, provides wood pigeon with roosting and nesting sights conveniently close to accessible food sources. Every advance in agricultural improvement seems, from a pigeon's point of view, to be done specifically for their benefit and numbers have increased accordingly. Turnips and a green leaf winter bounty provided the first expansion initiative, continually increasing arable production, another. Then came the introduction of clover to improve grass leys. Next came winter sowing and in 1976, oh bliss, subsidised oil seed rape. Something like a million acres of the stuff was planted in the UK, its succulent green leaves sustaining huge winter flocks. Anything from a pea to a potato is fair game to a pigeon. It has been estimated that a thousand pigeons eat, in a week, one ton of food intended for human consumption. Multiply this by a pigeon population, calculated at well over ten million in Britain alone, plus some winter migrants, and you have nearly four hundred thousand tons vanishing out of the food chain. Hardly surprising that pigeons are seen as European farming's principal pest or that man's ingenuity is stretched in attempts to find ways to protect his livelihood. For much of the year, the countryside resounds to the boom of gas operated bird scarers and everything from traditional scarecrows, reflectors that revolve in the wind, kites shaped like a hawk and banger rockets are used, more in hope than expectation, to keep pigeons away from crops. In the hilly countryside around Cava Dei Terreni in Italy, huge nets are suspended between ancient stone towers on either side of the valley tops and released when a flock of pigeons go by.

Shooting is the only really effective method of control, and wood pigeons provide high quality sport either free (most farmers are only too pleased to give responsible people with the right references permission to shoot) or for a fraction of the price game commands. As such, it gives the young and new entrants to shooting a chance to get started and it offers some three hundred thousand pigeon-shooting aficionados, supporting an industry manufacturing ever more sophisticated decoys and camouflaged hides, access to one of nature's finest foods. Wood pigeon are also one of the quarry species attractions on offer from the sporting tourism industries that have become so important to the old Eastern Bloc countries.

Except in the far north, wood pigeon have a distribution that extends into India, with vast flocks of them migrating across central and western Europe to winter in Spain, Italy and north Africa. For about two months, from the middle of September, millions of birds head for the south, many of them travelling through France to cross the Pyrenees. One of the main flight paths is over the great wooded area of Les Landes, in the south of France. French sportsmen, devoted to shooting pigeon during the migratory period, have built cosy huts in clearings among the pine trees called *palombières* – the French for wood pigeon is *palombe*. From these, a system of tunnels, about 1.5m (5ft) high and covered with bracken or brush wood, extend for considerable distances. Up trees adjacent to the tunnels, hooded tame pigeons are placed, attached to boards which will tilt at the tug of a cord running back to the *palombière*.

Wearied by his tree climbing, the French pigeon shooter totters back to the *palombière* for a *dégustation – palombières* are notoriously well stocked. Once recovered, a trap door in the roof of the *palombière* is raised through which the pigeon shooter watches the birds flying over. If he thinks there may be a flight line near one of the captive birds, he tugs the respective cord and that particular board tilts. The captive bird flaps its wings and with luck, *des palombes* decide to land. This is the moment when the *chasseur* tip-toes down the tunnel, gun in hand, hoping for that lucky shot.

The other extreme to this immensely civilised, but incredibly complicated method of shooting, is the French equivalent of what I consider the most thrilling of all sports – shooting pigeons from a platform erected in the top of a tall tree. A little to the south of Les Landes and west of St. Engrace is the Orgambidexha pass, high in the Pyrenees. Here, in a landscape stripped bare by the howling wind, among boulders and at the edge of terrifying chasms, hides have been built. Inside these, *palombe* fanatics (and there are lots of them) wait for the ultimate challenge – a woody on his way to Spain, hurtling through the pass with the wind under his tail, going like a rocket.

Pigeons are at their best between late Spring and early autumn when they have been at the farmer's crops; this of course is the period when they are most often shot. I love pigeon; when I was a child my father used to have squabs flown in from Cairo, and when I look at the empty doocots all over Scotland I mourn for the passing of this part of the living larder. It is a tradition still found In Europe and the Middle East and I have tried to select a variety of recipes to give this delicious bird its true variety.

### Ageing

Young pigeons have softer, pinker legs and a round plump breast.

### Hanging

Pigeons don't need hanging, and it is important to empty the crops as soon as possible.

### Plucking

Pigeons are the easiest birds to pluck; the feathers simply float off them and float everywhere, so pluck them outside or in a barn.

### Drawing

As for pheasant (see page 24–25).

### Roasting

Place a piece of seasoned butter in each bird and a piece of apple. Wrap the birds in streaky bacon or barding fat. Roast at 200°C/400°F/gas 6 for 20–25 minutes, basting as you go. Remove the bacon to brown the breast 10 minutes before the end. Allow one large pigeon per person.

## andalucian **pigeons**

The Spanish eat a lot of pigeon, and I think this is a very good way of doing them. I have halved the oil, toasted the bread and added capers which I always think add colour and a bit of bite.

4 young pigeons
8 anchovy fillets
175ml (6fl oz) olive oil
8 small onions
300ml (10fl oz) dry white wine
2 cloves garlic
1 sprig of parsley
1 tablespoon capers
4 triangles of good sourdough bread
salt

Rub the pigeons with salt and stuff them each with 2 anchovies. Heat half the oil in a large pan. Add the pigeons and cook over a low heat for 15 minutes, turning them until they are lightly browned all over. Fry the onions separately in the rest of the oil for about 5 minutes until golden all over. Then add them to the pigeons together with the wine, garlic and parsley. Simmer for 45 minutes until the sauce is reduced by half and the pigeons are tender.

Remove the parsley and garlic and skim off any surface fat. Arrange the pigeons on a serving dish, strain the sauce and pour it over the birds. Surround them with the onions and sprinkle with capers. Serve with the toasted sourdough bread.

## jellied **pigeons**

This is a very tasty dish for a cold table or a picnic. I tend to add a pig's trotter whilst cooking for extra jelly. If you want to use one, cut it in two and add to the pigeons while they are cooking, remove it when the pigeons are cooked and eat it separately cold for your tea! When the pigeons are cooked, I take the meat off the bone and return it to the stock to set. The original is a bit messy to eat but probably more fun!

110g (4oz) butter
3 young pigeons
6 sprigs of tarragon
150ml (5fl oz) dry sherry
game stock
salt and pepper

Preheat the oven to 170°C/325°F/gas 3.

Mix the butter with some salt and pepper to season it, and put a knob in each pigeon with 2 sprigs of tarragon. Put in an oven dish, pour over the sherry and add enough stock to cover them.

Cover tightly and cook in the oven for about 2 hours, or until the birds are tender. If necessary add more stock as the pigeons must be covered during cooking.

Leave to cool so that the butter rises and forms a solid seal before serving.

# pigeons from emilia romana

This is a rather complicated party dish from Emilia Romana, but it really does repay the effort and will amaze your friends whilst using very cheap ingredients. Do try it. You can get it all ready to cook, keep it overnight and bake it for the party on the day. The Italians add sweetbreads to the mould – if you have a supply, try it. Just cook them slightly in melted butter first, then slice and layer them in to the mould.

200g (7oz) butter
2 onions, chopped
1.1kg (2$^1$/$_2$lb) pigeons, with giblets reserved
1 tablespoon tomato purée
1 large glass white wine
600ml (1 pint) game stock
350g (12oz) arborio rice
225g (8oz) parmesan, grated
110g (4oz) cooked peas
2 tablespoons dried breadcrumbs
salt and pepper

Heat 50g (2oz) of the butter and cook 1 onion until translucent. Add the pigeons and brown well; brown the giblets at the same time. Add half the tomato purée and cook, turning until the birds and onion are coated. Pour in the wine, reduce the heat and season. Add the stock, a little at a time, to prevent from drying. Cook until the birds are tender – about 1–1$^1$/$_2$ hours. Remove the birds and set aside.

In a heavy pan melt 50g (2oz) of the butter and cook the second onion until translucent. Add the rice, stirring until coated with butter. Cook gently for about 3 minutes. Add water and salt, and cook over a low heat until the rice is *al dente* – about 12 minutes, adding more water as needed.

Transfer the rice to a large bowl and gently stir in 300ml ($^1$/$_2$ pint) of strained broth from the cooked birds. Fold in gently the parmesan and cooked peas.

Preheat the oven to 170°C/325°F/gas 3.

Butter a large round mould, and shake in the breadcrumbs to coat. Layer the rice mixture with the meat from the pigeons, thinly slicing the remaining butter between the layers. Mix the remaining tomato purée with a little stock and pour in. Bake for 1 hour. Unmould and serve.

## pigeons with raisins

A warming dish with a bit of gusto about it. The raisins and sweet sherry give it a Regency feel and bring out the richness of the meat.

50g (2oz) butter
1 onion, chopped
4 pigeons
50g (2oz) flour
300ml (1/2 pint) game stock
2 tablespoons red wine vinegar
2 tablespoons honey
110g (4oz) raisins
1 glass sweet sherry
salt and pepper

Preheat the oven to 180°C/350°F/gas 4.

Melt the butter in a pan, and fry the onion until golden. Add the pigeons and brown all over, and then remove them. Stir the flour into the onions and cook until brown. Add the stock, gradually stirring as you go.

Put the pigeons into an oven pan, and add the stock mixture and all the rest of the ingredients. Cook, covered, for 1 hour, or until the pigeons are tender.

## pigeon in the hole

Originally toad in the hole was made with rump steak rolled up, and then Hannah Glasse in the eighteenth century made it with pigeons. It works very well and I am grateful to my friend, Maggie Burn, for the addition of onions and mixed herbs.

For the batter:
225g (8oz) plain flour
3 eggs
150ml (5fl oz) milk
pinch of salt

4 pigeons
75g (3oz) butter
75g (3oz) dripping
6 well seasoned game or venison sausages
salt and pepper

Mix all the batter ingredients together in a blender and stand for 1 hour, then stir well.

Preheat the oven to 200°C/400°F/gas 6.

Rub the pigeons with butter and season well. In a roasting pan heat the dripping until smoking hot. Pour in a third of the batter mix and cook for 15 minutes, or until it's set.

Place the pigeons and sausages on the layer of batter and pour the rest of the batter mix around them (the batter should cover three-quarters of the pigeons). Return to the oven and bake for another 30 minutes until the batter is well risen and the pigeons are cooked.

# pigeon with rice and aubergine

**Individual portions can be made in large ramekins, in which case cut the cooking time to 45 minutes.**

*2 medium aubergines, sliced into 1.2cm (1/2in) thick slices*
*5 tablespoons olive oil*
*1 large onion, chopped*
*4 pigeons, cut in half*
*1 teaspoon ground allspice*
*1 teaspoon ground nutmeg*
*1 teaspoon ground cinnamon*
*1 teaspoon black pepper*
*600ml (1 pint) water*
*oil for deep frying*
*350g (12oz) long grain rice*
*1 large cup boiling water*
*salt*

Sprinkle the aubergines with salt and leave to drain for 30 minutes; pat dry. Heat the olive oil in a pan. Fry the onion until golden, and brown the pigeon halves. Add the spices and salt and pepper. Add the water, cover and simmer until the pigeons are tender – for about 1 hour. Remove the birds and onions from the liquid with a slotted spoon, and when they are cool enough to handle strip the meat from the birds.

Deep-fry the aubergine slices in a frying pan. Grease a large casserole (with a tight fitting lid) with a little olive oil. Arrange aubergine slices in a double layer on the bottom. Sprinkle a handful of rice over these. Layer the meat and onions on top, then the rest of the aubergine slices. Add the rest of the rice, spread evenly, and press down well. Sprinkle a little salt on top and add the boiling water. Cover tightly and cook until the rice is tender and the liquid absorbed –  about 1 hour over a very low heat (add more water if it's drying out). Invert onto a plate and serve.

# pigeon bistalia

You can see how this magnificent dish came out of the kitchens of the Ottoman Empire. It is a lot easier to make than it looks and will amaze your friends; you can even make mini ones. The trick is to use lots of oil on the pastry leaves. I have not attempted to tell you how to make leaves of *warka*, the traditional pastry used, which requires complicated things done on the back of a heated copper bowl with a flour and water paste. If you want to go there I recommend Robert Carrier's *A Taste of Morocco* as the only reliable recipe for this. I tried it once – try everything once has always been my motto – and it was interesting and probably that bit better but not so you would notice with the effort required.

For the *chermola*:
*1 large onion, grated*
*4 cloves garlic, chopped*
*1 teaspoon saffron*
*1 teaspoon powdered ginger*
*4 sprigs of parsley, chopped*
*6 sprigs of coriander, chopped*
*olive oil*
*salt and pepper*

For the almond mixture:
*450g (1lb) ground almonds*
*6 tablespoons icing sugar*
*4 tablespoons orange flower water*
*2 teaspoons ground cumin*

*6 young pigeons, boned and quartered with their giblets*
*225g (8oz) butter*
*850ml (1$^1$/$_2$ pints) water*
*generous $^1$/$_2$ teaspoon saffron*

*melted butter*
*6 hard-boiled eggs, shelled and chopped*
*pinch of cinnamon*
*23 leaves filo pastry*
*2 egg yolks, mixed with a little water*
*salt and pepper*

On the day before eating, mix all the *chermola* ingredients in a bowl. Add the pigeon quarters and giblets and rub in well. Leave overnight to absorb the flavours. Stir all the almond mixture ingredients together in a bowl, and set aside, covered.

The next day transfer the pigeons and *chermola* to a heavy casserole. Add the butter and water, season, cover and simmer for 20 minutes. Add the saffron, and cook for another 20 minutes. Transfer the pigeons to a dish, removing any loose bones, and reduce the stock by boiling hard over a high flame by two-thirds.

Preheat the oven to 220°C/425°F/gas 7. Brush the base and sides of a large flan tin with melted butter. Place 1 filo leaf in the centre of the tin, then place 5 more leaves overlapping the edges of the tin. Brush with butter and repeat with 5 more leaves. Sprinkle half the almond mixture in the centre of the tin, cover with 2 more pastry leaves, and melted butter.

Arrange the meat mixture in the centre of the tin, leaving the pastry round the edge clear. Put in the hard-boiled eggs, and sprinkle on the cinnamon. Sprinkle on the remaining almond mixture. Turn up the overlapping pastry sides, sealing with the beaten egg mixture. Add 2 more layers of 5 leaves and fold to the centre, brushing with a final layer of butter. Bake for 20 minutes or until the pastry is golden. Run a spatula under the pie and turn onto an inverted dish. Return to the oven for 10–15 minutes to brown the underside. Dust with cinnamon and serve.

# egyptian **pigeon** with green wheat

This was a favourite dish of my father's who had his pigeons imported from Cairo. In Egypt they raise fat squab especially for the table and stuff them with green wheat which remains preserved inside them after their deaths. Anyone who has had their vegetable garden scoured by pigeons will know what scavengers they are, so this dish is the Egyptian farmer's revenge! Green wheat or *farik* can be bought in Middle Eastern shops throughout the country, but if you live in wheat-growing country I'm sure the farmer will spare you a dozen heads, especially if you ask him to dinner. In Egypt the spinach that accompanies the pigeons is cooked to a slop, but at home we preferred it firm.

1 teaspoon coriander seeds, freshly ground

1 teaspoon cumin seeds

2 teaspoons mixed salt, pepper and chilli powder

110g (4oz) clarified butter

275g (10oz) fresh coriander

450g (1lb) farik or husked green wheat

6 pigeons or large squab

2 shallots, cut in half

2 tablespoons butter

8 cloves garlic, peeled,

1 teaspoon fennel seeds

4 tomatoes, quartered

900g (2lb) spinach

salt

Bring a pan of water to the boil and put in the ground coriander seeds, cumin and seasoning. Cook for 12 minutes, stirring occasionally, and drain.

Heat half the clarified butter in a frying pan. Add the fresh coriander, coriander seeds, cumin, salt, pepper, chilli and the *farik* and cook for about 5 minutes until the *farik* is *al dente*. Stuff the pigeons with the *farik*, pushing it in tightly and truss well.

Boil a large pan of water, add 2 teaspoons of salt and the shallots. Add the birds and simmer (do not allow to boil) for about 35–40 minutes. Drain and pat dry; save the water.

Heat the rest of the clarified butter in the frying pan and pan-fry the birds for about 10 minutes, turning as you go until they are golden brown; set aside to rest.

Heat the 2 tablespoons of butter in the frying pan. Mash the garlic. Fry the garlic, fennel seeds and tomatoes in the butter for 2–3 minutes; add the spinach and about 3 tablespoons of broth from the pigeons. Cover and cook until the spinach is just softened.

Put the spinach on a dish and arrange the pigeons on top. Eat with Arab flatbread.

# woodcock

All game birds are beautiful, but to me woodcock, whom the French have christened *mordoree*, 'the golden queen of the woodland', combine both beauty and mystery. A woodcock's rich coppery back and wings, with lighter, buff-striped head and underparts, will glow golden for a moment, when it flits through a beam of winter sunlight in a woodland glade.

Woodcock (*Scalopax rusticola)* are waders that have adapted to damp woods with rides, open clearings and soft ground in which to feed. They stand four square, on short, sturdy legs whilst they probe for worms and insect larvae with their long, delicate beaks, stamping their feet from time to time. They feed at dusk or just before dawn, flying with slow, leisurely wing beats, like some gigantic moth, to their favourite feeding place. They lie up by day, completely camouflaged among the bracken on a sunny south facing bank or the dry undergrowth at the edge of a woodland glade. Woodcock are solitary, silent birds except during the breeding season (from around the middle of March), when the cocks become vocal, emitting strange grunting, frog-like croaks as they patrol their breeding territory, a display known as 'roding'. In times of danger or scarcity of food, these extraordinary birds transport their chicks to safety, clutching them between their thighs.

They have an enormous range of distribution, from Britain across Europe, along the southern edge of Russia and through to Japan. Some birds are resident in Britain all year round in the south and west, Ireland, and where the Gulf Stream touches the coast of Scotland. Most fly to Britain from Scandinavia and Northern Germany, arriving as soon as the ground at their summering quarters becomes frozen and their food source disappears.

Our ancestors believed that woodcock only flew with the full moon. The first 'fall' always came with the one nearest to All Hallows' Eve and no doubt, their ghostly shapes seen against the moonlight did much to endorse the superstition that the dead were on the move that night. The next, and larger fall came with the following moon. In point of fact, woodcock fly in throughout October, November and December, depending on the weather and wind direction.

The conviction that woodcock were guided here by moonlight was the principal argument of the lunar migration theorists. A body of academics who reasoned that, when most woodcock disappeared in March and April, they flew to the moon, spending three months enjoying the lunar landscape and four months travelling there and back. Opposing them was an equally erudite party who knew, without any shadow of doubt, that woodcock burrowed into the sand of the sea shore and hibernated there for the summer. Why else were groups of them to be found in a state of almost bloodless exhaustion along our coastlines in early winter? Furthermore, there were fishermen willing to testify that woodcock washed out to sea, were sometimes caught in their nets. This controversy erupted every spring and winter until well into the eighteenth century, when the concept of migration began to be understood.

Woodcock rely on a north-easterly wind to carry them over the North Sea, and the reason they are sometimes found with their feathers puffed up, almost too weak to move, is because they are caught in strong offshore winds that prevents them from landing. Their digestion is so rapid and their intake of food normally so frequent, that they are quite unsuited for prolonged flight. However, there is usually a plentiful supply of food in early winter and they

quickly recover to press on inland and establish feeding territories. The extremes in condition between woodcock that had an easy or difficult flight over, led people to believe that there were two distinct species.

Before lighter shotguns (built on continental lines in the eighteenth century) made shooting birds on the wing feasible, woodcock were trapped in nets. They will generally follow the same route to their dawn and dusk feeding places, and these were quickly identified. A fine net hung suspended across a ride or the entrance to some airy clearing would guarantee a catch. In fact, they were so easily caught, there was a view prevalent for many centuries that woodcock had no brains and the name was commonly used to describe a fool.

The behaviour of a woodcock when disturbed could not be more different from its lolloping roding flight or the lazy journey to feeding grounds. When flushed, it leaves cover at deceptive speed, immediately twisting and turning from left to right, emptying its bowels and flying more erratically the faster it goes. Moving as tortuously in the open as they do in woodland, where they jinx between trees, in an incredible display of aerial dexterity. Colonel Peter Hawker, one of the early nineteenth century's finest shots, observed, 'the pursuit of woodcocks with a couple of good spaniels may be termed the fox hunting of shooting.' They are, next to snipe, the most challenging and difficult birds to shoot.

This, coupled with their scarcity, unpredictable behaviour and exquisite flavour has made them the most sought after game bird in Europe, and in Canada and America, where a subspecies, *Scalopax minor,* otherwise known as the timber doodle, is found from Manitoba to Newfoundland to Labrador, and south to the Gulf of Mexico.

In France, shooting woodcock over pointers, or Brittany spaniels wearing little bells on their collars, is almost a religion. The great culinary bible, *Larousse Gastronomique*, lists over thirty recipes and the sheer volume of literature – Colin McKelvie, the author and sporting columnist, mentions ninety-two popular titles and over two thousand scientific publications – gives an indication of the degree of fascination the French have for this strange little bird. Several countries in Europe have woodcock clubs, France has a particularly large and enthusiastic one called the Club National de Bécassins whose motto 'hunt as much as you can but shoot as little as possible' reflects the attitude of sportsmen everywhere, and there are similar clubs in America and Canada. In Britain, membership of our Woodcock Club is restricted to those who have achieved the near impossible – a successful left and right.

Anyone who shoots a woodcock plucks the pin feathers, a small, sharp- pointed, almost rigid feather from the elbow edge of either wing, and keeps them as mementoes. Some put them in their hatbands, a habit which is the origin of the expression, 'he's got a feather in his hat,' or like my son and I, paste them into our game book. Even before Victorians used them for painting the exquisite miniatures which were so popular at the time, artists painted with pin feathers for really delicate work. One of our leading wildlife artists, Colin Woolf, started using the same technique twelve years ago, to paint the most beautiful pictures of woodcock (see below). One of these paintings, auctioned for charity in 2000, was painted with a hundred-and-fifty-year-old feather found in a paint box belonging to the miniaturist, Lady Letitia Kerr (c1800–1868).

According to Colin, aficionados in the Far East use the pin feather of a woodcock, mounted on a silver stick, as a sex toy. The woodcock is what you might call a Sybarite's all purpose bird!

The most delicious of birds and honoured wherever they are found by shots the world over. My godfather, Rudi Jurgens – one of the best shots in Europe – retired to the Neimeigen Marshes in the south of Holland as he thought snipe and woodcock the only birds worth shooting. Both should be cooked with the innards left in as both shit as they fly away and therefore empty their gut.

### Ageing
If you've got them, eat them.

### Hanging
How ripe you like them is a matter for you, anything from 3–15 days depending on the weather. Snipe should be hung for 3–4 days unless it is very cold.

### Plucking
I pluck mine when the stomach feathers give way at the first pull. Be very careful when plucking snipe so as not to tear the skin.

### Drawing
As for pheasant (see page 24–25).

### Roasting
Rub the birds generously with softened butter and place a piece of barding fat over the breast. Place in a very hot oven at 220°C/425°F/gas 7 for 10 –15 minutes – more if you must (for snipe 6–15 minutes). You can extract the entrails, season them and serve them on toast with the bird, but I just tend to serve sippets of toast with the birds. Alllow one per person.

# woodcock with polenta

This is an Italian way of serving woodcock and it is very agreeable, especially if you have a lot of them. I never have that many and resented testing the recipe!

2.4 litres (4 pints) salted water

450g (1lb) cornmeal/polenta

3 woodcocks

3 thin slices pancetta or unsmoked streaky bacon, chopped

50g (2oz) butter

50g (2oz) raw ham, finely chopped

50g (2oz) pancetta or unsmoked streaky bacon, finely chopped

1 tablespoon celery, finely chopped

1 tablespoon onion, finely chopped

2 sprigs of parsley, finely chopped

1 bay leaf

6 juniper berries, crushed

125ml (4fl oz) Marsala or medium dry sherry

1 tablespoon tomato purée

salt and pepper

**Serves 3**

Preheat the oven to 200°C/400°F/gas 6.

Boil the water and pour in the cornmeal/polenta. Reduce the heat and stir constantly for 30 minutes until the polenta comes away from the sides of the pan. Turn onto a work surface and flatten to 1cm (1/2in), then leave to cool for 30 minutes. Divide into 12 portions and bake on a greased sheet, in the oven, until lightly browned – about 15 minutes.

Season the woodcocks and tie the bacon strips around them. Melt the butter in a casserole. Add the ham, bacon, celery, onion, parsley, bay leaf and juniper berries, and cook until the onion is golden. Add the woodcocks and brown them all over, then lower the heat; mix the alcohol with the tomato purée and stir into the pan. Cover, and simmer for 20 minutes or until the woodcocks are tender.

Remove the woodcocks and put the remaining contents of the pan through a mouli or a blender. Untie the woodcocks and cut them in half through the backbone. Arrange on the toasted polenta and pour over the sauce.

# burnetts' **woodcock**

**This is a dish I invented for my friends Jane and George Burnett. George is a keen shot and commented he couldn't find different ways to cook woodcock. He shoots more than most – I don't have that problem myself!**

For the potato cakes:
*450g (1lb) waxy potatoes*
*2 egg whites*
*1 egg yolk*
*1 tablespoon capers, chopped*
*1 teaspoon French mustard*
*150ml (5fl oz) whipping cream*
*25g (1oz) butter*

To make the potato cakes, boil the potatoes, drain until they have stopped steaming and mash them. Beat the egg whites very stiffly. In a separate bowl mix the yolk, capers, mustard and cream into the mash and fold in the egg whites. Form small cakes and fry them in butter until brown.

*4 woodcock*
*110g (4oz) butter*
*4 rashers fat bacon*

For the sauce:
*4 livers, (woodcock, pigeon, pheasant or chicken)*
*50g (2oz) butter*
*1 glass white wine*
*2 tablespoons game stock*
*6 juniper berries, crushed*
*squeeze of lemon*
*salt and pepper*

Preheat the oven to 220°C/425°F/gas 7.

Spread each woodcock with butter and cover with a bacon rasher. Roast for 10–15 minutes, depending how you like your birds.

To make the sauce, sauté the livers in the butter, then mash and sieve them. Put the purée in a pan with the white wine and stock, and add the juniper berries, seasoning and lemon juice, and simmer for a few minutes. Stir in any pan juices from the woodcock.

Put the woodcock on the potato cakes and serve with the sauce.

# woodcock with truffles

This French dish, which can also be made with snipe, comes from a happier age when both truffles and woodcock were plentiful. If you have a truffle and are happy to use it, it is a delicious dish. Strangely the garlic does not overpower the truffle. The original recipe calls for six truffles so be aware lottery winners everywhere!

4 woodcocks
25g (1oz) butter
2 cloves garlic, halved
as many truffles as you can afford, preferably black, thinly sliced
game stock
salt and pepper

Preheat the oven to 220°C/425°F/gas 7.

Rub the birds with the butter, season and roast for 10 minutes, so they are still very rare.

Rub an oven dish, preferably earthenware, with the garlic cloves. Put the birds in the dish and surround with truffle slices. Season and add the stock. Put the dish back in the oven and cook for a further 12 minutes.

# snipe

Sometimes, towards the end of February, walking home across a boggy area where heather gave way to rushes and reed grasses, I would be startled by an eerie throbbing, bleating sound rising to a soft fluting crescendo. Over the years, I have heard it hundreds of times and it never ceases to make the hairs stir on the back of my neck. This beautiful wind music is a cock snipe 'drumming', performing its spectacular courtship and territorial display by climbing to a hundred or more feet and diving with its outer tail feathers spread. This hauntingly lovely sound, created by the feathers vibrating through the air stream when the snipe reaches a certain speed, is the first promise of spring.

Various colloquial names are associated with this strange pulsating sound. Many believed it resembled a young goat crying for its mother. The Romans called them *campana caelostis* or *capella*, meaning little kid. The French, *chevre volant*. In southern Scotland we call them heather bleaters. Until 1950, when laboratory tests proved the point, no-one was quite sure how the noise was made, largely because snipe are always, disconcertingly, some distance from where the sound is heard. During the nesting period I am certain the cock bird does it to confuse predators.

Common snipe are resident here all year round with numbers increased by flocks from northern Europe and Scandinavia, arriving as soon as the ground becomes too hard for the soft flexible tip at the end of their beak to penetrate. They have a virtually worldwide distribution, from Ireland to Japan, Siberia to the tip of Africa and most of the American continent, with Carolina being noted for spectacular shooting.

These mysterious little creatures are birds of bogs and damp empty places, of mists and reeds. The name for a quantity of them in flight, a wisp, is so descriptive. Seen briefly above a bed of rushes they soon melt away into the grey winter sky. A number of them, seen on the ground is called a walk. Their striped plumage, the varying shades of yellows and light and dark browns, with their long, pale green legs are the autumn colours of marshes and estuaries.

Common snipe weigh between 110–175g (4–6oz) and measure 25–30cm (10–12in) of which at least a third is the beak. The little Jack snipe or Judcock is half the size; these purely migratory birds were once game species, but have been protected since 1981. At one time, the purpose of the disproportionately long beak, which enables snipe to probe deep into the mud for worms and insect larvae, was thought to be the means by which snipe launched themselves into the air.

Snipe are the most delicious eating. In my view, better even than woodcock. A 'finger' of snipe (three, the number carried between the fingers of one hand) equated to one woodcock in culinary terms. Otherwise, like woodcock, the term is a couple. Snipe are wonderful converters of food and come to the table like little balls of fat. They were considered good invalid food as the fat was believed not to cloy the digestive system. Possibly the reasoning behind Churchill's reply, 'a finger of cold snipe and a pint of port', when asked if he had a sovereign hangover cure.

Like all rare food, a snipe's delicious flavour is enhanced by the sheer difficulty in shooting

them. They are so utterly unpredictable that they can fool even the best shot. Most people of experience agree the only way to approach marshes or damp patches in the corner of a field where you think they may be, is downwind. Snipe, when flushed will rise against the wind and hang in the air for a second before flying away. As with woodcock, snipe zigzag violently from side to side, straightening out after a couple of dozen yards. They do this to conquer the wind and control their power of flight, from then on they go like the clappers. This, and the fact you can never tell what distance they may rise from you – in some weather they lie so tight you practically tread on them, in others, consistently get up just out of range – make walking-up these elusive little people, both the most frustrating and rewarding shooting.

Ireland has the greatest concentration of domestic snipe. The countryside has not been eroded by post-war monoculture, which saw so many wetland areas and other habitat sights destroyed on mainland Britain. Driven snipe, a rarity at home is not uncommon in Ireland and provides a shooting challenge equal to none. Perhaps the finest is offered by Charlie Plunkett, the Duke of Abercorn's agent at Belle Isle on Lough Erne.

An enchanting jumble of hundreds of little wooded islands, Upper Lough Erne is a paradise for wildfowl and snipe. Guns are transported by boats to a succession of little islands. Some guns stand on *terra firma*, the rest shoot from boats. To shoot a high twisting snipe from a wobbling boat, leaves a sensation that is nothing short of ecstatic.

## snipe in a pie

I was served snipe pie in the Auvergne. It was an elaborate affair beautifully decorated with pastry cut outs of flying snipe, guns and dogs. It was very large – this is a much smaller version for use at home.

100g (3¹/₂oz) sultanas

cognac

200g (7oz) butter

1.8kg (4lb) sharp apples, not Bramleys, peeled, cored and chopped

1 shallot, finely chopped

6 juniper berries, crushed

6 snipe drawn, trussed and barded

700g (1¹/₂lb) shortcrust pastry

1 egg yolk, mixed with a little water

salt and pepper

**Serves 6**

Soak the sultanas overnight in cognac, then drain and reserve.

Preheat the oven to 220°C/425°F/gas 7. Melt half the butter and sauté the apples and shallot until golden. Stir in the sultanas and juniper berries. Roast the birds for 10 minutes, then season them. Roll out half the pastry and line a pie dish about 20cm (8in) across and 15cm (6in) deep.

Arrange the birds in the dish and then fill it with the apple mixture. Roll out the remaining pastry and cover the pie with it. Seal the edges and brush the top with the egg yolk, making a slit for the steam to escape. Turn down the oven to 200°C/400°F/gas 6 and bake for about 35 minutes or until the crust is golden. Melt the other half of the butter, stirring in the reserved cognac, and serve with the pie.

## snipe curry

The Indian estuarine marshes team with wildfowl, and game books of the Raj show large drifts of snipe being shot. The curries recorded are rather fierce and fiery so, whilst giving a recipe for snipe curry in memory of my step-grandfather, who was a keen shot, I have used a rather delicate variant.

2 tablespoons oil

2 onions, chopped

1 tablespoon coriander seeds, freshly ground

1 teaspoon ground turmeric

1 teaspoon cumin seed

1 teaspoon ginger, finely chopped or ¹/₂ teaspoon ground

1 small chilli, deseeded and chopped

¹/₂ teaspoon ground fenugreek

4 snipe or woodcock

300ml (10fl oz) tin coconut milk

salt

Heat the oil in a heavy pan and cook the onions until golden. Add the spices and cook for another 5 minutes. Add the birds and cook them until they are well coated. Pour over the coconut milk and add salt, cover, and simmer gently for 40 minutes or until the birds are cooked. Serve with rice and curry trimmings.

## snipe pudding

Johnny had heard that Rosa Lewis, doyenne of the Cavendish Hotel, used to cook Edward VII his favourite breakfast of snipe pudding; Johnny tried making a conventional suet pudding à la steak and kidney using snipe with entrecote steak wrapped round them – the steak was supposed to melt into the sauce! To our modern palates (not very some would say) it was a waste of snipe. However on reading Rosemary Wadey's excellent *The Pastry Book* I came across the statement that you could bake suet crust. Ah ha I thought and here we are. Not what Edward might have liked but perhaps for his great-great grandson a modern (not very) snipe pudding.

*225g (8oz) self-raising flour*
*1/2 teaspoon salt*
*110g (4oz) shredded suet*
*150ml (5fl oz) cold water*
*4 pieces sharp eating apple*
*4 snipe*
*4 dessertspoons white wine*
*110g (4oz) butter, softened*
*salt and pepper*

Sift the flour and salt and rub in the suet, then add enough cold water to make a dough. Using the heel of your hand flatten out the pastry on a floured board. Preheat the oven to 200°C/400°F/gas 6. Put a piece of apple in each snipe and pour in a spoonful of wine. Season the outside of the birds and rub each with a quarter of the softened butter. Place a bowl of hot water on the floor of the oven to stop the suet pastry drying out too quickly. Divide your pastry into 4 and wrap each snipe in pastry securing the edges with cold water. Brush with a little beaten egg and bake on a greased baking sheet for 20 minutes. Reduce to 180°C/350°F/gas 4 and cook for a further 30 minutes.

## snipe with lettuce and capers

My Belgian great Aunt who was such a gourmet that the measurement round her waist when she married was the measurement round her neck when she died, used to cook snipe like this. You can use woodcock as well, but cook it for a little longer.

*250g (8oz) green bacon, chopped*
*2 round heart lettuces, separated*
*4 snipe*
*6 shallots or 1 onion, finely chopped*
*1 tablespoon capers or caperberries, chopped*
*350ml (12fl oz) white game stock*
*salt and pepper*

Preheat the oven to 180°C/350°F/gas 4.

Put the bacon in the bottom of a casserole dish and arrange the lettuce leaves on top. Put the snipe on top of the lettuce and add the shallots and capers. Pour on the stock, season, and bake uncovered for 35–40 minutes until the birds are cooked.

wildfowl

# wildfowl

If I had to choose one category of shooting above all others, I would unhesitatingly pick wildfowling. To me, it offers everything that I love about wildlife and the countryside. It takes place in weather that keeps most of the nation firmly indoors and in areas that have remained unspoilt, remote and uncivilised. Even marshes, like those along the Thames estuary, now surrounded by urban development and industrialisation become isolated and very lonely when light begins to fade and cold river mist creeps over the sea wall. I know, I've been lost out there. But that is part of the magic of wildfowling, pitting oneself against nature and the vagaries of wildfowl, whose behaviour is determined by weather, tides and moon. There is a romance and mystique unique to wildfowling that has much to do with the antiquity of the sport and a feeling of *deja vu* that any marshland evokes; a sense that these places, empty now except for wildfowl and marsh sheep, once supported busy communities.

The earliest inhabitants of Britain, four thousand years before Christ, settled in the coastal marshes, building settlements on areas of dry land out of the reeds and willow and living off the wildfowl and fish. Salt was a vital element for winter survival and most coastal estuaries were producing salt when the Romans arrived. With typical efficiency they set about building sea walls, draining marshes and creating productive salt pans. On the Cooling Marshes that run up to the Thames on the Isle of Grain, where I used to farm years ago, remains of salt pans and pottery kilns can be seen just beside one of the Kent Wildfowler's more productive flight ponds. Baskets of eels, pike and perch, bundles of reeds and every sort of wildfowl, netted as they flighted into the marsh pools, would have gone upriver to the major Roman settlements like London and Colchester.

The Anglo Saxons built settlements round the edges of the marshes and reclaimed more land, creating valuable summer grazings for cattle and sheep but there were still enormous areas where remote isolated communities lived on islands, sharing their existence with vast flocks of every conceivable marsh and sea bird. These glorious wildernesses of mists and bird life were viewed with a mixture of horror and suspicion by cosy upland farmers. The fens and marshes were dangerous places, a world apart, populated by strange, uncivilised, fever ridden, interbred people, possibly semi-amphibian, who were as wild and unpredictable as the pike, eels and birds with whom they lived.

The birds themselves gave rise to more marshland mythology. Bitterns not only boomed by day, an alarming enough sound with its eerily ventriloqual effect but also at night. This strange bumping noise struck terror into the hearts of those that heard it and is supposed to be the origin of 'things that go bump in the night'. Furthermore, it was generally believed that bitterns boomed, by thrusting their beaks into the ground and blowing hard. Most duck, mallard, gadwall, pochard and so on made identifying quacks. wigeon, although clearly a duck, whistled. Some, tufted duck and scaup for example, swam under water like fish. Other birds like avocets, red-shanks and godwits, yelped. Shell duck had a disconcertingly human laugh. Snipe moaned, whimbrel whimpered and water rail screamed and grunted. None of these sounds were remotely similar to the comforting bird song of the uplands.

Another anxiety was the curious way the marsh bird population fluctuated and changed between summer and winter. This was particularly noticeable among geese. Enough muddled mythology survived from pre-Roman times about the sexual symbolism of geese, but the fact that geese appeared in the skies in late autumn and left again in the spring required explanation. Geese seen flying by the light of a full moon provided it. Like woodcock, they too shared the lunar landscape, except in the case of barnacle geese. Superstitious minds reserved a real corker for this – the loveliest of all migratory geese – believing they evolved from a chrysalis emerging from the white lace-like growths a marine insect builds on drift wood and barnacle shells. This myth, which persisted among fishermen until well into the nineteenth century, was perpetuated by the clergy who were able to claim that, since barnacle geese were born of a sea creature, it was permissible to eat them on Fridays and during Lent.

Whatever prejudices may have developed about the marshes, it didn't stop people eating their wildlife. As the population grew, fishermen trapped and speared the eels and pike, reed cutters harvested reeds for thatching and flooring and wildfowlers trapped and netted to their heart's content. Marsh reclamation continued with the Normans and through successive monarchies without appearing to have any impact of the vast wildfowl population or much impression on the massive total wetland acreage. In the early Middle Ages, wildfowl and, in particular, herons and cranes, became a popular hawking sport among landowners and their guests along the marsh fringes.

The majority of wildfowl were caught in clap nets, designed to spring into the air as duck were spooked off pools. They were particularly effective on diving duck like pochard, scaup and goldeneye, that leave water with a low trajectory. Other species like, mallard, teal, and wigeon were trapped as they dropped into a pool by fine nets stretched between two poles. Geese were netted when they landed to graze. Greylag, who were the only goose to breed in Britain when all the others had migrated, were the ancestor of our white farmyard goose. Clap netting was gradually replaced by the more effective duck decoy, a series of netted pipes running back seventy yards from a pool, down a curved connecting dyke, wide and high at the end protruding into the pool, narrowing to a dead end as it rounded the corner. Duck were lured down the pipes, either by tame decoy ducks or the surprisingly effective decoy dog. This small reddish brown spaniel type, was trained to move in such a way that that duck would follow it down the pipe out of curiosity.

The drawback to netting was its semi-permanency. Frustratingly, wildfowlers saw opportunities to increase bags every day without being able to do much about it. Hail shot, small pieces of lead rattled around in a metal box until roughly spherical, was invented in 1520, and provided the means they had been waiting for. Military matchlocks had been finding their way into civilian hands for some time and both poachers and gentry, with their finer wheellocks, had achieved limited success on deer with solid bullets. Hail shot came into its own with wildfowling. Whilst the upland gunner stumbled after partridge leading his stalking horse, weighed down with matclock, gun stand and all the paraphernalia of powder horn and shot, the wildfowler settled himself deep in the rushes beside a carefully selected pool, matchlock balanced on its tripod and waited for the dawn.

The limitation to matchlocks was the method of powder ignition. A spluttering slow match held in the jaws of a spring loaded hammer, was thrust into a hole beside the breech when the trigger was pressed, igniting the powder charge. The whole art of wildfowling hinges on concealment and silence – neither criteria were achieved by matchlocks. Lighting the slow match with flint and tinder was a weather dependant, noisy business and once lit, gave off a plume of evil smelling smoke, enough to frighten away duck and geese. It is curious to think that over the next two hundred and fifty years, there were only two adopted revolutionary improvements in firearm design, both the invention of wildfowlers. The first was the snaphaunce, an ignition system where flint striking steel dropped sparks into a small quantity of powder which ignited the main charge. This invention of Dutch wildfowlers was to become the flintlock, which remained the only ignition mechanism until the early 1800s when the Reverend Alexander Forsyth developed the percussion cap.

The agricultural revolution is always understood to be the period from 1750 to 1900, but it started more than a hundred years earlier in the wetlands. Most noticeably on the Bedfordshire Levels, where Cornelius Vermuyden, the great Dutch drainage engineer designed a breath-takingly complex scheme of river diversions and drainage canals in the Lincolnshire peat marshes. Drainage and marsh reclamation became the craze, with armies of Dutch drain diggers swarming all over the country. Some of these reclamations were successful in agricultural terms, others, like Thorne Waste on the Lincolnshire borders, a complete failure. All were fiercely resisted by the wildfowlers and fishermen and all had a detrimental effect on the wildfowl population.

As land reclamation continued in the eighteenth century reducing wetlands and wildfowl habitat, the demand for wildfowl increased as the urban population expanded and toll roads provided a vastly improved transport system. Duck decoys became extremely lucrative, either as rental

AVANT NOEL
Le marché des dindes et des oies en Normandie

income or from direct sales. Some were constructed over natural pools out on accessible marshes, others were artificially built and often included the decoy keeper's house. By the end of the century, there were over two hundred commercial decoys in operation to say nothing of hundreds of smaller decoys supplying rural areas. One commercial decoy, on the Ouse near St Ives in Huntingdonshire, was sending three thousand brace a week to London. Wildfowlers netted and shot as they had for the previous two hundred years, but guns were lighter and more manoeu-verable and bags of wildfowl, bigger. The end of the eighteenth century also saw a new phenomena – the gentleman gunner.

Inland duck shooting had always been a gentleman's sport, often with duck lured into ornamental lakes by tame ones pinioned to posts sunk into the water, a method brought back from France by those who had been on the Grand

Tour. Wildfowling was the work and livelihood of professionals. Lighter shotguns, ease of travel and a genuine fascination with wildlife, drew a handful of sportsmen out onto the saltings to see what the professionals were up to. Those that did, immediately became hooked. The most notable of these was the grandfather of wildfowling, Colonel Peter Hawker.

Hawker was a truly remarkable man. He had written his first book on shooting by the age of fifteen in 1801, the same year that he was commissioned into, my father's old regiment, the 1st Royal Dragoons. He would almost certainly have written more on the subject, but for preventing circumstances created by Napoleon. However, time soldiering was not

wasted, he managed to become the hero of Talavera in 1809, receiving wounds that were to burden him for the rest of his life and wrote *The Journal of a Regimental Officer during the Recent Campaign in Spain and Portugal* whilst recuperating. Back in civilian life and his beloved wildfowling, he published *Instructions to Young Sportsmen* in 1814. This book was unrivalled as a manual on guns and wildfowling for the next fifty years and was into its tenth reprint by 1852, just after he died. He was an adviser to parliament at the time the game laws were rationalised in 1831, wrote music, published another book, *Instructions for the best Position on the Pianoforte*, and invented an ingenious hand mould for use on pianos. Above all, Hawker was a wildfowler and competed with

the professionals on land and at sea. His love of natural history and wildfowl, coupled with his enthusiasm and energy are reflected in the entertaining diaries he kept from 1802–1852.

Wildfowling captured the imagination of sportsmen seeking a step closer to nature. Perhaps a dozen books had touched on the subject before Hawker, at the end of the nineteenth century a further hundred and thirty had been written, by people so moved by their experiences that they discovered a talent for evocative writing. Sir Ralph Payne Gallwey, John Guille Millais, Lewis Clement, the Rev. H. Hely Hutchinson and the great Abel Chapman. These were some of the sportsmen naturalists who deplored what was happening out on the marshes – the continued reclamations, the Victorian passion for taxidermy and egg collecting that led to the extinction of rarer species and the wanton slaughter of mixed wildfowl to supply the consumer market. Worse was a strange anomaly in the 1831 game laws. Under the Act, a landlord could invite whom he chose to shoot or rent the shooting over his land to others. The foreshores (areas between high and low tide) belonged to the Crown and could be shot by anyone. A law intended to give the working man access to fish and a few wildfowl quickly became abused, particularly on marshes anywhere near large cities. With the railways, few marshes were far away and there was no-one to control the numbers or stop the unscrupulous digging of hides on the shore and the indiscriminate shooting of geese as they came in to roost.

In 1908 concerned wildfowlers, led by Stanley Duncan, founded the Wildfowlers Association of Great Britain and Ireland. Wildfowlers were encouraged to form themselves into clubs and acquire the shooting rights on the Crown foreshore and any neighbouring marshes. Their aim was to bring the foreshore and the marshes under the control of responsible people, whose love of wildfowl would ensure the conservation of bird life whilst enabling a traditional pot hunting sport to continue. From small beginnings in Stanley Duncan's black hut at Patrington Haven, which he used when hunting the marshes around Sunk Island on the Humber, WAGBI grew into an organisation which set standards for wetland conservation that have since been emulated in Europe, America, Canada, Australia and New Zealand.

The first hundred years have seen not only an expanding interest in wildfowling and wildfowl conservation, it has also given us another two

hundred and forty wonderful works of literature by luminaries like A. H. Patterson, J. Wentworth Day, D. J. Watkins-Pritchard ( B.B.), L. Brockbank, A. A. Cadman and A. Jarrett. Hundreds of articles are written every year in the sporting press, here, in Europe, America, Australia and New Zealand. The salt marshes, sand dunes, mud flats and endless horizons have inspired artists like Peter Scott and Archibald Thorburn. In 1981, WAGBI expanded to encompass all shooting and conservation issues, changing its name to the British Association of Great Britain and Ireland. BASC now has a membership of a hundred and thirty thousand, with over one thousand, six hundred affiliated clubs and shooting syndicates, of which two hundred are wildfowling clubs. The Association is represented on or works in partnership, with all other major conservation bodies, (particularly the Wildlife Habitat Trust here), in Europe, America and Australasia.

There are no professional wildfowlers left and wildfowling clubs impose bag limits on the number of birds that may be shot per person on any day during the season. Under the Wildlife and Countryside Act 1981, the geese and duck that may be legally shot are restricted to Canada, greylag, and pink-footed geese, with white-fronted geese in England and Wales only. Duck are restricted to: common pochard, gadwall, goldeneye, mallard, pintail, shoveller, teal, tufted duck and wigeon. Some, like pink-footed and teal I find better eating than greylag or pochard but each have gastronomic qualities of their own and none of them find their way into the bag without a great deal of careful assessment of the weather, position of the moon and its influence on the tides.

Sometimes, when I am crouched, deep in the crab grass beside a tidal creek, waiting for the

dawn and listening to the eerie, distant, welling sound of thousands geese stirring on their shore roosts, I can feel the presence of the old wildfowlers. Men that tramped out on to the marshes in their seal skin caps and leather waders, stinking of the goose fat they used to protect themselves against the cold. As the slither of dawn breaks into a lapis lazuli sky above the Norfolk coast and skein after skein of pink-foot pour over to their inland grazing, filling the air with the breath taking sound of their wings and ceaseless 'ang- ang- anging', I see my spectral companion nod with approval.

Wild goose is not allowed to be sold in this country, a conservation measure which is now largely out of date due to political measures in other parts of the world and the conservation work of the wildfowlers. So unless you are friends or more with a goose-shot you may never have eaten them. If not, make friends with those who shoot pink-foot at once. I had never eaten a pink-foot until the first programme in the *Clarissa and the Countryman* series and I must tell you it is one of the most delicious things I have eaten; I now drive through the park in Edinburgh looking longingly at the pink-feet on the loch. Previously I had only eaten Canada goose, the young of this species is good if it has been feeding on grass, but if it has been feeding on the foreshore you need the potato trick I used for duck (see page 80), or plunge the bird into boiling water and then dry carefully. Old Canadas are useless. Brent geese are now protected and greylags really aren't good eating, to put it politely. If you are lucky enough to have a pink-foot the best thing is to roast it, otherwise there follow some recipes (see pages 93–95). If you have more than you can usefully use, cut the breasts off them.

# duck

The ducks most usually eaten are mallard, widgeon and teal. Widgeon are held superior as they are grass feeders, but less common, so unless your lover is a wildfowler, you will find they are not usually available. Teal are quite small and make a single portion, although I tend to allow a duck per person unless they are very large. Wild duck adapts also to casserolling and other similar dishes. The North Kent Wildfowlers complained that you never find recipes for pochard so I have included two but all the duck recipes are pretty much interchangeable, allowing for the size of teal and adapting accordingly. The last meal I ate at the Connaught whilst it was the last great Belle Epoque French Restaurant left, and before the management turned it into yet another part of the Gordon Ramsey Machine, was teal cooked beautifully in a little chaffing dish and ignited with armagnac – the taste was sensational.

## Ageing

The webbing of a young duck can be torn easily, and the feet and bills are brighter on a young bird.

## Hanging

2–3 days are all that is needed. In warm weather ducks are better hung without their innards; the guts can be removed with a button hook without tearing the vent. If a duck has been feeding on the foreshore it may smell fishy, in which case insert a potato and a teaspoon of salt in the cavity and place the bird in a pan with 1cm ($^1/_2$in) boiling water, and bake at 180°C/350°F/gas 4 for 10 minutes. Drain the bird, remove the potato and proceed with the chosen recipe, remembering to deduct 10 minutes from the cooking time.

## Roasting

*Mallard* – place a piece of seasoned butter with herbs or crushed juniper berries or even an onion into the cavity. Smear the breast with butter and roast in a very hot oven (230°C/450°F/gas 8), basting with the butter and some red wine or port or orange juice for 20 minutes. This gives a fairly rare bird, but don't cook for more than 30 minutes in any event or they will sole shoes!

*Pochard* and *Widgeon* – as above.

*Teal* – as above but only cook for 12 minutes and no more than 20 minutes.

## Carving

Carve exactly as for goose (see page 92). Being smaller, the thigh and drumsticks may also be served unless the bird is very rare.

## orange and herb **duck**

Although this recipe is designed for mallard, it works perfectly well with any wild duck, even pochard! If using the small duck you may need more than one breast per person. This recipe serves two.

*breasts from 2 wild duck*
*salt and pepper*

For the stuffing:
*50g (2oz) butter*
*1 teaspoon brown sugar*
*1/2 teaspoon each salt and pepper*
*110g (4oz) thyme, sage and parsley, chopped*
*175g (6oz) breadcrumbs*
*1 shallot, chopped*
*rind and juice of 2 oranges*

Preheat the oven to 180°C/350°F/gas 4.

Carefully slice the duck breasts so that you can open them flat and place them on a piece of tinfoil and lightly season them.

Melt the butter in a frying pan and sauté all the stuffing ingredients, except the orange juice. When the stuffing looks done, add the juice and check the seasoning. Place the stuffing on one half of each duck breast and fold over.

Wrap each one in tinfoil and bake for 40 minutes in the oven. Open each package carefully onto a hot plate so as not to lose the juices.

## **duck** casserole

There are many ways of casserolling ducks and really the ingredients are a matter of choice and can vary to your taste. This is one I really like as the aniseed taste of the fennel goes very well with the duck. There are usually broad beans knocking around in the freezer and unless they are small, I suggest you peel them.

*3 tablespoons olive oil*
*1 onion, chopped*
*3 mallard, cut in half*
*salt and pepper*
*225g (1/2lb) broad beans, blanched and drained*
*juice of 1/2 orange*
*juice of 1/2 lemon*
*12 black olives, cut in half and stoned*
*2 heads of fennel, sliced*
*300ml (1/2 pint) red wine*
*450g (1lb) new potatoes, brought to the boil in cold water cooked*
  *for 20 minutes and drained*
*salt and pepper*

Preheat the oven to 180°C/350°F/gas 4.

Heat the oil in a heavy casserole and fry the onion. Add the duck halves and brown well. Season them, add all the ingredients, except the potatoes and bring to the boil.

Cover and cook in the oven for about 1 hour, or until the ducks are tender. Serve with the new potatoes.

This is an adaptation of a Roman dish, and I have dedicated it to Allan Jarrett, Chairman of BASC and President of the Kent Wildfowlers. The Kentish marshes were frequented by the Romans and they gathered a wild harvest from the land the Wildfowlers cherish so carefully today. Allan challenged me to find a recipe for pochard and this one works very well. However it is advisable to immerse the pochard in warm water, bring to the boil and simmer for 5 minutes, then take it out, dry it and then proceed as below. This is to remove possible fishiness as it is a shore feeder.

For the stuffing:
2 spicy sausages, (Polish, Spanish or Italian)
4 dates or preserved damsons
50g (2oz) ground almonds

salt and pepper
1/4 teaspoon aniseed
2 tablespoons butter
600ml (1 pint) duck stock
1 teaspoon oregano
1 teaspoon thyme

2 mallard or other wild duck
1 glass red wine

For the sauce:
1 teaspoon celery or cumin seeds
1 teaspoon fennel seeds
1/2 teaspoon rosemary
dash of wine vinegar

Preheat the oven to 190°C/375°F/gas 5.

Take the skin off the sausages, and mix all the stuffing ingredients together, and insert it into the cavity of the ducks.

Roast the duck for 45 minutes, basting from time to time. After 30 minutes bring the wine to the boil and pour it over the ducks.

Pound together the celery or cumin seeds, fennel seeds and rosemary; add the vinegar. Remove the cooked ducks to a warm platter, and add the pan juices and wine to the spices. Bring to the boil and reduce slightly. Serve with the duck.

## mallard with sausage and chestnut stew

This is an adaptation of a Roman dish from Apicius's cookery book from the 1st century AD. I am a fan of the author, for when he was down to his last million sesterces (which he considered the price of a good party) he killed himself so that the money would pay for his wake! Now that's what I call a real hedonist.

*50g (2oz) butter*
*110g (4oz) salt pork, diced*
*3 mallard, cut in pieces*
*1 onion, coarsely chopped*
*1 large carrot, sliced*
*2 cloves garlic, crushed*
*375ml (¹/₂ bottle) red wine*
*300ml (¹/₂ pint) stock*
*1 bouquet garni of parsley, thyme and a bay leaf*
*1 large spicy sausage, sliced*
*20 chestnuts, shelled*
*salt and pepper*

In a large casserole melt the butter and brown the salt pork for 5 minutes. Remove the pork and brown the duck pieces in the fat. Remove the duck and sauté the onion and carrot until soft and add the garlic. Pour off the remaining fat. Add the wine to the casserole and boil for 15 minutes until it has reduced by a third.

Return the duck and pork to the pan, add the stock and the bouquet garni and simmer for 1 hour. Remove the duck pieces to a dish and discard the pork pieces. Purée the stock and skim the fat from the top.

Return the duck and stock to the casserole, and add the sausage and chestnuts. Season. Cover and simmer until it is heated through – about 20–30 minutes. Serve with mashed potatoes.

## duck with gin-soaked sloes

In all the years of my drinking I sadly threw away the sloes from yet another finished bottle of sloe gin. I had to be sober to read Prue Coats' lovely *Poacher's Cookbook* and discover finally what to do with them. I no longer make sloe gin so I have to go round begging them off my friends!

*2 rashers streaky bacon, chopped*
*1 onion, chopped*
*1 stick celery, chopped*
*2 tablespoons gin-soaked sloes*
*2 wild duck*
*2 tablespoons sloe gin*
*salt and pepper*

Preheat the oven to 180°C/350°F/gas 4.

Put the bacon, onion and celery into a casserole. Stuff the sloes into the cavities of the ducks and place the birds on top of the vegetables, breast side down. Season. Cover and cook for 1 hour. Remove the lid, turn the ducks breast side up, and cook for a further 15 minutes to brown. Remove to a warm dish and put the vegetables through a mouli. Add the gin to the pan juices and ignite with a match to deglaze. Stir in the vegetable purée and serve with the ducks. Add water or more gin if the sauce is too thick.

## mallard with port

**Duck and port and oranges are a combination made in heaven – I hope you enjoy this dish.**

2 wild ducks
50g (2oz) butter
225g (8oz) streaky bacon rashers
juice of 1 lemon
110g (4oz) orange marmalade
300ml (1/2 pint) game stock
125ml (4fl oz) port
1 teaspoon tomato ketchup
salt, pepper and cayenne

Preheat the oven to 170°C/325°F/gas 3.

Brush the duck breasts with melted butter and cover with bacon rashers. Roast the ducks for 45 minutes. Then zap the oven to 200°C/400°F/gas 6. Remove the bacon, score the breasts and sprinkle with salt, pepper and cayenne. Pour over the lemon juice and return to the oven for 10 minutes. Carve the birds and arrange on a serving dish, and keep warm.

Add the marmalade, stock, port and ketchup to the pan juices and boil to reduce to a thickish sauce. Finish the sauce by adding a little butter and cooking for a few minutes longer to give a lovely glaze to the sauce, then serve with the duck.

## pochard with parsley and blackberries

**This is actually a Swedish dish designed for eider – as much of a challenge as pochard. The Swedes eat all types of wild duck including eiders, which are a huge nuisance to mussel farmers in the Scottish lochs where they can strip a mussel rope in minutes. They are protected in Britain.**

110g (4oz) parsley, chopped
1 tablespoon fresh cream cheese
1 large shallot, chopped
4 pochard breasts
salt and pepper

Preheat the oven to 180°C/350°F/gas 4.

Process the parsley and cream cheese together in a magimix until it's totally green. With a spoon, mix in the shallot and season well. Split the breasts without cutting through them. Spread a layer of the mixture on each breast and fold over again. Bake in the oven for 15 minutes. Rest in a warm place.

For the sauce:
1 tablespoon oil
1 small onion, chopped
1 small carrot, chopped
200ml (7fl oz) beef stock
110g (4oz) blackberries
salt and pepper

Heat the oil and sauté the onion and carrot until soft. Add the stock and blackberries and simmer. Sieve, season and serve with the pochard.

# duck pizzas with caramelised pineapple

This dish was inspired by a delicious starter I had at Bonnars Restaurant in Haddington in East Lothian; the chef whipped it up for me as I am allergic to mushrooms. It is quite delicious, and you can make your pizzas bigger or smaller at will. *Concasse* of tomato is merely home-made tomato purée, made by peeling and deseeding tomatoes and cooking them very slowly with a little oil and seasoning until the juice is first expelled, then evaporated.

For the dough:
*1 packet active dry yeast*
*$1/2$ teaspoon sugar*
*250ml (9fl oz) warm water*
*450g (1lb) strong white flour*
*pinch salt*
*oil*

Mix the yeast and sugar in a bowl. Add half the water and leave to become frothy – about 10–15 minutes. Add the flour, salt and 3 tablespoons of oil and mix well together. Add enough water to make a firm dough and knead well. Rub all over with some oil and leave covered for 2 hours to rise.

For the filling:
*110g (4oz) sugar*
*$1/2$ fresh pineapple or 1 tin pineapple chunks*
*4 tablespoons concasse of tomato or tomato purée*
*the meat from 1 roast mallard*

Put the sugar in a heavy pan and just cover with water. Without stirring, cook over a low heat until a caramel is formed; allow to reduce until it is treacly and a good colour.

Cut the pineapple into small pieces and put in a bowl. Pour over the caramel and toss until all the pineapple pieces are well coated. Put on a wire rack and allow to cool, making sure they are all separated, or they will stick.

Preheat the oven to 240ºC/475ºF/gas 9.

Break the dough into 20 small balls and flatten each ball to 1cm ($1/2$in) thick. Spread with the concasse or purée and place strips of duck on each pizza and then bits of pineapple on top. Cook for 10 minutes in the oven on an oiled baking sheet.

## Other suggested pizza toppings

Pheasant lightly coated with devil sauce (a mixture of worcestershire sauce, Harvey's sauce, dry mustard and whipped double cream) with red onion and capers
Partridge with celery strips and finely chopped walnuts
Strips of venison with thinly pared celeriac (just blanched)
Carpaccio of venison with thyme, oil and balsamic vinegar and slivers of shallot
Roe deer liver cut in very thin strips, tossed in butter with pinenuts
Salmon flakes with blue cheese and sliced gherkins

## salmis of wild **duck**

**This is a good dish to make if you have a mixed bag of different duck.**

*4 young ducks, including the livers*
*75g (3oz) green streaky bacon, chopped*
*1 onion, chopped*
*1 clove, crushed*
*5 juniper berries, crushed*
*1 stick celery, chopped*
*1 bay leaf*
*350ml (12fl oz) red wine*
*25g (1oz) butter*
*3 slices toast soaked in stock and squeezed dry*
*salt and pepper*

Season the ducks and roast in a preheated oven at 220°C/425°F/gas 7 for 30–40 minutes, until they are browned and tender. When they are cool enough to handle, joint the ducks, and cut away the rib cages.

Transfer all the roasting juices into a pan, and add the bacon, onion, clove, juniper berries and celery. Season, then add a bay leaf and the wine. Bring to the boil and cook for about 30 minutes, or until the sauce has reduced by half.

Melt the butter and sauté the livers quickly, then put them and the toast through a mouli or food processor.

Strain the sauce and simmer a little longer, skimming as you go. Stir in the liver mixture and, without boiling, heat the sauce stirring until it has a creamy consistency. Arrange the jointed ducks on a dish and pour over the sauce.

## roast **mallard** with quinces

**In my village there lives an erudite Professor who despite the Scottish climate grows very good quinces. Two years ago his tree produced two hundred or so and I was the grateful recipient of a box. The fruit filled the house with their wonderful smell and I bottled some and baked some, and, as it was a year I received quite a lot of duck, I did this:**

*2 mallard*
*6 x 75–110g (3–4oz) quinces*
*50g (2oz) melted butter*
*glass of white wine*
*salt and pepper*

Preheat the oven to 180°C/350°F/gas 4.

Wipe the duck with a damp cloth and season inside and out. Peel, core and quarter the quinces and stuff them into the cavity of the ducks.

Put the ducks in a roasting pan, melt the butter and pour over the birds. Roast them for 10 minutes.

Pour the wine over the duck and return them to the oven to cook for 40 minutes, basting as you go.

Zap up the temperature as high as it will go. Return the ducks for a few minutes to crisp the skin.

## teal with oranges

**A nice little dish for a splendid little bird, not quite the Connaught but in memory of its splendid food...**

*2 Seville oranges*
*2 strips barding fat*
*2 teal*
*4 shallots, finely chopped*
*1 tablespoon Grand Marnier or cognac*
*salt and pepper*

Preheat the oven to 220°C/450°F/gas 8.

Peel the rind from the oranges and cut the rind into thin strips. Squeeze the oranges and keep the juice.

Bard the birds and roast for about 12 minutes. Remove the barding fat, making several long slits along the breasts to allow the juices to flow. Season and add the shallots, the rind and the orange juice. Return to the oven for another 5–10 minutes, depending on the size of the birds and how rare you like them.

Transfer the birds to a dish. Heat the contents of the roasting pan and pour in a little Grand Marnier or cognac, and then ignite with a match to deglaze. Pour over the birds.

## cold duck salad with lucy's dressing

**This is a great way of using up leftover duck and is delicious as a starter or lunch dish. The dressing is named after my young friend Lucy Tibbitts who helped me invent it at one of her mother's lunch parties.**

*150g (5oz) cooked duck meat*
*2 red peppers*
*225g (8oz) cooked broad beans (unless they are very young remove the skins, the bright green is attractive with the peppers)*
*1 dessertspoon French mustard*
*1 clove garlic, crushed*
*juice of 1/2 lemon*
*1 dessertspoon ginger syrup*
*olive oil*
*salt and pepper*

Cut the duck into enticing pieces; grill your peppers, remove the skins and slice into strips.

Make a dressing by mixing the mustard, garlic, lemon juice, salt and pepper and ginger syrup together, trickling in the olive oil to form a smooth dressing – use a lot of muscle!

Mix the pepper strips and the broad beans together and dress with two thirds of the dressing. Arrange the duck strips on the top and pour over the rest of the dressing. Serve with good bread.

# goose

### Carving

Assuming you are, like me, right handed, position the bird so that the thigh bones are facing towards you. Place the prongs of the carving fork on either side of the breast bone and, using the flat of the blade, prise open the right hand thigh.

With the curved point of the carving knife, separate the thigh where it attaches to the body at the hip socket. This will almost certainly be very stiff and will require a certain amount of manual twisting. The thigh and drumstick of a wild bird are sure to be tough and should either be put back in the oven and served as a second helping or set aside for devilling, or converting into confit, at a later stage.

Do the same with the wing and repeat on the opposite side. Once the thighs and wings are removed the bird is ready for carving.

Begin by making an incision down the length of one side of the dividing breast bone. Make a second incision exactly parallel to the first and 3–5mm (1/8–1/4in) from it, turning the blade of the knife in towards the breast bone as it nears the bone and cutting inwards to free the slice. Lift it out and lay it on the plate. Continue taking long strips of meat in this manner until the breast bone drops down towards the wing and thigh joints. Then turn the carcase on its side with your fork and remove the last few slices by carving towards you from the wing joint to the thigh joint. Turn the bird over and repeat on the other side.

### Ageing

At the beginning of the season a useful clue is the notch in the tail feathers where the downy juvenile plumage has fallen out and not yet been replaced. This is a V-shaped notch about 3mm (1/2in) deep and wide. In a young pink-foot the bill is a blotchy flesh colour, the legs pale pink and the head pale and brownish; the plumage on the breast and belly is speckled and looks immature. In the adult the beak is banded pink on black, the head is dark almost black, and the breast and belly plumage is clear, and the legs the pink that gives the bird its name.

With greylags the bill of the juvenile is pale orange, the breast and belly slightly speckled and the legs a greyish pink. The beak of the adult is a clear orange, the plumage is spotted on the breast, but the belly is not speckled and the legs are a darker pink. With Canadas the cheek patches of the juveniles are greyer turning to white in the adult bird. Size is the main indication with Canadas.

### Hanging
3 weeks for Canadas and greylags, 2 weeks for pink-feet.

### Plucking
Geese are difficult to pluck as the feathers are very stiff, and so you will have sore thumbs. Find a friendly butcher or bribe a nice young man. You will need to singe after plucking as the carcase is unlikely to be clean unless you are very proficient.

### Roasting
Wild goose being dry, benefits from stuffing. There are many variants for stuffing, from foie gras to potatoes, but the important thing is to make sure it contains plenty of butter to keep it moist. I like to fry an onion in butter, and mix in apple, lemon rind, lemon juice, breadcrumbs, salt and pepper, herbs, anchovies, pickled walnuts and about 110g (4oz) butter in all, but use your imagination.

Stuff the goose, rub with butter and roast, breast down or on a trivet. Put in at 230°C/450°F/gas 8 for about 10 minutes, then reduce to 170°C/325°F/gas 3. Baste frequently, adding wine, orange juice or stock if the pan juices dry out. In total it will take 1–1 1/2 hours depending on size. Test with a skewer. Give 3–4 slices to each person. A wild goose will serve 4 people.

## goose with red cabbage and treacle

The front cover of our book *Sunday Roast* shows Johnny and me looking like something from a Norman Rockwell picture but on the table in front of us is a pink-footed goose with red cabbage; it is a lovely combination.

*1 goose (pink-foot or young Canada)*
*caster sugar*
*1 tablespoon olive oil*
*1 onion, chopped*
*3 sharp apples (not Bramleys as they collapse)*
*1 good sized red cabbage*
*2 tablespoons black treacle*
*1 wine glass sharp cider*
*salt and pepper*

Preheat the oven to 180°C/350°F/gas 4.

Rub the goose fiercely with salt, pepper and sugar.

In a heavy casserole heat the oil and fry the onion until golden.

Core and roughly slice the apples, shred the cabbage and add these to the onion. Add the treacle and cider, stir well and allow to cook for 10 minutes. Place the goose on top of this, cover and put in the oven for 45 minutes. Remove the lid and cook uncovered for another 25 minutes, or until the goose is cooked.

## canada goose stuffed with olives and prunes

Old Canada geese are pretty horrible and not much use for anything, but young Canadas can be quite good eating. This is a dish I invented when working for Rebeka Hardy at Danehill; her husband had shot it on the Solway and we were determined to eat it.

*175g (6oz) stoned prunes*
*armagnac or cognac*
*1 young Canada goose*
*225g (8oz) stoned green olives*
*barding fat*
*1 onion, chopped*
*3 sticks celery, chopped*
*rind of 1 orange, cut into strips*
*salt and pepper*

Marinate the prunes overnight in armagnac or cognac. Drain them (but keep the marinade), and stuff the olives with slices of prune; reserving some of the prunes. Stuff the cavity of the goose with the stuffed olives and leftover prunes. Season the goose and bard the breast.

Preheat the oven to 180°C/350°F/gas 4.

Arrange the onion, celery and orange peel in the bottom of a roasting dish. Put the goose on top and cook for 1 hour in the oven. Remove the fat. Take a ladle full of armagnac or cognac, add the prune brandy, set fire to it and pour over the goose. When it has finished burning return the goose to the oven and roast for a further 15 minutes. Strain the pan juices, reduce a little and serve with the goose, as well as the stuffing.

# roast **goose** with dumplings

**This is a Hungarian recipe. I used to go every year to the Gay Hussar in Soho to eat pike, wild cherry soup and roast goose, indeed it was the last meal I shared with my mother before her death. Lake Balikon is black with wildfowl during the autumn migration and much goose is consumed.**

110g (4oz) smoked bacon, finely chopped

110g (4oz) lard or goose fat

1 onion, chopped

1 parsnip, chopped

1 heel celery, chopped

1 carrot, peeled and sliced

1 clove garlic, crushed

1 goose

2 tablespoons flour

600ml (1 pint) white game stock

1 teaspoon paprika

1 bay leaf

1 teaspoon marjoram

10 peppercorns

1/2 glass of Hock or fruity white wine

1 teaspoon French mustard

1/2 teaspoon sugar

juice of 1 lemon

salt

For the dumplings:

1 egg

3 tablespoons lard, chicken fat or butter

2–3 tablespoons water

350g (12oz) flour

salt

Preheat the oven to 250°C/500°F/gas 10, or as high as it will go.

In a large roasting pan cook the bacon gently, then add the lard and melt. Add the vegetables and garlic and cook gently for a few minutes. Put the goose on top of the vegetables and roast in the oven for 20 minutes.

Remove the goose, sprinkle flour on the vegetables, and then add the stock and paprika. Bring to the boil and simmer for a few minutes. Carve the goose and place the pieces on top of the vegetables, and then add the herbs, peppercorns and the wine. Cover and cook over a low heat on top of the stove until the goose is cooked – about 1 hour.

Remove the goose joints and keep warm; then push everything else through a sieve or mouli. To the purée add the mustard, sugar, lemon juice and salt.

To make the dumplings, mix together the egg, 1 tablespoon of your chosen fat, the water and salt. Mix in the flour. Do not work the mixture too much and allow it to rest for 10 minutes covered with a damp cloth. Boil a large pan of water and add salt. When the dumplings have all risen to the surface, remove them with a slotted spoon, rinse in cold water and drain.

Before serving, fry the dumplings in the remaining 1 tablespoon of fat and serve with the goose.

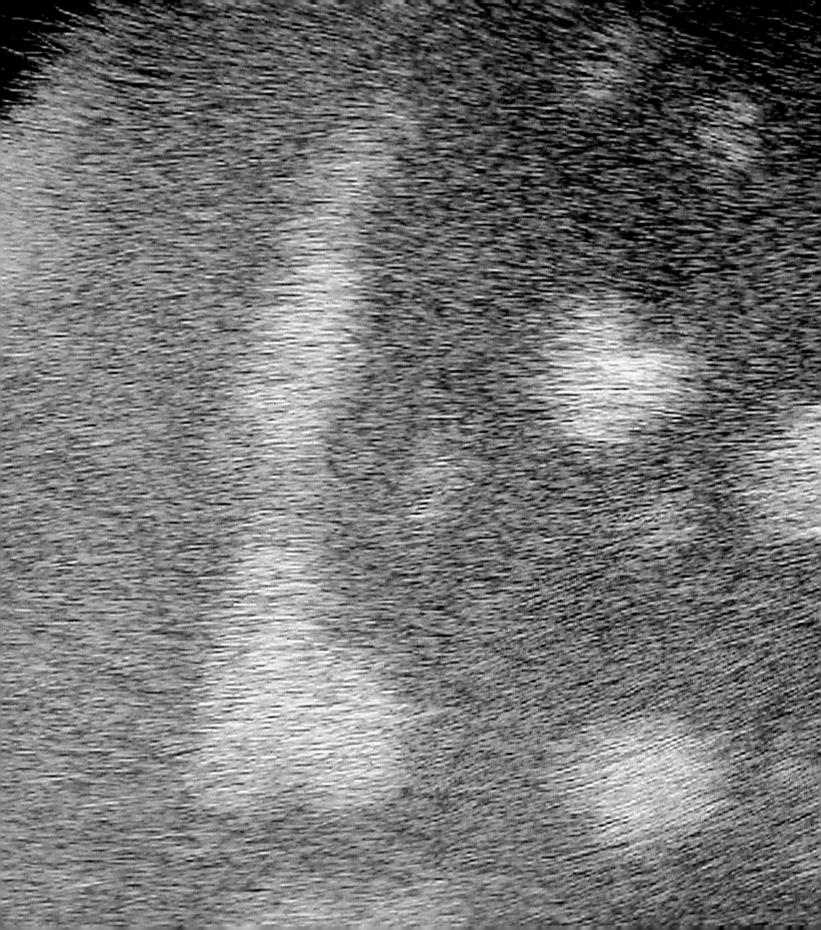

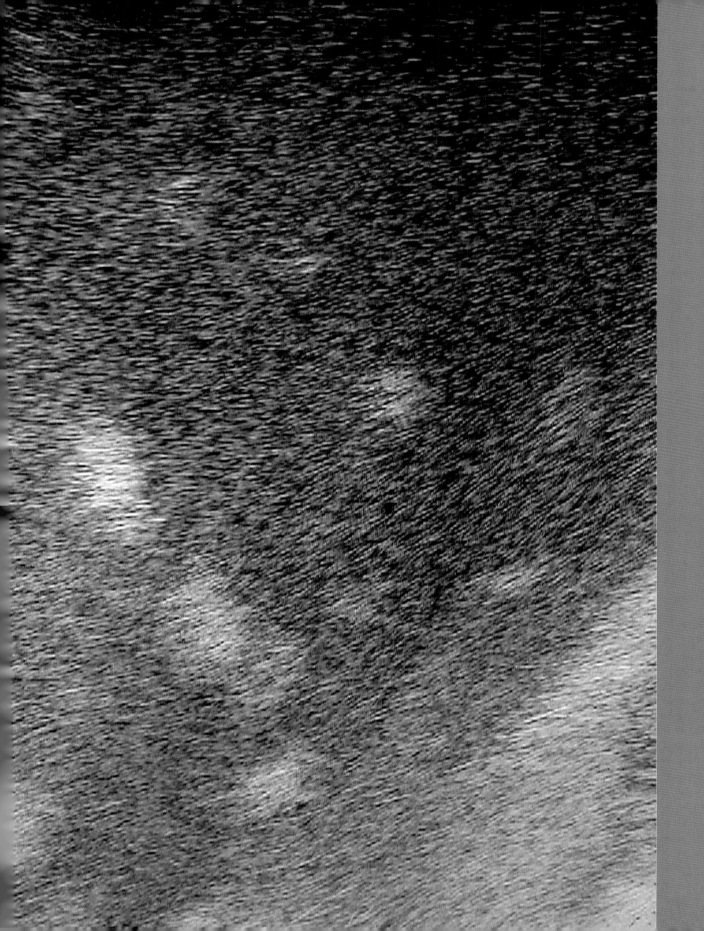

cloven hoof

# cloven hoof

Since the end of the Ice Age, deer, which includes any member of the *Cervidae* family including moose, elk and reindeer, have always been the principal game quarry. Size made them the most obvious target. There were and still are an enormous number living in the wild and they provided both meat and valuable hide.

More venison, the flesh of any deer species, is eaten today than all the other game species put together. To meet the consumer demand an increasing volume of venison is farmed in Europe, Scandinavia, North America, Australia and New Zealand. The rest comes from the management of wild deer species in their natural environment, a responsibility that is necessary for animal welfare and to protect farmland; it also brings wild venison into the food chain and provides an essential input to rural economies from sporting tourism.

The forests of Saxon Britain teamed with majestic red deer (*Cervus elaphus*), little roe deer, ferocious wild boar, wolves and possibly fallow deer (*Dama dama*). There is a school of thought that believes the Romans introduced fallow deer. All of these were first beaten out of cover into the open, and then hunted with gaze hounds that were probably not unlike the Scottish deer hound or Irish wolf hound of today. Most deer were taken in what were known as hayes, which were funnel-shaped stockades, sometimes incorporating a natural feature of the landscape, like a narrow, deadened valley. Whole herds of deer were driven into the hayes and ambushed. The meat was salted and the hides, an extremely valuable commodity, were tanned. This system, known by the gaelic name *tainchell*, continued in Scotland until the end of the eighteenth century.

The Normans introduced an entirely different method of hunting, based on selective culling, using packs of scenting hounds trained to hunt the scent of an individual beast – this was the precursor of modern hunting. They introduced a form of deer management which, although intensely unpopular with the vanquished Saxons and in time, with the Norman nobles as well, was nevertheless highly efficient. William the Conqueror and his successors declared huge areas of land, known as Royal Forests, their personal hunting preserves. These were franchised out, subject to certain rents in kind, to the nobility and clergy. The wild animals within the Forests were strictly categorised in terms of their ability to provide sport as well as their carcase value. Beasts of Forest were the noble beasts of Venery: the hart, the hind (red deer), the hare, the boar, and the wolf who made up for being inedible by his extreme sporting challenge. Less noble were the Beasts of Chase: the buck, the doe (fallow deer), the fox, the marten and the roe. Beasts of warren, which were the coney (rabbit), pheasant, partridge and hare, were not hunted. These animals were kept in enormous enclosures and more or less farmed, in commercial enterprises called warrens. All game belonged to the monarch and he would generally retain the beasts of venery for himself and particularly favoured nobility. However the franchise holder could sublet the rights of Chase or Warren to others, although he was always held responsible for seeing that game stocks were maintained and improved. Game within the forests and the conservation of their habitat were protected by ferociously brutal forest laws.

By the thirteenth century, the Royal hunting preserves covered a staggering thirty percent of England, at which point the Barons, in their confrontation with King John, grabbed most of it

for themselves, with land owners doing the same thing to the Barons a century and a half later. During the Age of Chivalry, the terminology, traditions and ceremonies of hunting became increasingly elaborate. Concentrating on courtesy and respect for the quarry, knowledge of the intricacies of hunting played a major role in the life of every gentleman's son.

A parkland of deer was an essential part of every Tudor landlord's establishment. These were socially competitive times and many had two parks, one for red deer and the other for fallow, which combined the convenience of a readily available food source with the ability to provide entertainment for one's guests. Apart from the hunting element, these deer parks were little different from modern deer farms. Outside deer parks, the wild red deer population had been largely removed because of the damage they caused to farmland. There were exceptions, most notably in the north, and down in the West Country where Exmoor was still a royal forest and the red deer population was controlled by staghounds in the same way as they are today. In Scotland there were any number in the great forests of Caledonia, Jed and Ettrick. Except for a wild population in the New Forest, most fallow were in the parks. Roe had little stature in terms of venery, having been demoted from a Beast of Chase to a Beast of Warren in 1338, and were pretty ruthlessly eradicated as pests. The majority lived in the great northern woods and in Scotland. Wild boar were extinct and the last wolf in England had been killed, reputedly by John of Gaunt. Both were still hunted with great enthusiasm in Europe though.

All deer went through a period of great disruption in the seventeenth and eighteenth centuries. During the Civil War, Cromwell's troops slaughtered whole herds of park deer. They also found park railings a convenient source of firewood, and large numbers of deer escaped into the wild. Some deer parks were re-established after the Commonwealth but many of the old Royalist landowners were obliged to sell their park timber to pay debts. Soon the wild deer found their habitat disappearing as deforestation, which had been happening invidiously for centuries, suddenly accelerated with the beginning of the Industrial Revolution. At the same time, vast acreages of heath and moorland – about two million acres between 1700 and 1800 – were enclosed to meet the demands of an expanding urban population, and the needs of an army on active duty abroad, for much of the period.

The most dramatic effect was on red deer, particularly in Scotland. All deer are forest dwellers, and as their woodland strongholds in the forests of Jed, Ettrick and Caledonia disappeared they were forced to seek new habitat in the open hill ranges of the Highlands. The same thing happened in England, with most red deer living on Exmoor, Dartmoor and the Quantocks. As a forest animal red deer lived singly or in small family groups depending on the season. With their cover gone, the homeless deer herded together for safety, with stags and hinds in separate groups, except during the rut.

It is this imposed behavioural pattern and the spectacular landscape of Europe's last great wilderness, that was to make the management of Scottish deer forests absolutely unique. Not however, for another hundred years. Hardly had the red deer established themselves in their new habitat than flock masters, offering huge rents for grazings, appeared in Scotland. In 1750 the red deer population was described as substantial. With the arrival of sheep, this population was to decline dramatically and, by 1810 only a handful of the now recognised four hundred and fifty deer forests carried any quantity of deer. Even T. B. Johnson in his *Sportsman's Cyclopedia* of 1831 referred to them as scarce and localised. However, the soil depth in the Highlands is too shallow to sustain large flocks of sheep for long, and numbers were already falling when the bottom fell out of the wool market in the middle of the century. As the sheep left, red deer started to come back. Some sportsmen were making the long journey north by coach in the early part of the century, to fish, walk-up grouse and black game, and try their luck stalking red deer.

Improvements in rifle making, Lefaucheux's breech loader, Eley's cartridge, a rapidly expanding railway system and Queen Victoria's passion for Scotland, led to the development of deer forests as prime land use on many Highland estates. By the end of the nineteenth century the area covered by deer forests, on land that would otherwise have been valueless, had risen to two million hectares.

All wild deer are unintentionally, extremely destructive. However, their welfare is our responsibility and deer forest management is, allowing for the difficulties of the landscape, exactly the same as any other form of stock farming. The health of a group of animals is determined by their number relative to available herbage, and a stalker's job is to ensure that this delicate balance is achieved. It is sporting tourism that enables deer forest management to be viable. Today, deer forests cover thirty-seven percent of Scotland's land mass, support a red deer population of 350,00 and play a vital part in maintaining the rural infrastructure.

The same management policies apply to our other deer species, which are roe, fallow, sika, muntjac and Chinese water deer. Agricultural improvements, woodland planting for game bird and fox cover, and even the hideous blocks of post-war conifer plantations, have created a perfect habitat for deer. The dwindling roe and fallow population began to expand in the late nineteenth century as they were joined by escapees from German stock introduced as park deer in the 1850s. This feral population is now distributed throughout Britain. Japanese sika have flourished in the West Country since the early twentieth century, particularly in Hampshire and are now spreading across Britain. These deer are descendants of those that swam ashore from Brownsea Island in

1896, and the pair that hopped over the fence the day after Edward VII gave them to Lord Montague of Beaulieu. In just eighty years, since the release of a few pairs from Woburn Abbey in the 1920s, little Chinese muntjac have become the most widely distributed of all deer in England. There are so many in East Anglia that they are predating into the suburbs of London. A relative newcomer, the curiously tusked Chinese water deer, found mainly in the south but spreading, is with us courtesy of the keeper who left the gates of Whipsnade open one night during the war.

The cloven hoofed are big business worldwide. Across Europe and Scandinavia, red, fallow, sika, reindeer, elk, roe and wild boar are all stalked, or in the case of France depending on species, hunted with hounds. The Finns use elkhounds to locate and drive from cover the eighty thousand or so that are culled annually. In New Zealand, sambar, red deer, wapiti, fallow, Himalayan tahr, chamois, sika, and American white-tailed deer, have been introduced and provide a burgeoning commercial and recreational industry. Which, apart from sport and venison, supplies the Far East homeopathic medicine market with by-products – antler velvet, blood, sinews, tail and pizzles. Pig hunting in New Zealand with dogs especially bred for the job is the national pastime in rural areas. Australia has chital, fallow, hog deer, red deer, sambar and like New Zealand, domestic pigs turned feral, in the less arid areas. The United States and Canada have got the lot. Their own indigenous species – moose, caribou, white-tailed deer, mule deer, and lovely prong horned antelope, to which have been added red, sika, fallow, Columbian black-tail, and chital. There are now more deer in North America than when the Pilgrim Fathers arrived. Down in Alabamy, hog hunting is practically a religion.

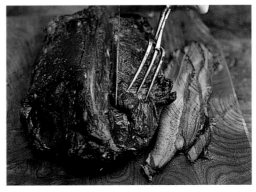

## Carving

The method of carving venison is determined by the size of the carcase, but is basically the same as for lamb or mutton. Roe, muntjac and Chinese water deer are carved like lamb.

### Saddle

Here the carver has a chance to show off. Allow yourself plenty of room as you will be carving slices from the rump, saddle and fillet for each plate. The joint will require turning to get at the fillet and you will be working at speed. Insert the fork in the joint to the left of the backbone and run the point of the knife down the length of the back bone until it meets the hip bone. Remove the knife and cut straight down over the ribs beside the hip bone. This leaves a clear right-angled incision separating the saddle meat from the rump. Make another incision 4mm ($1/6$th in) thick, parallel with the first, angling your knife towards the chine when it meets the ribs to free the meat. Lift out the long delicate pink slice and place on the plate. Move the fork to the left side of the rump and insert. Carve horizontally across the rump towards the hip bone, adding the slice of rump to the plate. Now, ensuring your knife is firmly fixed beside the backbone, lever the joint over, cut a slice of fillet towards the chine and serve.

### Leg

For a leg of roe, carve as for a large leg of lamb or mutton. Take the knuckle end wrapped in a cloth in the left hand, cut right across the joint at the meatiest part, down to the bone levelling the knife when the edge of the meat is reached on either side. Make a second, 4mm ($1/6$in) thick, parallel with the first making sure that the knife is angled so that the first slice is a thin wedge. Continue taking slices on either side of the original maintaining the wedge shape until this side is completed. Turn the joint over and proceed as before. With the little legs of muntjac and water deer,

position the leg so that the thickest area at the hip end is uppermost and insert fork. Cut a small wedge at the point where the meat at the knuckle end begins to widen. Angle your knife at 35° and carve slices 4mm ($1/2$) thick until you reach the pelvic bone. Then turn the joint and carve the remainder in slices parallel to the bone.

Saddle of sika and fallow are carved depending on their size, does are smaller than bucks. Smaller joints are carved as lamb, larger ones like a loin of pork. Make an incision along the back bone but instead of carving parallel strips, carve slices across the saddle and over the ribs 4mm ($1/6$in) thick, angling the knife as you touch bone to free each slice. Be sure to keep the knife at an angle of 35°.

A saddle from the Monarch of the Glen, elk or moose would be carved like a sirloin of beef, across the ribs from the chine. In this instance, keep your slices to an 3mm ($1/8$in), there will be no shortage of flavour. A haunch will be carved like a leg of mutton, either as a whole or divided into a shank end gigot or rump. To carve these, start at the point where the joint has been divided and carve back towards the knuckle with a shank end, and towards the pelvis for the rump, remembering always to keep a slight angle to the joint.

---

It is unlikely that you will shoot a red deer without the aid of a stalker, but I can conceive of some circumstances where you might have to dispatch of one. The first thing you must do, and quickly, is to paunch it – meat goes off very quickly or at best is tainted if the entrails are not removed. You will need a very sharp knife as deer hide is tough. Make a slit from the vent up to the thorax and handle the deer so that the paunch comes out, it is then easy to cut it free. Keep the liver and

kidneys as they are delicious but, unless you are intending to make haggis or humble pie with the lights and lungs, leave the rest out on the hill, carefully buried. Your deer will need hanging in a cool larder, and if it's not fly-proof, wrap the carcase in muslin and put some bog myrtle around the anus. Remove the head before hanging. Flay the deer which really only needs a sharp knife and attention to detail and butcher it as for a sheep. I suggest you may need professional help at this stage or at least a butchery book. A red deer is quite large and not for the faint-hearted. For our overseas friends, recipes for red deer will translate happily for Elk, Moose, Reindeer and Caribou.

### Red Deer

*To Roast:* Marinade your joint overnight in red wine and olive oil. Remove from the marinade and dry. Rub the meat all over with salt and pepper. Preheat oven to 220°C/425°F/gas 7. Bard the joint with fat pork and cook for 15 minutes per 450g (1lb). Roasting joints are the haunch, shoulder or saddle.

### Roe Deer

I find roe meat totally delicious and could exist happily on this beast and no other for all of my declining years. A sporting farmer, hearing of my passion for its offal, recently sent me a parcel of kidneys, livers, hearts and sweetbreads; bless you, Tommy, what a feast I had! Roe deer are vermin and do immense damage so one can eat them with virtue as well as relish. If you find yourself with a carcase treat it as for red deer, although it is smaller and easier to handle. Our American cousins should use the roe recipes for white tail and antelope. Roast as for red deer.

### Muntjac

Hang it for 3–5 days paunched but in its skin and then skin it and cook it.

# west country **venison** with cider

# texas **hash**

There is a great deal of venison in the West Country. At the time of writing, existing legislation maintains that the stag hunting south of the Bristol Channel is the most effective and humane way of keeping the population under control in the heavily wooded coombs and open moors of the region. Those of you who dispute this statement, go out and see for yourself. Cider is also a great product of the region so it is an obvious meld.

900g–1.3kg (2–3lb) of venison
600ml (1 pint) cider
50g (2oz) flour
50g (2oz) melted butter
1/2 teaspoon ground allspice
a bunch of mixed herbs
2 onions, finely chopped
110g (4oz) carrots, diced
75ml (3fl oz) venison stock
salt and pepper

Marinate the venison for 8 hours in the cider, turning it from time to time. Remove, dry and sprinkle with flour, salt and pepper. Reserve the cider.

Preheat the oven to 180°C/350°F/gas 4.

Brown the venison in the butter, sprinkle with allspice and add the herbs and vegetables. Pour over the cider and the stock. Cover tightly and cook for 2 hours.

Traditionally this dish is served with watercress, I wilt mine in a little melted butter, and season it with salt and pepper, and serve as a vegetable.

Again hash is a good way of using up venison mince, of which there always seems to be a lot of from the forequarter. You can, if you prefer, chop it very finely rather than mince it which I feel gives a nicer texture, but hey – what the hell! Life's too short.

450g (1lb) minced venison
3 tablespoons oil or bacon fat
3 large onions, chopped
450g (1lb) cooked tomatoes (tinned will do)
2 jalepeno chillies, chopped
1 teaspoon chilli powder
2 medium potatoes, thinly sliced
175g (6oz) Monterrey cheese, grated (use cheddar as a substitute)
salt and pepper

Preheat the oven to 180°C/350°F/gas 4.

Brown the meat in the oil or fat. Add the onions and cook until they are soft. Stir in the tomatoes, chillies, chilli powder and the seasoning and cook for about 5 minutes longer. Spread into a flat oven dish, layer the sliced potatoes on top and sprinkle with the grated cheese.

Cover and bake for 45 minutes. Remove the cover and cook for a further 15 minutes or until nicely browned.

## venison with wild mushroom stew

## red deer with beetroot

This is a central European recipe; I can't remember whether it came from a Polish or a Hungarian friend, but it is jolly good. Use a mixture of wild mushrooms – whatever is growing. If you have none, use field mushrooms but the colour may suffer!

450g (1lb) venison
400g (14oz) leanish pork
olive oil
150g (5oz) Polish boiling sausage, roughly sliced
2 large onions
2 cloves garlic
3/4 teaspoon paprika
400g (14oz) sauerkraut
225g (8oz) dried mushrooms
570g (20oz) fresh mushrooms
225ml (8fl oz) game stock
225ml (8fl oz) white wine
3/4 teaspoon caraway seeds
bouquet garni of marjoram and thyme
600ml (1 pint) single cream
salt and pepper

Cube the meats and brown them in olive oil. Transfer to a large casserole with the sausage. Chop the onions and garlic and sauté until golden. Mix in the paprika and add to the meat. Add all the remaining ingredients, except the cream. Bring to the boil, stir in the cream, cover and simmer for 1 hour. Check the seasoning and serve with flat noodles or mashed potatoes and greens.

The brilliant food writer Claire Macdonald discovered there is an enzyme in beetroot that breaks down the fibres in venison. When I was staying at Kinloch Lodge, the blissful hotel on Skye, she told me it would tenderise even the toughest old stag.

900g (2lb) venison, cut in cubes
seasoned flour
oil
2 strong onions, chopped
10 juniper berries, crushed
3 medium beetroots, chopped
1 tablespoon redcurrant jelly
300ml (1/2 pint) burgundy or other strong red wine
150ml (5fl oz) game stock
3 sprigs of thyme (dried will do)

Preheat the oven to 170°C/325°F/gas 3.

Toss the venison chunks in the seasoned flour, heat some oil and brown the meat in the oil. Transfer it to a casserole. Fry the onions in the same pan and then add to the venison.

Add all the other ingredients to the venison. Bring to the boil and put in a slow oven for 2 hours, or until the venison is tender. Serve with mashed potatoes or colcannon.

## red wine **venison** burgers

## **venison** liver with puréed peas

**Burgers are a good way of using up surplus rare venison; here the red wine in the burger gives a nice rich flavour. You can make a lot at once and freeze them for barbecues.**

*450g (1lb) venison*
*175g (6oz) streaky bacon*
*1 small glass dry red wine*
*2 tablespoons finely chopped shallot (use onion if no shallot)*
*olive oil*
*2 tablespoons parsley, finely chopped*
*1 tablespoon redcurrant jelly*
*salt and pepper*

Put the meat and bacon through the grinder together, or chop in the magimix. Add half the red wine and the shallot to the meats, mix well and season.

Form into 4 burgers, pressing hard so they are tightly formed, and rest in a cool place for at least 30 minutes. Heat a little oil in a frying pan and fry the burgers – don't turn until they are browned on the first side. Cook for about 5 minutes each side, more if you like them well done. Remove the burgers and keep them warm. Pour off any surplus fat.

Pour the rest of the wine into the pan, raise the heat and stir in the redcurrant jelly. Cook until the sauce is hot and the jelly melted. Add the parsley, pour the sauce over the burgers and serve.

**This is a very simple way of serving venison liver, but slightly different. I think it works rather well.**

*750g (1lb 10oz) peas, fresh, frozen or bottled*
*3 tablespoons single cream*
*700g (1 1/2 lb) liver*
*75g (3oz) seasoned flour: salt, pepper, dried mustard and*
 *a little cayenne*
*butter*
*salt and pepper*

Cook the peas and purée them until they are almost smooth. Add the cream and season.

Slice the liver finely, and toss in seasoned flour. Heat a little butter in a heavy pan and quickly sauté the liver so that it is still pink.

Put the peas on a dish, lay the liver slices on top and pour over the pan juices.

# venison pastie

This is what Robin Hood took on his picnics! I love pasties and indeed when I am making mine I usually don't cook the venison first. However I am the first to admit that this is chewy and, in the interests of harmony, I am offering you the more conventional method. Add anything that amuses you to your pasties but do use lard in the pastry – I can't understand people who will happily eat bacon but gasp in horror at the thought of lard.

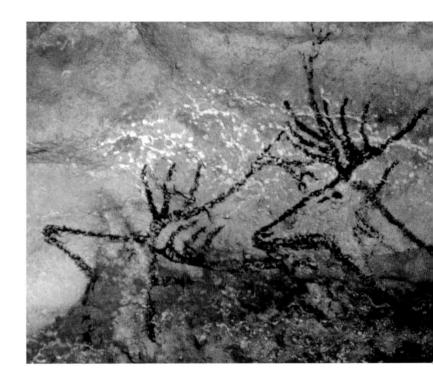

For the pastry:
*225g (8oz) plain flour*
*50g (2oz) butter*
*50g (2oz) lard*
*4 teaspoons cold water*
*pinch of salt*

Sift the flour and salt into a bowl. Cut the butter and lard into small pieces and rub them into the flour using your hands until the mixture resembles breadcrumbs. Add enough water to make pliable dough. Knead lightly, form into a ball and wrap in a damp cloth; chill for 30 minutes.

For the filling:
*450g (1lb) venison, cut from haunch or saddle*
*2 medium onions, chopped*
*1 glass red wine*
*150ml (5fl oz) stock*
*bouquet garni of thyme, parsley and a bay leaf*
*2 tablespoons redcurrant jelly*
*cornflour*
*a sliver of apple or a few redcurrants*
*1 egg yolk, mixed with a little milk*
*salt and pepper*

Cut the venison in small pieces, and put in a saucepan with the onion, wine, stock, salt and pepper, bouquet garni and jelly. Bring to the boil and simmer until the meat is tender – about 40 minutes. Strain the liquid, then boil it hard to reduce to 200ml (7fl oz). Thicken with a little cornflour mixed in cold water.

Roll out the pastry and cut into 4 circles, about 10 x17.5cm (4 x 7in) each. Put the meat mixture onto one half of the pastry circles, and add a sliver of apple or a few redcurrants to each one. Damp the pastry edges, fold over and crimp firmly together.

Preheat the oven to 200°C/400°F/gas 6. Place on a greased baking sheet and brush with a little egg. Make a slit in the top of each pastie, and bake for about 30 minutes.

Reheat the sauce, and pour a little into each pastie through a funnel. Serve hot or cold.

# norwegian **venison** with sour cream

I was served this dish by a Norwegian friend I had at the time called Ninni; it struck me as quite delicious. Since then I have seen a similar Russian recipe for hare done in much the same way which I expect would be rather good. In Norway the dish would be made with elk or moose but I make it with venison. The Scandinavians use a white malt vinegar, but I use wine vinegar. I have to confess that I stir the cream in at the beginning, but it doesn't look so appealing, but you have to reduce the sauce at the end in any event. I leave it to you, gentle reader.

For the marinade:
225ml (8fl oz) wine vinegar
450ml (16fl oz) water

1.8kg (4lb) venison, chopped into 5cm (2in) cubes
seasoned flour
2 carrots, sliced
2 Hamburg parsley root, sliced (or use celery)
2 onions, sliced
40g (1$^1$/$_2$oz) butter
600ml (1 pint) strong ale
450ml (16fl oz) sour cream
1 tablespoon dill, chopped

Marinade the meat for at least 2 hours. Drain the meat, dry it and dust it with seasoned flour.

Preheat the oven to 180°C/350°F/gas 4. Put the meat in a casserole with all the vegetables. Melt the butter and pour it over the meat and vegetables. Then pour over the ale. Cook, covered, for about 1 hour. Strain the roasting juices into a clean pan and reduce by half over a high heat. Mix in the soured cream, pour over the meat and cook for a further 1 hour. Sprinkle with dill and serve.

# **venison** hotpot

Hotpot was designed for the long bones of the Lancastrian sheep which acted as a frame to hold in the other ingredients. Sheep breeds have changed so much that you can't really often find that effect with mutton, but venison chops do very well instead. As far as I know no-one nowadays makes black pudding with deer's blood but in Orkney and the Isle of Harris they make theirs with sheep's blood. It is quite delicious and really suited to this venison dish but any good black pudding will do. Stewart Higginson at Grange-over-Sands makes a wonderful one which I stock up with when I am visiting lovely Holker Hall.

8 venison chops, with bone shortened
4 venison kidneys (use lamb's if none available)
900g (2lb) potatoes, sliced
4 slices black pudding
2 onions, sliced
300ml ($^1$/$_2$ pint) stock
25g (1oz) oil or butter
salt and pepper

Preheat the oven to 180°C/350°F/gas 4. Trim any fat from the chops. Heat a little oil in a pan and brown the chops and the kidneys over a high heat for 3–4 minutes.

Put a layer of potatoes in a deep ovenproof dish, lay some of the chops over the top, then a layer of kidneys and then a layer of onions. Continue with a layer of potatoes, then black pudding and so on, seasoning each layer with salt and pepper. Add the stock. Finish with a layer of potatoes, and brush the top with oil or dot with butter.

Cover and cook for 2 hours. Remove the lid, increase the heat and cook for a further 30 minutes to brown.

## roe fillet with red onion marmalade

Roe deer fillet, like all deer meat, should be eaten on the rare side unless it is stewed. Like squid it should be cooked a little or a lot but medium cooking doesn't suit. Do not cook your fillet to anything beyond medium rare or it will be like boot leather.

For the marmalade:

*3 red onions*

*50g (2oz) butter*

*5 tablespoons treacle*

*2 tablespoons red wine vinegar*

Slice the onions and lightly sauté them in melted butter. Add the treacle and the vinegar and simmer for 40 minutes. Adjust the sweet and sour balance to your personal taste.

*1 medium leek*

*1 roe deer fillet*

*salt and pepper*

*caul fat or fat bacon*

Preheat the oven to 180°C/350°F/gas 4.

Halve the leek lengthways, rinse and simmer in a little boiling salted water until flexible.

Seal the fillet on a hot pan, and season with salt and pepper. Wrap in leek leaves and bind with caul fat or fat bacon.

Roast the fillet for 15–20 minutes. Leave to rest for 10 minutes and serve with marmalade.

## roe deer with fresh pear chutney

I was recently a witness at the wedding of my friends Michael and Neillia Graham-Stewart and I pointed out to Michael that, now that he was a married man, he should give up his vegetarian ways. He admitted he couldn't even remember why he had become a 'veggie' and so I offered to cook him anything his heart desired. He chose fillet of roe deer and had three helpings so they should now live happily ever after!

For the chutney:

*2 pears*

*1 small chilli*

*1 clove garlic*

*1 small piece ginger*

*1 cinnamon stick*

*pinch of ground cloves*

*50g (2oz) sugar*

*2 tablespoons apple cider vinegar*

Peel, core and chop the pears roughly. Put all the ingredients together in a small pan and cook gently, stirring until the sugar has dissolved, and then simmer until the pears are soft. This takes about 15 minutes.

*1 teaspoon thyme*

*1 bay leaf*

*900g (2lb) roe deer fillet or boned leg*

*salt and pepper*

Preheat the oven to 180°C/350°F/gas 4. Roll and tie the meat, if needed. Mix the herbs and pepper together and rub them into the meat. Heat the oil and brown the meat to seal on all sides. Season with salt and roast for 15–20 minutes. Serve with the chutney, and potato and white bean cakes (see p115).

# roe **deer** fillet benedict

This is a very handy supper dish or for the more robust breakfast. The Benedict who invented this was Benedict Astor who, descending to the dining room of the Waldorf Astoria in New York with a crushing hangover, invented his breakfast. It does adapt very well to roe deer.

For the Hollandaise sauce:

*3 egg yolks*

*1 tablespoon cold water*

*225g (8oz) unsalted butter, cut in small cubes*

*1 tablespoon lemon juice*

*salt and pepper*

*1 poached egg per muffin*

*1 thin slice roe deer fillet per muffin*

*1 English muffin or 2 crumpets per person*

*1 or 2 spring onions per muffin*

*salt and pepper*

Place a bowl over a pan of boiling water. Put the yolks, water, salt and pepper in the bowl, and beat until the yolks are smooth. Whisk a handful of butter cubes into the yolks, beat until the butter is absorbed, and keep going until all the butter is used and the sauce begins to thicken. Stir in the lemon juice.

You can also do it in a microwave: melt the butter and keep in a jug. Put the egg yolks in a bowl with the water and beat until smooth. Pour in the butter, beating as you go. Put in a bowl in the microwave at power 5 and run for 3 seconds, remove and stir vigorously. Return for another 5 seconds and repeat. Once the required thickness is reached, add a few drops of cold water to stop it cooking.

Poach the eggs and drain them well.

Heat a little butter in a frying pan and flash-fry the roe slices, seasoning as you turn.

Toast the muffins or crumpets and lay some slices of spring onion on the muffins, and lay one slice of meat on top of each. Put a poached egg on top, and pour over the Hollandaise sauce.

## german roast roe **deer** with brussels sprouts and walnuts

For the marinade:

2 glasses robust red wine

2 onions, sliced thickly

2 carrots, sliced

4 sprigs of thyme

2 bay leaves

10 peppercorns

4 whole cloves

2 tablespoons flour

1 haunch roe deer

7 strips of salt pork or fat bacon

2 tablespoons olive oil

450g (1lb) Brussels sprouts

75g (3oz) chopped walnuts

175g (6oz) butter

Mix the marinade ingredients together, put in the haunch and marinate for 24 hours, turning from time to time. Remove the venison and pat dry; strain and reserve the marinade liquor.

Preheat the oven to 230°C/450°F/gas 8. Place the venison in a roasting pan and cover it with strips of pork or bacon and the oil. Roast for 25 minutes, reduce the temperature to 170°C/325°F/gas 3 and roast, allowing 15 minutes per 450g (1lb) in total. Remove to a dish and keep warm. In a pan combine the roasting juices and the remainder of the marinade, bring to the boil and reduce by one third.

Cook the Brussels sprouts and the chopped walnuts together in butter until the sprouts are tender, and then blend them together. Carve the meat, arrange slices on a plate alongside some of the sprouts and ladle over the sauce.

## bollocks to **blair**

Over the last four years Johnny and I have travelled many miles and signed thousands of books at Game Fairs, Hunt Supporters' Suppers, Wildfowling Dinners et al. Ninety-nine times in a hundred Johnny has inscribed below his name the phrase 'bollocks to Blair', a sentiment heartily echoed by the sporting and farming types at these dos, and indeed by very many townies as well. I feel my dear friend deserves a delicious recipe for giving such a morale boost to so many, so here is a recipe for him. I have turned down several invitations to cook at Downing Street for Mr Blair; I hope one day I may cook this in their kitchens to celebrate his departure. Sweetbreads are also good cooked this way.

75g (3oz) butter

6 roe deer testicles, split in half

225ml (8fl oz) game stock

75ml (3fl oz) double cream

2 tablespoons green peppercorns

1 teaspoon cayenne

salt

Heat the butter in a sauté pan and fry the testicles, turning them as you go, until they are lightly coloured. Remove from the heat and salt lightly.

In a separate pan heat the stock and bring to the boil. Add the cream and green peppercorns, and cook over a good flame for 10 minutes, stirring as you go.

Pour the sauce over the testicles, and return to the sauté pan and simmer for 7–8 minutes. Add the cayenne and check the seasoning. Serve with rice or with toast made from good country bread.

## flank of **elk** stuffed and rolled

The Swedes eat a large quantity of game, and they cull 100,000 elk each year, all of which are consumed within the country. Flank steaks are a neglected cut from most beasts and they taste very good; it is a cut I tend to use for Stroganoff recipes. Here is a simple but yummy way of preparing flank. Obviously you can use venison if you don't have elk. Serve with whatever roast vegetables you wish, I have used parsnips and baby turnips.

900g (2lb) flank in a piece
110g (4oz) oyster mushrooms
25g (1oz) butter
3 tablespoons tapenade (black olive paste)
6 anchovy fillets
butter

Preheat the oven to 200°C/400°F/gas 6.

Start slicing the elk through the centre, and two thirds of the way through open out and flatten to 3.75cm (1¹/₂in) thick.

Cut the mushrooms into strips and sauté them in the butter until they are just soft. Spread the meat with tapenade and arrange strips of mushroom and anchovy on one half. Fold the meat closed and tie tightly with string. Rub the venison well with butter and roast for 40 minutes.

Remove from the oven and rest for 10 minutes.

## **potato** and white bean cakes

This dish came about because I tried a Croatian recipe for bean and potato mash, which to put it politely wasn't very nice; not wanting to throw away the result I decided to make cakes of it and was pleased with the result. Once the cakes are made you can freeze them and take them out to fry. They do best in lard or pork fat but if you eschew this use oil. Let them be well done before you turn them.

110g (4oz) dried white beans
8 sprigs of sage
900g (2lb) potatoes
2 tablespoons olive oil
1 medium onion, finely chopped
110g (4oz) pork fat or lard
1 teaspoon salt
black pepper

Put the beans and sage into cold, salted water and simmer for 1–1¹/₂ hours or until the beans are tender, and then drain. Put the potatoes, unpeeled, into cold, salted water and cook until they are done – about 20 minutes; drain and peel. Mash the beans and potatoes together and mix in the onion; taste for seasoning. Form into small flat cakes. Heat the lard and fry the cakes on both sides until golden.

## fallow ciste

The word *ciste* is the Welsh for coffyn, the original term for meat cooked in a pastry case or, as we call it, a pie.

8 chops
50g (2oz) butter
4 deer kidneys (use lambs if none available), sliced
1 onion, sliced
110g (4oz) carrots, sliced
1 teaspoon parsley, chopped
1/2 teaspoon thyme, chopped
1 bay leaf
700ml (1 1/4 pints) game stock
225g (8oz) shortcrust pastry
salt and pepper

Trim the chops, stripping the end bones free of fat and gristle. Heat the butter and brown the chops and the sliced kidneys. Add the onion and carrots. Put the chops round a medium saucepan with the bone ends sticking up. Arrange the kidneys and vegetables in the centre, season with the parsley, thyme, bay leaf, salt and pepper, and add enough stock to just cover the vegetables.

Cook, covered, for 30 minutes, then adjust the seasoning. Roll out the pastry to fit the saucepan, press down over top of the casserole so that the bones protrude though the pastry. Cover tightly leaving space for the ciste to rise and simmer for 1 hour.

## venison chilli with lemon, beans and a tomato sauce

There was a time in my life, whilst I was cooking at Wildes club, when I made chilli 5 days a week for several years. I made a lot of changes and found venison makes a good substitute for beef. The lemon juice adds a certain *je ne sais quoi*, as does the beer.

juice of 1 lemon
900g (2lb) minced venison
olive oil
2 onions, chopped
2 cloves garlic, finely chopped
1/2 teaspoon thyme
2 x 400g (14oz) tins of chopped tomatoes
400g (14oz) tin of kidney beans
1 bottle of beer (not lager) or stout
2 tablespoons chilli powder
1 tablespoon sweet chilli sauce (or use ordinary chilli sauce or Tabasco sauce with a little added sugar)
salt and pepper

Pour the lemon juice over the mince, mix in and allow to stand for 30 minutes. Heat the oil and fry the onions and garlic; add the venison and brown well. Season. Add all the other ingredients, stir well, cover and cook slowly for 4 hours. Add more beer if it becomes too dry.

# loin of **fallow** with spiced blood oranges

**This is a dish I invented at Nantwich Food Festival where
I came across spiced blood oranges made by a farmer's
wife whose company is called Cahoon. They are such a
wonderful invention and go very well with duck and all
types of deer, as well as making a delicious pudding
with meringues.**

For spiced oranges:

*10 oranges*

*600ml (1 pint) white wine vinegar*

*1.1kg (2$\frac{1}{2}$lb) sugar*

*1$\frac{1}{2}$ cinnamon sticks*

*50g (2oz) cloves*

Slice the oranges and put them in a pan, barely cover with water
and simmer, partly covered, until the peel is tender.

Slowly cook the vinegar, sugar, cinamon sticks and cloves together
in a pan until the sugar has dissolved and  then boil for 5 minutes
to create a syrup.

Drain the oranges and reserve the cooking liquor. Lay half the
oranges in enough syrup to cover them and simmer for 30–40
minutes until the oranges look clear. Add the remaining oranges,
and if they are not covered, add some of the reserved liquor.
Cook as before, cover with syrup and leave to stand overnight. If
there is not enough syrup boil up some more. If the syrup is too
thin, pour it into a pan, reboil, and then return it to the oranges.

Put in jars and leave for eight weeks before using.

*25g (1oz) butter*

*450g (1lb) fallow loin*

*1 shallot, chopped*

*2 tablespoons of oranges, with their juice*

*1 glass red wine*

*salt and pepper*

Melt the butter in a heavy sauté pan and seal the loin properly all
the way round. Season and set aside. Fry the shallot in the butter
until soft, then stir in the oranges. Return the meat to the pan and
pour on the wine. Keep the heat fairly high and cook, turning the
meat frequently for 10 minutes. Add more wine if necessary.

Remove the pan from the heat and the meat from the pan; slice
the meat and if it is too rare return the slices to the pan to cook
a little more – the meat should be rare. Arrange on a dish and
pour the oranges and pan juices over. Serve with potatoes and
strong greens.

## saddle of **fallow** with anchovies

Saddle of fallow is a splendid cut for a dinner party as it looks most impressive. Meat larded with anchovies as a form of adding salt also brings a depth of flavour and has no fishy taste.

1 saddle venison
2 tins of anchovy fillets
50g (2oz) lard or pork fat for barding
lard or olive oil for frying
3 onions, sliced
300ml (1/2 pint) red wine
salt and pepper

Preheat the oven to 220°C/425°F/gas 7.

With a very sharp pointed knife make insertions all over the meat, into which put an anchovy fillet. Season with pepper. Cover the meat with barding fat and secure it well.

In a heavy oven dish melt the lard, and fry the onions until coloured. Place the meat on top of the onions, add salt and pour over the wine. Roast for 15 minutes to seal the meat, and then reduce the heat to 170°C/325°F/gas 3, allowing 15 minutes per 450g (1lb).

**Serves 6–8.**

## **fallow** glazed and stuffed from cremona

450g (1lb) strips of venison flank

For the marinade:
125ml (4fl oz) olive oil
1 glass red wine
ground black pepper

For the stuffing:
25g (1oz) butter
2 shallots, finely chopped
50g (2oz) black olives, stoned and chopped
1 tablespoon chopped fruit from the cremona mustard
2 tablespoons breadcrumbs
1 egg

For the glaze:
2 tablespoons syrup from Cremona mustard mixed with 1 teaspoon dried mustard powder or flour

Mix the marinade ingredients and marinate the venison for 2–3 hours, turning occasionally. Remove from the marinade and pat dry. Reserve the marinade.

Preheat the oven to 180°C/350°F/gas 4. Melt the butter and fry the stuffing ingredients together, breaking in the egg to bind, and mix well. Flatten out your venison making a slit in the meat if necessary to flatten it. Spread the stuffing on the meat and roll up like a Swiss roll. Tie with string at various points to secure. Place in a covered casserole, pour in the marinade and pot roast in the oven for 45 minutes. Remove and transfer to a roasting pan and paint the joint with the glaze, return to the oven for a further 10–15 minutes continuing to baste with the syrup.

## moose carpaccio with cheese and lingonberry compôte

This is a Swedish recipe designed for moose. Obviously otherwise use venison. You can buy lingonberries in IKEA if you are lucky enough to have one, or use cranberries or redcurrants. The cheese in this recipe was originally hard cheese spiked with aquavit, but in its absence use pecorino. If you like, soak the cheese in a little brandy, then leave it to dry before slicing it with a potato peeler.

275g (10oz) strip of loin or fillet of moose
olive oil
1/2 red onion, chopped
4 tablespoons lingonberries
1 tablespoon honey
sprig of fresh thyme
110g (4oz) pecorino
fleur de sel (or sea salt)
ground pepper

Freeze the meat. Defrost slightly and slice as thinly as possible. Allow to thaw, arrange it on plates and brush with olive oil, and sprinkle with salt and pepper.

Shred the onion and simmer gently with the berries and the honey for 5 minutes. Season with salt and pepper and freshly chopped thyme. Cool, divide between each plate and add slivered cheese.

## muntjac stewed with blackcurrants

This funny little beast not much bigger than a hare has become a great pest in the south of England and is gradually creeping north. There are some who swear that it is their favourite of the deer tribe and some, myself included, who feel it is much ado about nothing. However, if you kill it, you must cook it and I am quite pleased with this recipe for doing so.

900g (2lb) boneless meat
seasoned flour
olive oil
400ml (14fl oz) game stock
225g (1/2lb) blackcurrants, destalked
12 shallots, peeled
1 teaspoon thyme
1 bay leaf
salt and pepper

Cut the meat into chunks and roll in the seasoned flour. Heat a little oil and brown the meat.

In a casserole bring the stock to the boil and add the blackcurrants. Bring back to the boil and add the meat, a few pieces at a time so the liquid stays at the boil. Add salt and pepper, the whole shallots, thyme and bay leaf, and simmer for 45 minutes.

# muntjac meatloaf

**Meatloaf is a great invention; you can serve it hot with potatoes or mashed swedes or carrots, or cold with a salad.**

700g (1¹/₂lb) minced muntjac
350g (12oz) cream crackers, crushed
1 onion, chopped
110g (4oz) olives, stoned and sliced
2 eggs, lightly beaten
2 tablespoons cream of horseradish
150ml (5fl oz) tomato juice
1 tablespoon dry sherry
salt and pepper

Preheat the oven to 190°C/375°F/gas 5.

Mix all the ingredients well in a bowl. Grease a 23 x 12.5cm (9 x 5in) loaf tin and press the mixture well into it. Bake for I hour.

Turn out onto a warm dish and serve.

# sage cobbler

**A cobbler is a dish I am very fond of. It is mostly found in America where it has survived modernisation.**

900g (2lb) boned muntjac
25g (1oz) seasoned self-raising flour (or plain with a pinch of baking powder)
2 tablespoons oil
3 onions, thinly sliced
50g (2oz) dried peas (soaked overnight and drained)
600ml (1 pint) game stock
salt and pepper

For the scone topping:
225g (¹/₂lb) plain flour
1¹/₂ teaspoons baking powder
¹/₂ teaspoon dried sage (or 1 teaspoon fresh)
50g (2oz) butter
1 egg, lightly beaten
2 tablespoons milk

Preheat the oven to 170°C/225°F/gas 3. Cut the meat into 2.5cm (1in) cubes and dust with seasoned flour. Heat the oil and fry the onions until golden, and then add the peas. Add the meat, brown it and then transfer everything to a 1.2–1.8 litre (2–3 pint) casserole. Season and add the stock. Cover and cook for 2 hours.

To make the scone topping, sift the flour into a bowl, add the baking powder, a pinch of salt and the sage. Rub in the butter. Mix to a soft dough by adding egg and as much milk as necessary. Knead and roll out to 1cm (¹/₂in) thick. Cut into 8 rounds. Arrange these on top of the casserole and brush with milk. Zap the oven up to 220°C/425°F/gas 7 and bake for 20–30 minutes until the scone dough is risen and golden brown.

# persian **meatballs**

I used to have a cigarette case exquisitely enamelled with Persian riders pursuing a deer across an open plain. I have long since drunk it away but the image remains. If you don't have access to sumac or white mulberries use dried cherries, or at a pinch raisins soaked in a little lemon juice. For muntjac use leg meat and roast the saddle, but for other deer meat, just use whatever you have. I have used beef fat in deference to Persia's Muslim state, but bacon fat will do.

*1 1/4 teaspoons cumin seeds (roasted in a hot pan until they pop)*
*700g (1 1/2 lb) muntjac*
*50g (2oz) beef fat*
*2 onions, finely chopped*
*2 teaspoons dried mulberries or sumac berries, chopped*
*600ml (1 pint) game stock*
*dash of red wine vinegar*
*1 tablespoon olive oil*
*2 cloves garlic*
*600g (1 1/4 lb) cooked chick peas*
*1.3kg (3lb) spinach*
*salt and pepper*

In a food processor mix the meat, fat, onion, salt and pepper, cumin seeds and half the berries together. Grind until they are all blended, but not too smooth, then make into small balls. Sprinkle a teaspoon of salt into a heavy pan, put in the meatballs and cook for 5 minutes until they are brown all over. Add stock and a dash of red wine vinegar and cook for another 15 minutes at a gentle simmer. In another pan heat a little oil and cook the garlic cloves until they start to brown, then discard them. Stir the chickpeas into the oil and the remaining berries, and put the spinach on top. Season well, and add a little stock. Cover and cook for about 5 minutes or until the spinach has wilted. Drain the spinach and chickpeas, lay them on a dish and place the meatballs on top.

# venison sausages

Talking to my butcher, Colin Peat of Haddington, I asked about the availability of sausage casings for less privileged customers than myself! He replied that if anyone wanted to make a few pounds of sausages he would happily sell them some, but if they wanted them in bulk they would have to buy through the trade. Natural sausage casings are the best and in Britain lamb casings are used, beef casings being imported currently from Germany. You will need to soak your casings in warm water (about 90°F) for an hour or two to remove excess salt and soften them. This has the added benefit of stopping them bursting when cooking or smoking them and also allows them to stretch better to take more filling. A 1.2m (4ft) length of sheep casing makes 700g (1 1/2 lb) sausages, the same amount of pork casing, which is wider and more elastic, makes 1.1kg (2 1/2 lb) sausages. Venison is a very dry meat so it is necessary to add fat, pork fat or beef suet being the most favoured.

Machines: if you have a Kenwood mixer or some such you can buy a sausage filling attachment. I have a hand pump rather like an outsize syringe which Johnny gave me, or you can simply stuff by hand using the handle of a wooden spoon. When I was a child we used to kill our own pigs and spent forever making sausages. One useful tips is if you are butchering your own beast, freeze the meat you have earmarked for sausages and make them at a more serene time. If you wish you can sort out the intestine and wash them through for sausage casings, but having done this for years when young I tend to buy my casings nowadays.

You can make sausages with any game and make changes to your heart's content – rabbit and pear goes well – adding fruit allows you to reduce the fat input, as does mushrooms; add half the quantity of fruit or mushrooms to that of meat.

Flavourings or spices are yours to choose. You can even make fish ballotines. Grind the meat and the fat together to save mixing it later. However, remember that uncooked sausages don't have a long shelf life so freeze them at once and individually, and then put in a bag or you won't be able to take out just a few as needed. Have fun and let me know your successes if and when we meet!

Basic Recipe:
*900g (2lb) ground venison*
*450g (1lb) ground pork fat or beef suet*
*2 teaspoons of the herb or spice of your choice, finely ground*
  *(try half thyme half bay leaf for starters)*
*2 teaspoons salt*
*1 teaspoon black pepper*

Chill the venison and fat and then grind together; mix in your herbs or spices and seasonings. Fry a small piece of the mixture and taste it – if necessary adjust the flavourings. Stuff it into the casings and eat or freeze.

*3.6kg (4lb) caribou from the shoulder, haunch or brisket*
*50g (2oz) seasoned flour, made with cayenne, English mustard*
  *powder, salt and pepper*
*50g (2oz) beef dripping*
*3 carrots, chopped*
*2 onions, chopped*
*1/2 small jar redcurrant jelly*
*4 cloves*
*1 stick cinnamon*
*600ml (1 pint) milk*
*600ml (1 pint) game stock*

Rub the meat with seasoned flour. Melt the dripping in a heavy casserole, add the meat and brown it slowly. Remove the meat, and fry the onions and carrots in the fat. Add about 2 tablespoons of water, and the meat, redcurrant jelly, cloves and cinnamon. Cover, and simmer very slowly, either in a slow oven (170ºC/325ºF/gas 3) or on top, turning from time to time and adding a little water. It will take about 3 hours. Remove the meat to a warmed serving dish in a very low oven to rest.

Make the pan gravy with half milk, half stock and serve with dumplings (see page 126) and boiled vegetables.

# caribou as sauerbraten

The thought of caribou always sets me off reciting the poems of Robert Service. However it is a delicious meat. Recently someone tried raising it in Scotland but, in a land with so much venison, I thing the venture failed. You must be careful when cooking it as it can go stringy quite easily but it lends itself beautifully to braising and pot roasting.

1.3kg (3lb) caribou, round or rump
300ml (1/2 pint) strong game stock
6 peppercorns, crushed
6 juniper berries, crushed
dry English mustard powder
1/2 tablespoon dried thyme
1 bay leaf
125ml (4fl oz) red wine vinegar
3 tablespoons butter
1 onion, sliced
3 tablespoons flour
175g (6oz) tomato purée
1 tablespoon Madeira or medium dry sherry

Put the meat in an enamel or earthenware casserole with a tight fitting lid. Mix the stock, seasonings and vinegar and pour over the meat. Leave in a cool place for 3 days, turning daily. On the fourth day remove the meat, and reserve the liquor.

In a heavy pan melt the butter and fry the onion, then add the meat and brown it all over. Remove the meat and stir in the flour. Add the marinade liquor and stir until it has thickened. Put the meat in the gravy and season with salt. Simmer, covered, for 3 hours, or until tender. Remove the meat and carve. Mix the Madeira and tomato purée into the pan juices and serve with the potato dumplings.

For the dumplings:
225g (1/2 lb) mashed potatoes
225g (1/2 lb) flour
1 teaspoon baking powder
1 teaspoon salt
1 onion, minced
1 tablespoon hard cheese, grated
1 tablespoon melted butter
3 egg yolks, beaten

Mix all the ingredients together well. Shape into 16 balls. Drop into boiling salted water, cover and cook for 12 minutes.

# wild boar

The gamey, close grained meat of these notoriously savage and unpredictable creatures has been prized for centuries across the whole of Europe, Scandanavia and southern Russia. In America, wild boar introduced at the beginning of the nineteenth century for sport, have crossed with domestic pigs turned feral to create a wild hybrid. Domestic pigs turn feral very quickly and the bush country of Australia and New Zealand have large populations of those that escaped from the early settlers. In the last twenty years, a number of enterprising British farmers have diversified into farming European wild boar with surprising success. Consumers have taken to boar meat as an alternative food source where ostrich, bison and guinea fowl have failed to gain much popularity. A joint of wild boar will be much smaller than domestic pork and should be carved like fallow venison. The leg in the same way as mutton and the saddle or loin from the chine over the ribs.

My friend Peter Gott raises one-hundred-and-twenty wild boar at a time in his woods in Cumbria so I have had access to quite a lot of this meat. When buying boar make sure it is purebred as some of the crosses have a very coarse flavour. Boar is not counted as game in Britain as it had died out by the time the Victorian game laws were drawn up and therefore has to be taken to the abbatoir! On the continent it is both hunted and shot. It is a very dangerous beast indeed and its death is treated with respect and pageantry. I remember being in a friend's garden in Tuscany and seeing the damage a pair of boars had done. The beast is excellent eating and has a surprisingly subtle flavour, not strong at all. When I was a child, my father kept pigs and we used to kill them and have a sweinfest. If you shoot one bring in the experts as it is quite a carry on. To debristle the beast requires much time, effort and boiling of water. The blood should be saved for black pudding and blood sausage and the intestines, which make excellent sausage skins, are very extensive.

# wild boar with red beans and sour plums

There is a variety of sour plum which grows in southern Russia and Iran which you can occasionally buy in Middle Eastern shops. However ripe plums with a little lemon juice will do, and I tend to supplement these with the Japanese Umeboshi plums which you can find quite widely. I often bottle just ripe plums in wine vinegar which works very well for cooking. If you are using tinned beans put them together with the boar after you have browned it.

*450g (1lb) red kidney beans*
*olive oil*
*900g (2lb) shoulder or leg of boar, cut into cubes*
*seasoned flour*
*2 onions, chopped*
*1 clove garlic, crushed*
*450g (1lb) plums*
*6 Umeboshi plums*
*1/2 teaspoon cayenne*
*1 bottle of beer*
*salt and pepper*

Soak the beans overnight in cold, unsalted water. Drain and put them into a large pan of water, bring to the boil and cook hard for 10–15 minutes, then lower the heat and cook for 1 hour.

In a frying pan heat the oil, dust the meat with seasoned flour and brown it in the oil. Add the onions and garlic to the pan and cook until coloured. Cut the plums into pieces and add them with the cayenne.

Drain the beans and put them in a casserole with the boar and plum concoction. Season, add the beer and cook covered at a very low heat in the oven at 170°C/325°F/gas 3 or on top of the stove for another hour.

For the marinade:

*2 carrots, chopped*

*3 onions, chopped*

*3 cloves garlic, crushed*

*4 tablespoons olive oil*

*thyme*

*1 bay leaf*

*6 black peppercorns, crushed*

*125ml (4fl oz) Marc or some form of aquavit*

*600ml (1 pint) red wine*

*125ml (4fl oz) red wine vinegar*

Cook the carrots, onion and garlic in the olive oil gently for 5 minutes. Add all the rest of the ingredients and simmer for 20 minutes. Allow the marinade to cool and pour over the boar. Keep in a cool larder for 6 days turning as you go, or in a fridge for a fortnight.

*1 haunch boar*

*40 cloves*

*50g (2oz) lard*

*juice of 1/2 lemon*

*cayenne*

*salt and pepper*

Preheat the oven to 240°C/475°F/gas 9.

Remove the boar from the marinade and stick the cloves all over it. Season with salt and pepper and smear with the lard. Put the boar in the oven in a roasting tin and turn the joint after 15 minutes. After 30 minutes reduce the heat to 220°C/425°F/gas 7 and cook for about 2 hours, turning every 30 minutes. Remove the boar, strain the marinade and add flour to the pan scrapings. Cook for 2 minutes and then stir in the strained liquor to the sauce and lift it with lemon juice and a little cayenne to taste.

**Serves 6–8.**

## boar with red wine and coriander seeds

This is another Cypriot recipe used to cook the half wild pigs that run loose in the hills. I really like the combination. Don't be put off by the amount of coriander seeds and remember, only pulvrise it as you need it.

1.3kg (3lb) piece boar loin
6 teaspoons coriander seeds, pounded in a mortar
300ml (1/2 pint) strong red wine
2 tablespoons olive oil
salt and pepper

Cut the rind from the meat, score the fat, cut the skin into small pieces and keep. Rub the meat vigorously with half the ground coriander and a generous sprinkling of pepper. Cover and leave for 3 hours, then pour on the wine, cover again and leave overnight. Remove from the marinade and dry well.

Preheat the oven to 180°C/350°F/gas 4.

Heat the olive oil in an ovenproof dish and brown the pork well all round. Pour over the marinade and sprinkle on the rest of the coriander and add some salt. Cook in the oven for 2 hours, basting as you go.

## cumberland boar pie

This is my adaption of the original Cumberland pie, the forerunner of mince pies, which was originally made with mutton. I have adapted it to boar for my friend Peter Gott who raises wild boar in Cumbria and does such wonderful things with them. His partner Christine also makes wonderful pies, so this is for them. These pies were designed to be made in bulk and stored for several months, the sugar being a preservative. I have given a recipe for 2 large Christmas-size pies but you can make them any size you want. It is a typical medieval pie but don't knock it until you've tried it. Serves 8–10.

700g (1 1/2 b) pie boar
900g (2lb) stoned raisins
900g (2lb) currants
110g (4oz) candied peel
pinch of nutmeg
pinch of mixed spice
900g (2lb) soft brown sugar
125ml (4fl oz) rum
1.8kg (4lb) crust pastry
1 egg
salt and pepper

Put the meat, raisins, currants and peel through the mincer, and then mix with the nutmeg, mixed spice, sugar, salt and pepper, and the rum. Make the pastry and line 2 raised pie moulds, setting enough pastry aside for lids. Fill the pies with the mixture and cover with the pastry lids. Crimp the edges and make a hole in the top. Brush with beaten egg and bake for 2 1/2 hours at 220°C/425°F/gas 7 for 30 minutes, and reducing to 170°C/325°F/gas 3 for the remaining 2 hours. Serve hot or cold. You can store it in a cold stone larder.

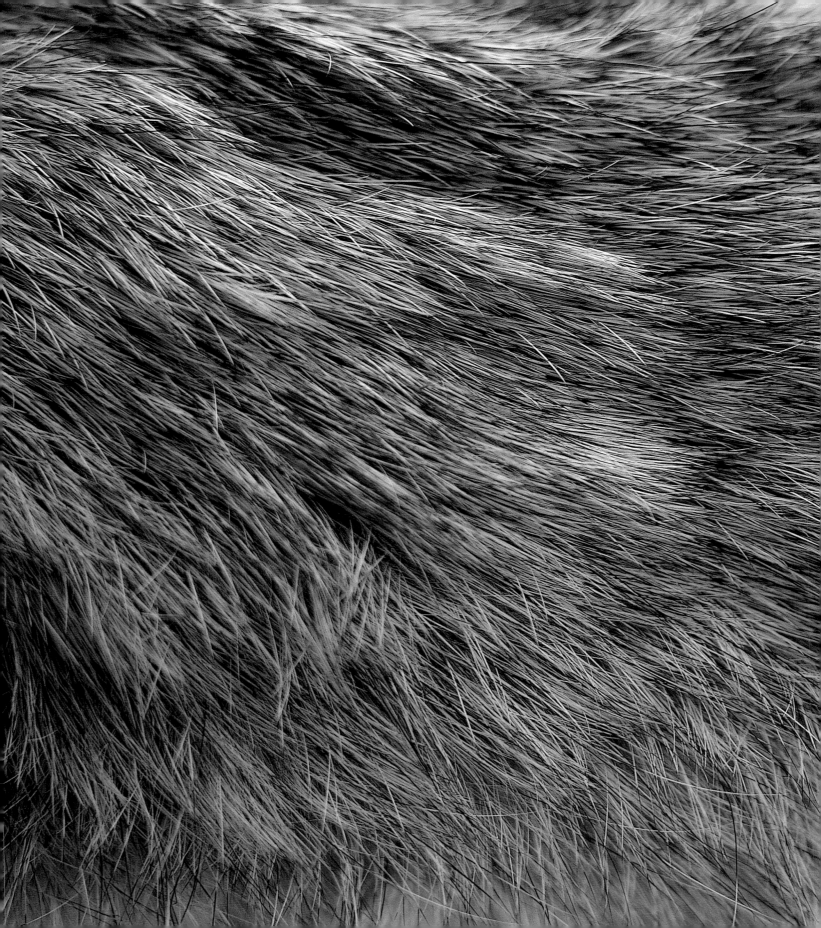

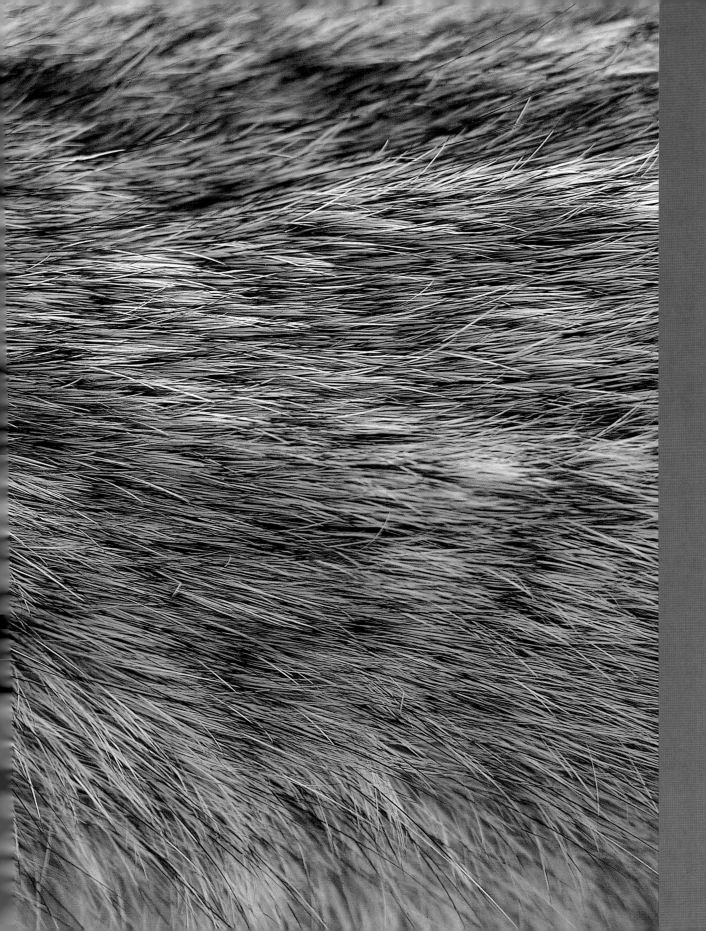

hares and rabbits

# hares

There are two species of hare in England and Scotland, the blue or mountain hare which is indigenous, turns white in winter and lives on the high moorlands, and the larger brown hare of low ground, which was introduced. The Irish hare, a recognised species in its own right, combines some of the characteristics of both. It is larger than a mountain hare and its coat turns partially white in winter. Mountain hares can be found in mountainous and northern parts of Europe, and across the Arctic regions. Brown hares have a distribution that extends across the whole of Europe and central Asia. They were also introduced during the nineteenth and early twentieth centuries to Canada, North and South America, Australia and New Zealand.

No other creature is more surrounded by myths and legends, or commands such respect among sportsmen, than the hare. Most of it attached to brown hares, partly because they are bigger, faster, and more extreme in every way than their mountain cousins but, also I suspect, because they were more familiar to the Celts, who regarded them as sacred. Oestre, the pagan Goddess of dawn, fertility and rebirth, whose festival was held at the vestal equinox (the start of spring fecundity), had as her favourite animal, light bearer and attendant spirit, a hare. Early Christian monks converted one of the hottest parties in the pagan calendar into a tame religious festival, but kept the name – Easter.

Hares are the fastest and most agile European animal, capable of speeds 70kph (45mph) and can turn on a sixpence in full flight. This in itself commanded considerable respect from the Celts, but their behaviour, which appears almost humanly irrational, and a scream when caught or injured hideously childlike, convinced them that hares were more than mere animals. As surface dwellers, hares have developed

elaborate defensive tactics to disguise their scent from predators, and protect their young. Hares live in 'forms' or 'seats' – shallow hollows scraped out of the ground in a position that gives them a clear view of the surrounding countryside. When a hare leaves or approaches its form, it doubles back and forth, making 90° turns and sudden leaps to break up the scent line. Does go to the buck from spring to early autumn and their exuberant, chaotic mating display with its gambolling, leaping and boxing is a phenomena of the countryside.

A doe can have four litters a year of between two to four leverets. For years, people believed hares were hermaphrodite and that both sexes bred. This was disproved in the nineteenth century, but what is almost unique is that does are capable of being pregnant and conceiving at the same time. Unlike most young animals that are born bald, blind and defenceless, leverets have fur and can see almost immediately. Once

the birthing process is over, the doe scrupulously cleans each one and moves it to a separate hiding place where they wait, silent and immobile for their daily feed. About an hour after sunset, breaking her scent trail in the usual way, the doe suckles each leveret in turn. Once fed, she stimulates the urinary area with her tongue, ingesting any discharge to ensure that the leveret remains scent free for the next twenty-four hours. She then moves them to different sights.

Paradoxically, the wildest of all animals is easily tamed if caught young enough. Legend has it that Boadicea had a hare which accompanied her on her campaigns against the Romans. This contradicts the accepted belief that brown hares were first introduced to Britain by the Romans, as part of their living larders. They were very partial to hare, according to Pliny, the flesh made those who ate it look 'fair, lovely and gracious, for a whole week afterwards'. The Romans certainly brought over hares from France, keeping them in walled gardens called 'leprosaria'. Country people call a hare 'puss', partly because they are cat-like in their fastidiousness, but largely because the latin name is *lepus*. The Romans were also mad keen on their coursing. The ethos upon which National Coursing Club rules are based, can be found in the writings of Arrian, a Roman living in the 1st century AD, 'the aim of every true sportsman with hounds is not to take the hare, but to engage her in a racing contest, or duel, and he is pleased if she escapes'.

Many superstitions about hares were started by Christian monks in their efforts to destroy paganism. Oestre became a witch, whose familiar was a hare. To get about by daylight unrecognised, witches turned themselves into hares. Not surprisingly, it was evil luck if a hare crossed your path, particularly if you were a pregnant woman or a fisherman on his way to launch his boat. There were variants on a general theme in practically every rural area, but the most abiding were that hares were the reincarnation of dead relations. This was particularly popular in East Anglia, but with a curious twist. Beagling and hunting with harriers or coursing them with greyhounds was perfectly acceptable, but to shoot one was considered the most appalling crime. When my father was at Cambridge just before the war and whipping-in to the Trinity Foot Beagles, he witnessed a mob of Fen farmers driving a man from his home and out of the Fens for shooting a hare.

Under Norman Forest Law, hares became one of the five Noble Beasts of Venery, joining the hart, hind, boar, and wolf. The Normans loved to watch hounds hunting. Deer, boar and wolves provided all the thrill, drama and pageantry of the chase, but for the complicated science of hound work there is still nothing to beat a hare.

They were keen on match coursing and greyhound breeding, and also kept hares in walled enclosures for the table.

Hares continued to be bred in captivity as a delicacy and fiercely protected in the wild through successive reigns. When the deer population diminished they became the principal hound quarry until they were usurped by the fox. During the great age of falconry, they were flown at by the prince of hawks, the goshawk. In Scotland, moorland hawking after blue hares was considered great sport. When shotguns became lighter and more manageable some were shot, but only by those entitled to under the restrictive game laws of the time. Hungary was one of the famous hare shooting destinations for international sportsmen, before the First World War. After the collapse of communism, like the other old Eastern Bloc countries, Hungary is now developing a lucrative sporting tourism industry.

Life for brown hares changed dramatically towards the end of the nineteenth century. A hundred years of agricultural improvements had created a paradise for all wildlife, hares in particular. The mixed farming policy of the time provided them with all the food and shelter they could possibly want. Their numbers increased dramatically and tenant farmers began to lobby parliament to be allowed to protect their crops. There was a certain amount of public sympathy. Not only were farmers suffering from a crippling agricultural depression, their livelihoods were being eaten before their eyes, and the current game laws restricted the shooting of any game to the landlord. In 1880 the Ground Game Act was passed, demoting hares to vermin and giving tenant farmers the right to protect their crops by whatever means. After seven hundred years as a noble beast of chase, hares could

now be killed at any time of the year. Brown hares were shot, snared, trapped and netted in huge numbers. With the collapse of grain prices, many farmers found the only way to keep afloat was by trapping rabbits and hares. Hare numbers had dropped so alarmingly in the first decade after the Act, that the Hare Preservation Act was introduced in 1892, forbidding the sale of hares between March and July. Small comfort if you happen to be a hare, but that is how the situation stands today.

A declining population suffered a further blow in the 1960s with the introduction of arable monoculture. Silage, cut so much earlier than hay, destroys breeding habitats and kills leverets born just before cutting. Blue hares on the moorlands of northern England and Scotland fared better, as heather management for sheep and grouse with its mix of different lengths and ages of heather, created a perfect habitat. An indication of a well managed moor is the number of hares it carries. Periodically, when the population grows too large, keepers hold hare shoots to avoid disease spread.

In the last ten years, EU set aside rules – subsidising farmers for land taken out of production and the more recent provision, permitting this allocation to be used as field margins creating wide headlands – has done much to replace lost habitat and hares are on the increase. Unfortunately, so are illegal coursing and organised poaching. The future of brown hares hangs under the black cloud of political bias. The present government is trying to ban all field sports, starting with hunting and coursing, handing a carte blanche to the poaching gangs. From a farmer and landowner's point of view, the simplest method of avoiding the threat of poachers and the property damage that goes with it, would be to get rid of the hare.

### Carving

A roast hare is presented with the legs drawn up into the body and secured with a wooden skewer. The best meat on a hare is the along the back bone and to ensure an even distribution of meat I like to carve a hare onto a serving dish, and have it taken to the table. Remove the meat from the saddle by carving slices not less than 3mm ($^1/_8$in) thick, parallel with the back bone. Detach the hind legs and slice off meat parallel with the thigh bone. Fore legs and shoulders have so little on them that they are served in one piece. Finally, turn the carcase over and remove the delicate little fillets. Because of their size, rabbit and blue hare are served jointed. Turn the carcase and sever the fore end just below the shoulder blade. Now, divide the saddle by cutting down the centre of the back bone.

---

When I was young there were hare shoots where a thousand hares would be killed in a day – a grown hare consumes 18kg (40lb) of vegetation in a week, thereby proving my point that there's not a lot of good in lettuce! When I first moved to Scotland I found a hare hanging on my door as a present from Johnny and it was the first beast in my game larder here.

### Ageing

A young hare has ears that tear easily, a smooth coat and small white teeth. Hares are best between autumn and early spring although, as vermin, can be taken any time; the medieval monastics used to eat them in Lent, using a curious argument that they didn't qualify as meat.

### Hanging and Skinning

A hare should be hung, head down, with a bowl below the head or its head in a plastic bag to catch the blood. Once the blood is drained mix it with vinegar and keep it in the fridge to add to the dish. Hang it for 1–2 weeks depending on the weather. I paunch it after it is skinned. I do this over the bath wearing a swimming costume but that is perhaps *de trop*... it is what my mother did so heredity will out. I once lost an admirer when I opened the door thus attired with blood to the elbows; he was a rather whimpy sort of chap. Sever all 4 legs at the first joint, then cut through the skin of the hind legs half way between the leg joint and the tail. Peel the skin from the hind legs. Tie them together and hang over a bowl with a little vinegar beneath to catch the blood. Pull the skin over the body and forelegs. I remove the head but you can skin it and keep it on. Cut the hare up the middle, but don't cut into the gall bladder. Tip the blood from the rib cage into the bowl. Discard the guts, keeping the liver. Rinse in cold water and dry with kitchen roll. Remove the blue membrane. A hare serves 4–6.

**My favourite pub is the Cholmondley Arms at the village of the same name on the A49 in Cheshire, where Guy and Carolyn Ross-Lowe win award after award for their pub and its food. They manage to keep a great pub atmosphere and wonderful food – not easily done. This is Carolyn's excellent hare terrine recipe.**

For the marinade:
*300ml ($^1/_2$ pint) red wine*
*1 tablespoon olive oil*
*6 juniper berries, crushed*

*1 hare, flesh removed and cut into longish strips*
*450g (1lb) fat pork, minced*
*450g (1lb) lean pork, minced*
*1 onion, finely sliced*
*25g (1oz) butter*
*1 clove garlic, crushed*
*1 dessertspoon fresh thyme and parsley, chopped and mixed*
*450g (1lb) streaky bacon*
*salt and pepper*

Mix the marinade ingredients together, add the hare strips and leave for 2 days. Mix the minced fat pork and lean pork together. Sweat the onion and the garlic in the butter for 5 minutes and then discard the garlic. Mix the onion with the pork, herbs and salt and pepper. Preheat the oven to 170ºC/325ºF/gas 3. Line a 900g (2lb) terrine with streaky bacon and put in half the minced pork mixture. Press down, then put some hare strips on top, and continue this until the mixture and the hare are used up – about 4 layers. Cover with streaky bacon. Cover the terrine and wrap in two layers of tinfoil. Cook in a *bain marie* or roasting tin of water for 45 minutes. Allow to cool. Press in the terrine under weights in the fridge until cold, leave for 24 hours and serve.

## hare swet

*Swet* is the Swedish for stew and this is a seventeenth century recipe I found when visiting Lekeslotte, a fantastic twelfth century castle on an inland sea 100 miles across. The summer exhibition at the castle was on hunting which in Sweden is mostly shooting or tracking moose or bear with hounds. There was even a room of different pelts for the children to feel, imagine trying such a exhibition in anti-ridden Britain. The Swedes are the nation that invented political correctness but they recognise the normality of hunting, shooting and fishing and, when they have eaten their own moose, elk and roe, they buy a vast amount of our venison.

1 hare
1 bottle red wine
olive oil
125g (4¹/₂oz) speck, cut into 5cm (2in) squares
12 onions, chopped
1 piece ginger the size of your thumb
4 cloves
4 teaspoons nutmeg, freshly grated
200ml (7fl oz) water
salt and pepper

Cut the hare into pieces and marinate it in the red wine for 8 hours. Then remove the hare from the wine and pat dry with kitchen roll.

Brown the hare in a little oil on both sides. Add everything to the hare, including 300ml (¹/₂ pint) of the wine from the marinade. Bring to the boil, cover and cook until tender – about 1¹/₂–2 hours, depending on the size and age of the hare.

## baron of hare

This is an Austrian recipe and I'm not sure where the name comes from, although I suppose it's some Hapsburg pretension to compare it to Baron of Beef. It is quite delicious and somewhat different.

1 saddle of hare
strips of fat pork for larding
1 teaspoon salt
¹/₂ teaspoon paprika
flour
110g (4oz) butter
225ml (8fl oz) sour cream, perhaps a little more
125ml (4fl oz) strong beef or game stock
50ml (2fl oz) vinegar
1 bay leaf
4 juniper berries, crushed
¹/₂ teaspoon thyme
juice of ¹/₂ lemon
2 tablespoons capers
pinch of sugar
1 tablespoon butter kneaded with 2 teaspoons flour

Preheat the oven to 190°C/375°F/gas 5. Lard the hare with the pork fat and rub it with the salt and the paprika and sprinkle well with flour. Brown the hare on all sides in melted butter. Pour over 175ml (6fl oz) of the sour cream and the stock and vinegar, and add the bay leaf, juniper berries and thyme. Roast for 1 hour or until tender – the meat should be pink and juicy – and baste from time to time, adding more sour cream if necessary. Transfer the meat to a dish and keep warm. Strain the pan juices, and measure them; add the lemon juice, capers, sugar and enough heated sour cream to make 600ml (1 pint) of sauce. Whisk in the butter and flour and bring it to the boil, stirring until it thickens. Adjust the seasoning and serve the sauce separately.

# jugged hare

The traditional way of cooking hare and a very good and rich dish. I remember the German restaurant Schmidts in Charlotte Street, Soho, used to serve it for lunch every Wednesday and it was hard to get a table on that day.

1 well-hung hare
1 teaspoon vinegar
olive oil
seasoned flour
game stock
1 onion, studded with cloves
bunch of thyme, marjoram and parsley
1 bay leaf
pinch of nutmeg
pinch of mace
2 tablespoons redcurrant jelly
150ml (5fl oz) port or claret
salt and pepper

Joint the hare, saving the blood and liver. Mix the blood with the vinegar to prevent it congealing. Preheat the oven to 180°C/350°F/gas 4. Heat some oil in a pan, dust the hare pieces with seasoned flour and brown them in the oil. Transfer to an oven-proof dish and pour over the stock to cover. Add the onion, herbs and spices. Cover tightly and place in the oven for about 3 hours.

Strain the liquid into a pan and return it to the boil. Add the redcurrant jelly. Pour a little liquid into the blood and stir until smooth. Add the blood to the gravy and cook to thicken, but do not boil. Add the wine and season to taste. Arrange the meat on a dish and pour over the sauce. Garnish with a forcemeat ball (see page 149) and heart shaped sippets of toast.

# lagas stifado

In Ancient Greece, if a man wanted to please his lover he went out hunting with greyhounds and brought her (or more probably him) back a hare. This event is recorded in Homer and other poets and is engraved and embossed on the sides of vases and drinking vessels. No-one sees fit to say how it was cooked, but this is most probably how:

1 hare, cut into 12 serving pieces
375ml (13fl oz) red wine vinegar
6 cloves garlic
6 juniper berries, crushed
6 myrtle berries
4 bay leaves
4 tablespoons olive oil
1 tablespoon honey
1 tablespoon dried crushed red bell peppers or of paprika
2 tablespoons ground coriander
450g (1lb) shallots, peeled
300ml (1/2 pint) strong red wine
1 tablespoon capers
1 sprig of thyme
salt to taste

Put the meat in a large bowl and add the vinegar, garlic, juniper and myrtle berries and the bay leaves. Cover and marinate for 24 hours, turning the meat in the marinade several times.

Preheat the oven to gas180°C/350°F/gas 4. Remove the meat to a casserole. Bring the marinade to the boil in a small saucepan and strain it over the meat. Add everything else, except the thyme, and keep back half the olive oil, and cook in the oven for 20 minutes. Reduce the heat to 150°C/300°F/gas 2, and cook for 2 1/2 hours. Add the thyme, salt and the remaining olive oil, and cook for another 15 minutes.

A good raised hare pie was usually eaten to celebrate the feast of the pagan goddess of spring whose name was Oestre and her symbols of fertility were the egg and the hare. Ring any bells? Christianity steals most things and the hare has now become the Easter bunny. There are still parts of the country where the tradition continues so here is a recipe for you to honour her too.

Many people are daunted by the thought of raising a hot water crust, it is like so many things in life, until you do it you will always fear it. The things to remember are that as soon as your pastry is cool enough to handle comfortably you must work it – you can not leave hot water pastry until later. Choose the mould to work with – a glass or a piece of wood – and raise the pie around it. It is rather like pottery, you can raise it free hand without a mould but until you are used to the process it may look a bit wonky, like your first attempts with clay. Try not to make it too thick, you will improve as you get less scared of it my first efforts would break a mammoth's tooth! And remember, when you are filling it, to leave room to pour in the stock to form jelly. Once you have got the hang of this you will be so proud.

For the pastry:
*450g (1lb) plain flour*
*1¹/₂ teaspoons salt*
*200ml (7fl oz) milk and water mixed, or plain water*
*110g (4oz) lard*

*225g (¹/₂lb) pie veal*
*225g (¹/₂lb) cooked ham*
*1 onion*
*mace*
*nutmeg*
*4 dried apricots*
*handful dried cherries or cranberries (soaked in cold tea to swell)*
*350g (12oz) hare, diced*
*beaten egg to glaze*
*1 pigs trotter or 2 level teaspoons gelatine*
*300ml (¹/₂ pint) game stock*
*salt and pepper*

I make my game stock with a pig's trotter and or a veal knuckle when making pies, but using gelatine is more usual. To make the pastry, sift the flour and salt into a bowl. Heat the water and lard together and bring to the boil, pour into the flour, mix together quickly to form a stiff paste and raise a pie from it.

Preheat the oven to 200°C/400°F/gas 6.

Chop the veal and ham together with the onion and add plenty of salt and pepper, mace and nutmeg. Put half the meat mixture in the bottom of the pie. Chop the fruit and mix it with the hare meat, and put on top of the veal mixture. Add the rest of the veal mixture, and put the lid on top. Decorate and brush with beaten egg and cook for 30 minutes.

Glaze again and reduce the heat to 180°C/350°F/gas 3 and continue to cook for 1¹/₂ hours, covering with greaseproof paper when it has sufficiently browned. Dissolve the gelatine in the stock, and as the pie cools pour in through a hole in the top. Chill until firm, preferably overnight, before de-tinning.

# rabbits

I have a great affection for rabbits. Yes, they have caused me a certain amount of grief as a farmer but I balance that against the hours of fun I have had ferreting. Ferreting rabbits was my introduction to the countryside I love, as it has been for my own children and countless others. Besides which I like to watch them sunning themselves outside their burrows, the bucks chasing the does in the spring and the young, crouching immobile as the shadow of a buzzard passes over them.

Rabbits (*Lepus cuniculus*) are so much a part of the landscape that it is easy to imagine them to be indigenous. Rabbits originated in the Iberian peninsular, gradually colonising Europe in the same way that they colonised Britain, Australia and anywhere else they could get a foothold. Exactly when they arrived in these islands has been the subject of heated academic dispute. One faction believe, as I do, that they were brought over with the Romans as part of their living larders. After all they introduced pheasants, possibly fallow deer and certainly brown hares, both for eating and coursing. They were well acquainted with rabbits and appreciated the value of their meat and skins. They recognised their prolificacy could be both an advantage – Linnaeus had a happy time working out that one pair would potentially multiply to eighteen thousand in four years – and a disadvantage – the Balearic islands became so overrun that the Emperor Augustus was obliged to divert a military force to exterminate them.

Proof enough, you might have thought, but not according to Barrett-Hamilton. 'The supposition that the rabbit was introduced by the Romans is without foundation' thunders his *History of the British Mammal* (1910), 'as it had no native name in any part of these Kingdoms until the Normans came over and named it'. To support this argument, is the first pictorial evidence of a rabbit as described by Dr Browne in his *Life of Bede*. Embroidered on the hem of robes used to wrap the apparently uncorrupted remains of St Cuthbert, when they were removed from Lindisfarne to the newly constructed Durham Cathedral in about 1100, was the scene of a mounted man with 'hawk on hand and a row of rabbits below'.

What we do know for certain is that the Normans brought with them a highly efficient and lucrative form of rabbit farming, that had obviously been tried and tested in Normandy. Thousands of rabbits were kept in enclosures and harvested for their meat and skins which were made into bed covers, caps, gloves, linings, trimmings – their uses and the demand for them was endless. These commercial warrens quickly became established all over the country wherever there was suitably sandy soil, as historic place names demonstrate, but particularly in East Anglia.

Rights to create a warren were the King's gift, and many of the warrens were doled out to keep the clergy happy. Some were enormous places – Lakenheath in the Breckland of East Anglia, set up by the Bishops of Ely towards the end of the eleventh century, covered nearly two and a half thousand acres surrounded by an earth bank ten miles long topped with gorse and patrolled by warreners. Warrens were fiercely protected, with the salted skins stored in fortified lodges, like the ruin of one still standing at Thetford Warren in Norfolk. The beauty of warrens was the speed with which they could be up and running. Once the earth banks were constructed, a warren was almost immediately into production. A doe breeds at six months and, depending on the weather, can have six litters of five young, known as kinder, a season.

Half of those will be does, reproducing within the same season.

There was a constant demand for rabbit meat, particularly through the winter, when warren bred rabbits were one of the few readily available sources of fresh meat, and the skins, with their rich grizzle grey fur, were extremely valuable. The hide of a bullock was estimated at one twentieth of the value of the carcase, a sheep skin one tenth, but a rabbit skin, twice the value of its meat. A warrener was highly respected and warren management an extremely sophisticated form of farming. Apart from protecting his warren and its produce from thieves, a warrener had to maintain the delicate balance between a healthy rabbit population and available herbage, whilst maximising output. He had to make hay for winter fodder, catch the rabbits, select the best to kill, process the meat and salt the skins. Ferrets were used to bolt rabbits but when a larger quantity was required, long nets were used, stretched between them and their burrows when they were out feeding at night. Once a year, in the early winter, the whole stock was gone through and the bucks reduced, leaving only the best on a ratio of one buck to seven does.

Inevitably, some rabbits escaped and gradually spread across England and southern Scotland. The Highlands they found less attractive, possibly because of predators, only reaching Invernesshire in the 1850s, but for the rural population elsewhere, rabbits were a welcome bonus, providing a supplement to a subsistence diet and the diversity of ferreting. Rabbits and bacon from the cottars' pig, were for centuries the countryman's staple food and the skins were always saleable. In time, every village had a rabbit catcher fully employed by local farmers to keep numbers under control.

In the seventeenth century a whole new industry sprang up creating a further demand for skins. Rabbit fur felt was now used instead of beaver to make hats. In the mid 1800s there were still many warrens up and down the east coast, selling rabbit meat into local markets and supplying fur to hat makers in London, Manchester and Bristol. Added to this was the incredible quantity of rabbit skins from independent rabbit catchers. Rabbits feed at a considerable distance away from their burrows, and a couple of men could catch hundreds a night by quietly running out long nets between the rabbits and their burrows, then frightening them into the nets. In fact, butchers and felt makers preferred wild rabbits. The flesh had better flavour and the fur contained more natural oils. With an industry as vibrant as this, it is small wonder that nineteenth century colonists took rabbits with them, which led to such disasters in Australia and New Zealand.

Warrens began to disappear as the input from rabbit catchers increased and land, previously considered only suitable for rabbits, was reclaimed for arable production. Perhaps the last commercial warren was the one at Lakenheath, which packed up after eight hundred years when the RAF built a runway through the middle of it in the Second World War. It was during the five years of war that rabbits here, on the continent, and in particular Australia and New Zealand, got completely out of hand. Thousands more acres going under the plough as part of the war effort and fewer people on the land, led to a massive increase in the rabbit population.

Ever since the deadly myxoma virus had been discovered among European grey rabbits introduced to Brazil in 1896, successive Australian governments had considered and rejected controlling rabbits biologically. The extent of post–war devastation by rabbits finally persuaded the government in 1950 to release the virus. France and Britain followed in 1952. The effect was horrific and initially, highly successful. The virus, carried by rabbit fleas, spread like wild fire in the confined space of their burrows and myxomotosis killed wild rabbits by the million. Yet, in a relatively short time they somehow developed an immunity to the disease. I was given my first ferret when I was seven years old in 1955 and found plenty of healthy rabbits to bolt, even though there might have been affected rabbits in the same locality. I suspect healthy rabbits soon learnt to segregate infected ones.

Perhaps the worst effect of myxomatosis was the prejudice against rabbits it created among consumers. Long after healthy animals have returned to the countryside, wild rabbit meat is still shunned and insipid supermarket chicken has become the cheap food of this generation. Equally tragic is the effect the anti-fur lobby has had on the fur trade. Hatters buy felt from rabbbits reared artificially on the continent and there is virtually no market for domestic rabbit skins. Rabbit numbers are escalating again and scientists are busy working on a new, deadlier form of virus. It is a tragedy that this wonderful natural product should be so wilfully wasted.

It is always a mystery to me why we don't eat more rabbit. Various excuses abound such as people ate too much during the war. Well the wartime population is not the dominant purchasing force now! I was born in1945, the year the war ended and am 4 years off the pension the government won't give me. The other great excuse is myxamatosis; well I remember the horror of mixi rabbits dying in the hedgerows in the 1960s but, in the same way

that foot and mouth or BSC haven't diminished the demand for beef or swine fever that for pork, mixi hasn't put me off rabbit. We import much of our rabbit from France, domestic and less tasty than wild, or much much worse from China, where the feed is polluted with human excrement which they use as manure for their vegetables; meanwhile we bury tonne upon tonne of our own rabbit. No Australian feels sentimental about rabbit and I am half Australian but I hate waste and I cannot understand why what was once a massive country industry is no more and perfectly good food is thrown away. A friend of mine when he was a boy used to sell a thousand wild rabbits a week into Smithfield and Leadenhall Markets. So please give rabbit a go, and I mean wild rabbit. When you kill a rabbit paunch it at once as it goes off quite quickly. Skin it in the same way as hare but do not hang it. Young rabbits have soft ears that will tear and sharp white teeth. A small rabbit feeds 2–3 people.

W.Kemble
·1884·

This is a Soanish rabbit stew, but it may be a bit oily for your palate, in which case reduce the amount of oil slightly. The anchovies are there in place of salt to add a deeper texture, but you can add salt instead.

4 tablespoons olive oil

1 large rabbit or 2 smaller ones, cut into pieces

1 large sprig of thyme

5 teaspoons black peppercorns, crushed in a mortar

3 cloves garlic, chopped

600ml (1 pint) game stock

3 anchovy fillets

pinch of cinnamon

1 tablespoon capers and/or lemon juice

Heat half the oil in a big, heavy bottomed pan and brown the rabbit pieces. Transfer them to a casserole to which you add the rest of the oil, the thyme, pepper and garlic. Cook over a low heat for 10 minutes. Add the stock, anchovy fillets (or salt), cinnamon, capers and lemon juice. Bring to the boil, reduce the heat and simmer for 1–1 1/2 hours, or alternatively transfer to a slow oven at 170°C/325°F/gas 3, once brought to the boil.

## fried **rabbit** with mustard

This is Eliza Acton's recipe written in 1840, and adapted by
Robin Weir and Caroline Liddell to include mustard, which
I think is a great improvement. I have added a few
tweakings of my own.

hind legs of 4 rabbits

home made breadcrumbs made from stale bread

1¹/₂ tablespoons mustard powder

1 large egg or 3 egg whites, beaten

75g (3oz) butter

300ml (¹/₂ pint) white game stock

3 strips lemon rind

1 rabbit liver (optional)

1 teaspoon flour

2 tablespoons cream

juice of ¹/₂ lemon

salt, pepper and cayenne

Put the joints in a pan of unsalted, boiling water and simmer for
5 minutes; drain and cool. Mix the breadcrumbs with 1 tablespoon
of mustard powder and season with salt, pepper and cayenne.
Dip the joints in the egg and then the breadcrumbs.

Melt 50g (2oz) of butter in a frying pan, and gently fry the joints for
15 minutes, turning them once or twice during cooking. In a
separate pan simmer the stock with the lemon rind and rabbit liver
(if you have it) for 5 minutes. Remove the liver and mash well with
the remaining butter and flour to form a thick paste, then add it
little by little to the stock whisking as you go, (if you have no liver
do this with flour and butter alone) until the sauce thickens. Take
¹/₂ teaspoon of mustard powder and mix it with the lemon juice.
Stir it into the sauce with the cream and let it bubble. Put the
rabbit pieces, nicely browned, on a serving dish and pour over
the sauce.

## **rabbit** brawn

I love a good brawn, and this is a Gloucestershire dish using
rabbits which is an excellent use of them and very good as
a starter or on a buffet table. I make my own setting agent
using stock from pigs' trotters which is very gelatinous or
use a leaf of gelatine, but powdered will do. Serves 8–10.

3 rabbits, skinned, cleaned and jointed

600ml –1.2litres (1–2 pints) sharp cider

2 carrots, sliced

1 onion, sliced

1 sprig of thyme

pinch of ground nutmeg

pinch of cloves

1 tablespoon cider vinegar or white wine vinegar

dash of Tabasco sauce

50g (2oz) gelatine

small bunch of parsley

2 hard-boiled eggs

salt and pepper

Cover the rabbits with the cider in a pan; if this doesn't cover
them, make up the difference with water. Add the carrots, onion,
salt and pepper, thyme, nutmeg and cloves. Bring to the boil and
simmer until the meat is tender – about 2 hours.

Remove the meat from the bones and dice into small pieces.
Strain the stock. Add the tablespoon of vinegar, and the Tabasco
sauce, and reduce by boiling to 1.2 litres (2 pints).

Season to taste and mix with the gelatine. Arrange the rabbit
pieces in a wetted mould, sprinkling with chopped parsley as you
go; add slices of hard-boiled egg and the stock and allow to set
overnight. Turn out and serve.

## rabbit in the dairy

**Wild rabbit can have a strong taste, and the way the country people overcame this was to soak it in milk. This is probably the origin of this delicate dish. It is very good if you are feeling poorly or in need of comfort.**

*2 rabbits, jointed*
*50g (2oz) bacon rashers, chopped*
*2 onions, chopped*
*mace or nutmeg*
*1.2 litres (2 pints) whole milk*
*salt and pepper*

Preheat the oven to 180°C/359°F/gas 4.

Wash and dry the rabbits and place in an ovenproof dish. Add all the other ingredients and cook, covered for 1¹/2 hours. Remove the rabbits and reduce the sauce by fast simmering or thicken with a little *beurre manie*. Serve with a colourful vegetable, such as carrots or kale.

## elizabethan rabbit

*50g (2oz) bacon fat or oil*
*2 rabbits, jointed*
*1 tablespoon seasoned flour*
*3 sliced Jerusalem artichokes or uncooked artichoke hearts*
*1 onion, finely chopped*
*50g (2oz) carrots, diced*
*300ml (¹/2 pint) red wine*
*50g (2oz) raisins*
*1 apple, finely diced*
*faggot of herbs*
*rind of 1 orange*
*150ml (5fl oz) stock*
*110g (4oz) seedless grapes, halved*
*salt and pepper*

Preheat the oven to 180°C/350°F/gas 4.

Heat the bacon fat or oil, dust the joints with flour and fry until brown. Remove to a casserole. Sauté the rest of the vegetables and add to the rabbit. Pour in the wine, bring to the boil and then reduce the heat. Add the raisins, apple, herbs and orange rind. Season. Pour over the stock, cover and cook in the oven for 2 hours; add the grapes for the last 30 minutes.

# fife pie

The rabbit came late to Scotland and later across the Firth of Forth to Fife – I think this is one of the earliest Scottish rabbit recipes.

With my usual reluctance to buy meat when game is plentiful, I have made the forcemeat balls with rabbit not veal. If you have the rabbits' livers and they are clean, substitute them for an equal quantity of meat and fry them in a little butter first. Pies of this date included anything from oysters to cockscombs so let your imagination run riot! I make rough puff pastry from habit but use packet puff for ease!

For the forcemeat balls:
*meat stripped from 1 rabbit*
*an equal quantity of fatty bacon*
*1 anchovy, chopped*
*grated rind of 1/2 lemon*
*1 egg, lightly beaten*
*grating of nutmeg*
*225g (8oz) breadcrumbs, made from stale white loaf*
*salt and pepper*

Chop the meat and bacon and then finely mix all the ingredients together, binding them with the egg. Roll the mixture into small balls and set aside.

*2 rabbits*
*450g (1lb) pickled belly of pork (use unpickled if you must)*
*nutmeg*
*2 medium onions, chopped*
*300ml (1/2 pint) game stock*
*2 tablespoons white wine*
*110g (4oz) rough puff pastry*
*1 egg*
*salt and pepper*

Preheat the oven to 220°C/425°F/gas 7.

Strip the meat from 2 rabbits and cut into 2.5cm (1in) cubes. Slice the pickled pork thinly and season both meats with salt and pepper and nutmeg.

In a 2.4 litre (4 pint) greased pie dish layer the meats with the forcemeat balls, sprinkling chopped onion on each layer as you go.

Pour in the stock and white wine. Cover with the pastry and brush the top with beaten egg, and bake in the oven for 15 minutes; reduce to 180°C/350°F/gas 4 and continue to bake until the pie is well risen and golden – about another 40–45 minutes.

# rabbit with chocolate and tomatoes

This recipe, like the chocolate and tomatoes it contains, is believed to have been brought back to Spain by the Conquistadors. The rabbit is not native to South America, but the origins of this dish are reputed to have been for cooking chihuahua which were bred especially for the table. Whatever its origins, it is delicious.

1 large rabbit cut into 4, liver reserved
3 cloves garlic
2 tablespoons olive oil
1 onion, chopped
450g (1lb) tomatoes or 1 tin 400g (14oz) chopped tomatoes
1 glass white wine
150ml (5fl oz) game stock
1 stale white bread roll, cut into small chunks
25g (1oz) bitter chocolate, broken into small pieces
6 almonds, roasted
small bunch of parsley, (including the stalks) finely chopped
salt and pepper

Rub the rabbit pieces with salt and pepper. Peel and crush the garlic in a mortar with the liver.

Brown the rabbit pieces in the oil, add the onion and cook until coloured. Pour in the tomatoes, white wine, stock and the bread roll. Cook, covered, for about 30 minutes. Add the liver, garlic, chocolate, almonds and the parsley leaves and stalks, and cook gently for another 2 hours, or until the rabbit is tender. Add a little water if the sauce appears to be drying out.

# rabbit saltimbocca

**This is a dish I made up when I was demonstrating at the Scone Game Fair. I took the ale from the lovely Heather Ale people, the bacon from Peter Gott, the sage from Scotherbs, someone shot the rabbit and away we went.**

Per person:
2 rabbit fillets
50g (2oz) butter
2 sage leaves
1 slice ham or back bacon
1 bottle Heather Ale or other good ale
salt and pepper

Lay the rabbit between two bits of greaseproof paper and flatten the fillets carefully with a meat hammer (or in my case just lean).

Melt the butter in a heavy sauté pan, lay 2 sage leaves and a slice of ham or bacon on one of each pair of fillets, place the other fillet on top and secure with tooth picks. Brown the rabbit in the butter, turning carefully. Season, then pour in half a bottle of beer, (what you do with the rest is up to you,) cover, lower the heat and cook, turning once, for about 10 minutes or until the rabbit is cooked.

# rabbit with apples and cider

2 tablespoons oil or butter or bacon fat
1 large or 2 smaller rabbits cut into pieces
seasoned flour
110g (4oz) back bacon, preferably in a piece and cut into
   small cubes
4 onions, chopped
900g (2lb) sharp apples (not Bramleys), peeled cored
   and chopped
600ml (1 pint) dry cider
salt and pepper

Preheat the oven to 170°C/325°F/gas 3.

Heat the oil or fat in a heavy frying pan, dust the rabbit pieces with seasoned flour and brown well. Transfer to a casserole. Fry the bacon and the onions until golden. Add the apples and cook a bit longer, and then transfer to the casserole with the rabbit. Season and pour on the cider. Bring to the boil, cover and transfer to the oven for 1–1 1/2 hours, or until the rabbit is tender.

## rabbit with a piquant sauce

**This is a curious dish that my mother used to make. The flavours combine very well and the crisp bread topping is rather comforting.**

*25g (1oz) seasoned flour*

*1 rabbit, cut into pieces*

*110g (4oz butter)*

*1 onion, chopped*

*1 tablespoon Tabasco sauce*

*1 tablespoon Worcestershire sauce*

*1 tablespoon dried mustard powder*

*1 tablespoon tomato ketchup*

*1 tablespoon some fruit sauce, such as HP*

*1 bottle lager*

*crumb of 1 small sandwich loaf, torn into hazelnut size pieces*

Preheat the oven to 180°C/350°F/gas 4. Dust the rabbit pieces with seasoned flour. Melt 75g (3oz) butter and brown the rabbit pieces.

Remove the rabbit to an oven dish and fry the onion until coloured, and add to the rabbit. Put all the ingredients except the bread into the pan and cook together. Pour the mixture over the rabbit. Scatter the bread pieces on top of the rabbit and dot with the remaining 25g (1oz) butter. Cover with tinfoil and cook for 1½ hours. If it appears to be drying out add more beer and butter. For the last 15 minutes remove the tinfoil to allow the bread to crisp up.

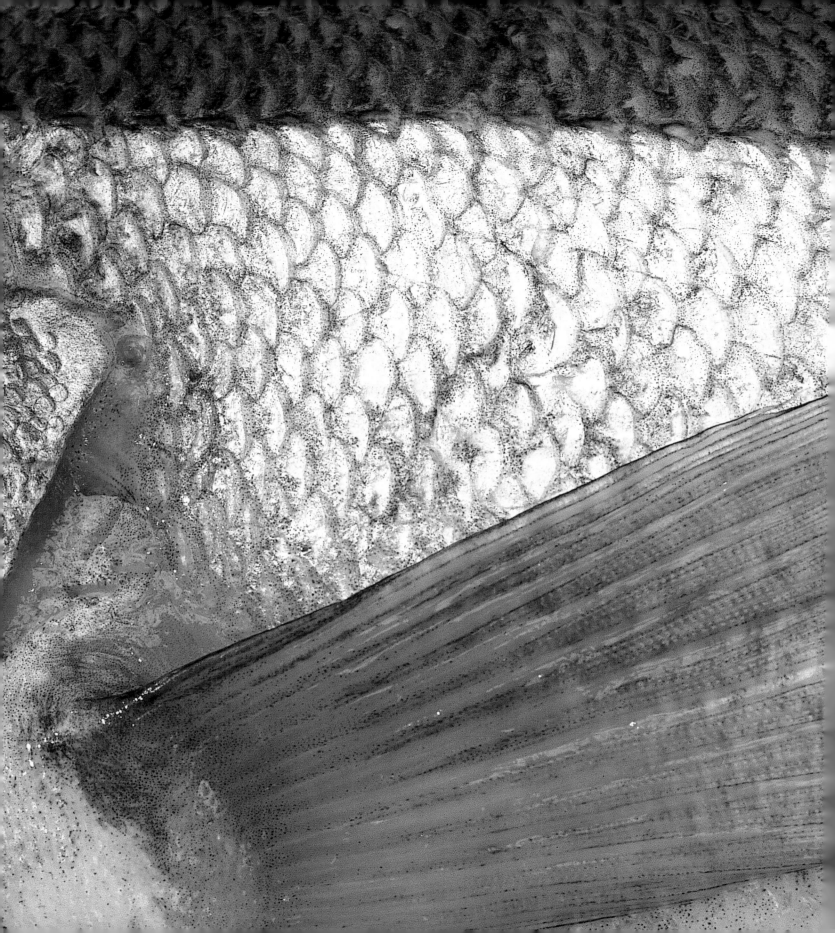

fish

# fish

A tributary of the river Teviot runs through the farm, its banks covered in mature alder and willow trees. These used to be coppiced a hundred years ago, with clogs for woollen mill workers made from alder wood and baskets from the willow rods. It is an enchanting, peaceful place; the motion of the water is as soothing as its mumbling sound, tumbling over the shallows. In the summer there are kingfishers and dippers scudding along the surface, mallard and ducklings creep under the over-hanging banks, iridescent dragon flies dart here and there and bees drone among cow parsley, pink campion and flowering wild garlic. I come down here with my old Sharpe's Parabolic, a 2.55m (8½ft) split cane rod designed by Cesar Ritz, the hotelier, and try roll casting for the little brown trout that lurk in the pools. I know that my chances of catching anything are pretty remote – there are far too many herons about – but like the three and a half million other fishermen in this country alone, I do love trying.

Angling is, like all other field sports, a vital contributor to the economy and a key part of the socio-economic fabric. Globally it is the most popular participant pastime, encompassing the whole spectrum of social backgrounds and every age, particularly children. Some six thousand people are employed by the manufacturing, retail and bait industry in this country, with an estimated turnover of three and a half billion pounds. Worldwide, this figure must run into hundreds of billions and involve enthusiasts of every nation. Possibly no other sport induces such passion, fascination and determination among devotees. I know any number of otherwise unadventurous people who think nothing of disappearing to the north of Norway in pursuit of Arctic char, sea trout in the Falklands, enormous brown trout in New Zealand, bone fish in the Bahamas, wild rainbow trout in Alaska,

steelhead salmon in Patagonia or the silver goddess herself, the arctic salmon, in Iceland. I recently met a young bride bitten to such an extent, she spurned the offered anniversary jewellery in favour of a classic Hardy Palakona split-bamboo trout rod.

I have seen a small boy about to leave on his first sea fishing trip, gazing in ecstasy at a heaving grey November sea and my own children spending hours trying to catch dog fish off Craignure pier, Isle of Mull. Enthusiasts, in the hope of catching a shark off the Cornish coast, will happily share a boat with the appalling stench of 'rubby dubby' – shark bait made from rotted mackerel. New quarry fish have been introduced to our still waters like zander, the voracious European perch, wels catfish, bullheads and of course, sloppy rainbow trout. And all because of that indescribable buzz, the heart stopping moment of excitement when that tentative tightening of a line turns into a screaming reel and quivering bent rod.

In the days when there were few domestic animals and the main food source derived from everything that swam, flew or ran, fish were a vital component in the survival chain and every-thing from a porpoise to a minnow was eaten. Coastal communities with their little inshore fishing boats and estuary netting, kept themselves supplied with fresh fish, and inland settlements with fish preserved in salt. Upriver, fish were netted, trapped, speared and guddled. Wherever there was a principal building, be it palace, castle, manor or monastery, moats were stocked and stew ponds dug. Carp, introduced by the Normans, were the most popular stocking fish. They are hardy, prolific and fertile. The monastic houses specialised in carp husbandry, and considerable efforts went into selectively breeding bigger and better strains. Protecting fish in the inland waterways was of enormous importance and otters, the principal predator, were kept under control by otter hound packs. Their role was sufficiently significant to be recorded by a charter of Henry II appointing one

Roger Follo the 'King's Otter Hunter', in 1175. Rod fishing as a sport had been popular with the Egyptians, Greeks and Romans. In Britain the need for food was such that fishing as a recreational pastime scarcely occurred to anyone until well into the fourteenth century, although it had evidently become popular on the continent before that date. Possibly the earliest publication on fishing, *The Treatyse of Fysshynge with an Angle* printed in 1496 contained material of French origin. Descriptions of the rods used – great cumbersome poles of willow and hazel topped with blackthorn to which a line of nine strand plaited horsehair was attached – leaves one wondering how anything was ever caught.

Bait fishing is more credible than the descriptions of suggested flies for trout and grayling, and yet the same patterns were still in use a hundred years later, when line and rod were both finer and lighter. The first real advances came in the seventeenth century. Fish were still of enormous economic importance. Fishing fleets were busier than ever and estuary fishing was particularly lucrative, with licencees on rivers like the Bann in Northern Ireland exporting hundreds of tons of salted salmon each year to Europe and as slave food for the West Indies. The massive growth in popularity for rod fishing had much, I suspect, to do with Cromwell's Commonwealth. Hunting and hawking were frowned on by the Puritans as smacking of Monarchist activities and the flood of seventeenth century angling literature, Walton's *The Compleat Angler* for example, was written during or shortly after that period. Rods and tackle were now becoming sophisticated enough for casting of a sort, lines were down to three strands of horse hair and by the end of the century, reels were commonplace for heavier fish. Fly making had become more scientific, varied and realistic in attempts to imitate insects that attracted fish to rise.

The majority of fish were still caught with bait and the fertile imagination of determined anglers was applied to improving bait recipes. Nicholas Cox, writing in 1679, devotes a considerable part of his book to the subject. For carp and tench he recommends feeding for a day or two by 'casting in garbage, chicken guts, pellets of honey and sugar mixed, livers of beasts, worms chopped in pieces, cow dung or grains steeped in blood and dried'. For the fishing itself, bait in the form of paste made from bean flour, cat's flesh and honey. Cox has a different bait for each fish: cheese and honey for barbel, grasshoppers with their legs cut off for bream, parmesan cheese with saffron for chub, wasp larvae with their heads dipped in blood for dace, wire worms for trout, and earthworms kept in moss for twenty days, minnows or lob-worms scented with oil of ivy berries for salmon. And so he goes on through the range of coarse and game fish, each different and most reflecting the brutality of the age. Special inventiveness was reserved for pike, for whom all anglers had a ghoulish admiration, based on stories of monsters attacking cattle as they went to drink, otters, dogs and small children as they paddled in the shallows. Attacks on humans were well documented; Cox knew of a maid who had been bitten, as he primly puts it, 'as she washed herself'. A fish capable of such behaviour needed a dramatic bait. Live frogs or young duckling were Cox's suggestions, others favoured a puppy or a kitten tied to bladders to keep them afloat. William Lauson swore by a paste of powdered mummy and human fat. All recommended the heaviest tackle for these prehistoric creatures which, until fly fishing for salmon became the vogue in the nineteenth century, were indisputably the most exciting fishing experience available.

Fishing continued its rise in popularity during the eighteenth century. There were significant

improvements in rod and tackle design. With the introduction of foreign woods, like greenheart and lancewood, rods became shorter and more flexible. Fly tying continued to be as adventurous, reels, common place and casting more scientific. Artificial lures replaced live bait, although coarse fishermen were reluctant to relinquish tried and tested bait recipes with kitten and puppy meat considered essential ingredients for most of them. England's great rivers, the Severn, Tamar, Derwent and Trent still produced enormous revenues from commercial salmon netting and stew ponds, harvested for carp as they had for the last five hundred years.

Immense changes took place during the nineteenth century, particularly in Scotland during the latter half of the century. Rods were now being made in split cane, dry flies came into use and oil dressed silk floating lines replaced horsehair. Reels even had adjustable ratchet systems that assisted playing a fish. There was another surge of fishing literature among which was William Scrope's D*ays and Nights of Salmon Fishing on the Tweed* published in 1843. The salmon rivers of England, except in the south-west, had become victims of industrial pollution and both commercial and rod fishing were but a fond memory. Scrope wrote mouth-wateringly of fishing on the Tweed and his book coincided with the sporting tourism revolution which was about to sweep Scotland. Fishing the northern rivers became initially, a component of the whole 'Glorious Twelfth' adventure, before becoming part of the annual migration to Scotland in its own right, with fishermen making pilgrimages to the Tweed, Tay, Dee, Spey, Nather, and Helmsdale to name only some of the wonderful salmon rivers.

This was the glorious age of game fishing with riparian owners making lucrative incomes from their rights on the salmon beats in Scotland and trout streams in England, like the Kennet and Itchen. It fuelled an industry that is still expanding to this day and gave us the names of the great rod and tackle makers – Hardy, Farlow, Grant and Sharpe. Because of the geography of many of the best game rivers, fishing brought incomes and employment to remote regions, particularly the Highlands, enabling other tourist industries like golf to develop in the area. At much the same time, Victorian sportsmen tried their luck on the great rivers of northern Scandinavia, the Alta, Tana and Stjordal in Norway and the mystical Kymijoki in Finland. This is reflected by the magnificent Imperial fishing lodge at Labinkoski on the Kymijoki built by Czar Alexander III in 1889.

Since the Second World War the history of our game rivers seems to have been one long battle to conserve fish stocks. Agricultural pollution and acidity from massive forestry plantations have done enormous damage, so too have the fish farms, although both agriculture and fish farming are now making concerted efforts to reduce pollutant risk. Nothing can be done about the forestry, sadly. Klondikers drift-net fishing off Ireland and up in the salmon feeding grounds around Iceland had a devastating effect, but international fishing agreements will now, hopefully, correct the balance. Conservation bodies like the Tweed River Authority, the West Country Rivers Trust and the Countryside Alliance Campaign for Angling are only three of the many that work to improve spawning grounds on the main river tributaries. We are winning the battle, which is just as well, a rod caught salmon is worth £10,000 to the local economy – £12 million in the Tweed Valley alone, in a reasonable year. Conservation is the central issue and fishermen are guardians of the world's waterways, from the small boy firing his bait

catapult full of maggots into the waters of a disused canal for tench, to the game fish enthusiast putting money into the Russian economy with his trip to the mighty Yokanga.

## Carving

All round fish are carved in the same way, whether they be the mighty salmon or the lowly tench. To use a salmon as an example, since most people make such a hash of it when a dressed one appears as part of a buffet. The fish is presented from the kitchen skinned and lying on its side. Once the decorations have been removed, the division where the flesh joins at the spine is clearly visible. Simply run a fish trowel down this division from head to tail, pressing from side to side to ease the flesh. Starting at the head, where the flesh is thickest and on the opposite side from the belly, insert the trowel about 1cm (1/2in) down from the head, at right angles to the spine and work the trowel through the flesh over the ribs. Now use the trowel to press the flesh off the bones onto a fish fork. If the fish is properly cooked, the flesh will come away easily. Increase the size of each section as you move towards the tail and the body of the fish becomes narrower. Repeat on the other side and once the backbone is completely exposed, lift free leaving the remaining fillets to be cut into sections and served.

## Game Fish

*Salmon*
Curiously the advent of farmed salmon, which has so much diminished the fish in modern eyes, has returned it to a commonplace fish as it was in the seventeenth century when the London apprentices rioted when fed Thames salmon more than three times a week. After World War Two stocks declined and salmon became a luxury. I can still remember the

excitement when some kind friend sent a salmon in its rush carrying bag, with bog myrtle to deter the flies, down by train overnight. I spend a good part of my life sitting on failed trains and yearn for the efficiency of those days. But just when I decide I don't like salmon someone gives me a wild, freshly caught one and again I declare it to be the finest of fish.

For perfect cold salmon. This is a lovely dish where the size of the fish dictates the cooking time. Clean and gut the fish, trim the tail and leave the head on. Put it in a fish kettle and fill the pan with cold water, add a handful of salt. Bring to the boil and allow to boil for exactly two minutes. Turn off and allow it to cool. Remove the fish to a dish, skin and decorate with slices of cucumber and lemon slivers, or as you like. I knew a Scottish doctor who used to surround it with laurel leaves as the king of fish. Gloomy and rather unattractive but *chacun à san gout*.

For hot salmon: rub the fish with oil, salt and pepper and season the cavity. Put in some melissa (lemon balm) or lemon thyme or just half a lemon and a dessertspoon of white wine. Wrap in tinfoil and cook at 180ºC/350ºF/gas 4 for 12 minutes per 450g (1lb).

In a dishwasher: though I didn't invent this I think I was the first person to do it for television with my friend Sue Crewe, who was then writing *Jennifer's Diary*, and is now editor of *House and Garden*. You must run your dishwasher through with the soap and rinse sections open to clear it. Rub your fish with oil, salt, pepper and wrap in several layers of tinfoil. Put on the top layer of the dishwasher, run on the glass wash and your salmon will be perfectly cooked.

*Trout*
When I worked for Rebeka Hardy, her husband

and son would often come up from the lake with freshly caught brown trout, which is the food of the gods. Pan-fry them in butter or wrap them in foil and cook them in the oven at 180°C/350°F/gas 4 for 8 minutes per 450g (1lb) or, best of all, make a fire by your trout stream and cook them over the open fire on a twig skewer.

## Coarse Fish

I have included this section for the thousands of lovely men of all ages who have asked me at fairs around the country, and for their long suffering wives who don't know what to do with the catch. In the Jewish community and in Europe, coarse fish are eaten much more and don't deserve their name.

### Carp

The fish of the Medieval stew ponds are part of the living larder complex. When I was a child in St John's Wood our fishmonger Mr Brown always sold carp for the large Jewish community, as among other things it is an intrinsic part of gefilte fish. If your carp are in muddy water take them alive and leave them with a running tap in fresh cold water for 24 hours.

### Pike

The best of all fresh water fish and one which we totally ignore in the eating stakes. Until I went to the West Indies and learnt how to fillet flying fish, which have the same three banded bone structure, I had terrible trouble fileting them but patience and a shape knife will get you there.

### Zander

Zander were the first fish I caught in the Piskers' pond in Sussex and I could never persuade anyone to cook them for me, so I had to learn. Zander are much eaten in Scandinavia, Germany and Switzerland where I had zander taken straight from the lake at Vevey.

## robert may's **salmon**

The phenomenon of celebrity chefs writing cookbooks is not new. It dates back to Ancient Greece, but the advent of the Stuart Court in England saw a greater sophistication in cooking, and Robert May was on a par with the Gordon Ramseys and Marco Pierre Whites of his day. This is an excellent dish as seen on TV cooked by me in the second year of *Two Fat Ladies*, and I unrepentantly repeat it here. The darne is the cut of salmon at the thickest part behind the head.

900g (2lb) darne of salmon
3 oranges, peeled and sliced
2 teaspoons nutmeg, freshly grated
red wine
juice 1 orange
salt

Skin the darne. In a pan large enough to accommodate the fish, spread a layer of sliced oranges. Place the fish on top and season with the salt and nutmeg. Put the remaining slices round the fish and on the top. Pour the wine and orange juice both inside and outside the cavity and bring to the boil. Cover and simmer for 15 minutes or until the salmon is just cooked. Serve with sippets of toast.

## **salmon** and cabbage rolls

3g (1/8oz) dried ceps
10g (1/2oz) dried chanterelles
600g (11/4lb) cooked salmon
50g (2oz) smoked salmon (optional)
125ml (4fl oz) whipping cream
2 tablespoons chives
1 cabbage
salt and pepper

For the sauce:
600ml (1 pint) fish stock
125ml (4fl oz) single cream
pinch of saffron

Soak the mushrooms for 1 hour. Purée the salmon in a food processor, with the optional smoked salmon. Add the cream, purée again and transfer to a bowl and mix in the chopped mushrooms and chives. Season.

Preheat the oven to 180°C/350°F/gas 4.

Select 8 cabbage leaves and blanch them for a couple of minutes in salted, boiling water and then drain them. Spread the salmon mixture on the leaves, roll into parcels and secure with string or tooth picks. Put in a greased ovenproof dish, pour on some fish stock and bake them in the oven for 30 minutes. Drain and keep the liquid.

In a pan mix together the remaining fish stock, the pan juices, the cream and the saffron. Bring to the boil and simmer to reduce by one third. Serve with the parcels.

## salmon mousse with cheese

This is a very good way of using up cooked salmon that is lying about, and it makes a splendid starter or buffet dish. I usually make my salmon mousse with blue cheese but you already have that recipe from *Full Throttle*, so this is another good one.

175g (6oz) cream cheese
125ml (4fl oz) sour cream
450g (1lb) cooked salmon
1 shallot, finely chopped
50g (2oz) baby broad beans or petit pois
1 sachet of gelatine
300ml (1/2 pint) cream
1 tablespoon summer savoury or lovage or flat parsley, chopped
juice of 1 lemon
1 teaspoon dry sherry
2 gherkins, finely chopped
salt and pepper

Mix the cream cheese and the sour cream together and put the mixture in a large bowl. Flake the salmon and stir it in with the cheese and cream and the shallot. If the peas or beans are large, cut them into pieces. Dissolve the gelatine according to the instructions and mix in well. Add the remaining ingredients. Put into a wetted mould or moulds and refrigerate for at least 2 hours. Serve with toast, oatcakes or salad.

## salmon fishcakes made with gnocchi

This is a dish I invented one day when I had some delicious cold salmon caught in a haaf-net on the Nith and for some reason some leftover gnocchi and decided to make some fishcakes. The gnocchi was commercial – no need to make your own for this – and gnocchi has of course already been mixed with eggs and flour. I preferred the texture to the usual mash used in fishcakes – I hope you enjoy them too.

175g (6oz) cooked gnocchi
225g (8oz) cooked salmon
4 spring onions
1 egg
olive oil
salt and pepper

Reboil your gnocchi until it floats, then drain it and roughly mash it (you want to keep it textured). Flake the salmon and finely chop the spring onions. Using your hands mix all the ingredients except the oil together in a bowl and season well. Form into patties.

Heat the oil in a heavy pan and fry the patties, don't turn them until they are cooked on the first side.

## salmon as cooked at the golden aur

The Golden Aur is a wonderful fish and chip shop in Bala, Wales. I first came across it on a golden weekend with dear friends, when I discovered camping at the age of forty. We laughed all weekend in the rain when 'grey were the skies over Cader Idris', and warmed ourselves up at the restaurant. On my second visit they were just closing, when Johnny, myself and Steve Sclair, our series producer of the first *Clarissa and the Countryman* arrived, but it was kept open just for us. On my third visit, the entire crew came as we had been thrown out of the dining room of a rather silly hotel for wearing jeans, (not me!) at which we were the only guests! During the war the only available fish were salmon from the River Dee. This is the only time I have had salmon deep fried in batter. It is very good.

Make a batter as for pigeon in the hole (see page 59). Cut the salmon into fillets, making each piece the size of an average cod fillet at your chippie. Season the fish and coat well with the batter and deep fry. Serve with pickled cucumbers and tartare sauce.

## salmon with pinenuts

This is something different for your buffet or picnic table. You don't have to use a whole fish, as it makes a good summer dish with salmon cutlets, or even trout. This recipe serves 10-12 people.

*4.4kg (10lb) salmon, cooked in tinfoil (juices reserved), skinned and backbone removed and reassembled as a whole fish*
*1/4 white sandwich loaf, crusts removed, soaked in water*
*400g (14oz) pinenuts*
*3 cloves garlic, crushed*
*juice of 3 lemons*
*175ml (6fl oz) olive oil*
*thin slices cucumber to decorate*
*salt and pepper*

Squeeze out the bread. Process the bread, pinenuts, garlic, lemon juice, salt and pepper in a food processor, adding enough fish juices to make a sauce the thickness of mayonnaise. Cover the fish with the sauce and decorate with cucumber.

# salmon with chicory and roquefort

**I really like the combination of chicory, Roquefort and salmon, but if you don't have chicory use spinach and just lightly blanch it, and then make sure it is well wrung out.**

*1.3kg (3lb) salmon, skinned and boned*
*110g (4oz) Roquefort cheese*
*50g (2oz) butter*
*juice of 1/2 lemon*
*1 head chicory*
*puff pastry*
*egg to glaze*
*salt and pepper*

Cut the piece of fish in half, lengthways though the middle to open up 2 fillet pieces.

Mix together the cheese, butter and lemon juice and season well. Spread over one half of the fish and place the other piece of salmon on top. Cut off the bottom of the chicory head and split it into leaves.

Preheat the oven to 220°C/475°F/gas 7.

Roll out the puff pastry, spread a layer of chicory onto the pastry and sprinkle on a little salt and pepper. Place the salmon on top, and then place more chicory around and on top of the fish. Fold over the pastry, crimp the edge and seal it with egg. Brush the top with egg and decorate as you like.

Bake for about 40 minutes, or until the pastry is golden brown. Serve with Hollandaise sauce (see page 112).

## salmon cooked in goose fat

*1 fillet salmon per person with the skin left on*
*small tin 100g (3¹/₂oz) goose fat*
*handful of fennel seeds*
*salt and ground black pepper*

Heat a skillet and roast the fennel seeds in a little goose fat until they start to pop. Remove the seeds from the pan and mix with the remaining goose fat.

Season the salmon pieces with salt and pepper and then rub well with the goose fat mixture. Heat your skillet until it is good and hot and then place the fillets, skin down, on the skillet and then lower the heat.

Cook for about 10 minutes, depending on the thickness of the fillet, and for the last 2 minutes flip them over to sear the skinless side.

Serve skin side up – the skin should be golden and crispy.

## trout in a cheese broth

**This is a Swedish recipe which I found adapts very well to trout. Allow 1–2 trout fillets per person, according to the size of your fish. Swedish cherry wine is not like cherry brandy, but is quite a light wine, so unless you have access to it use a light red wine. This can be served as a starter.**

*65g (2¹/₂oz) butter*
*2 tablespoons flour*
*1.2 litres (2 pints) fish stock (or chicken)*
*400ml (14fl oz) light cream*
*350g (12oz) aged hard cheese (use cheddar as a substitute)*
*4 fillets trout*
*2 eggs*
*1 glass cherry wine and 1 tablespoon kirsch*
*salt*

Make a roux in a large saucepan by melting the butter and stirring in the flour; cook for 2 minutes. Add the stock and simmer until smooth. Add the cream and cheese and bring to the boil. Stir thoroughly and then add the trout fillets and reduce the heat. Simmer gently for 3 minutes. Whisk the eggs, wine and kirsch together, add to the soup and simmer for a few minutes.

TROUT FISHING

## trout stuffed with confit

One year Johnny made some delicious *confit* from some geese that had not been sold before Christmas. It was a major labour of love and his friends got large jars. There comes a time when the contents are severely reduced and you want to finish it up. This is what I did and it is very good. Don't open a jar specially, but if you have some around and have caught some trout I recommend it.

fat from a jar of confit
1 onion, finely sliced
1 clove garlic, crushed
1 tablespoon parsley, chopped
6–7 tablespoons confit, finely chopped
2 tablespoons breadcrumbs
4 trout
1 lemon
salt and pepper

Take a dessertspoon of fat from the confit and fry the onion and garlic in it, until softened. Add the parsley and the meat from the confit and fry a little longer. Mix in the breadcrumbs and season generously.

Preheat the oven to 190°C/375°F/gas 5.

Clean the trout and dry them, inside and out. Divide the mixture in 4 and stuff each trout and then sew it up.

Cut 4 pieces of tinfoil or baking parchment and grease them lightly. Lay 1 fish on each and squeeze on a few drops of lemon juice. Fold the tinfoil and secure the parcels. Bake for 35 minutes.

## rainbow trout in red wine with tarragon

This is a Quercian dish which I acquired during a drunken visit to this lovely region of France. I begrudged the wine to the dish at the time, but it is a good dish and a useful way of cooking rainbow trout.

225g (8oz) mushrooms, finely chopped
2 shallots, finely chopped
50g (2oz) butter
2 tablespoons homemade breadcrumbs
4 sprigs of fresh tarragon or 1 teaspoon dried
4 rainbow trout
2 onions, sliced
2 carrots, sliced
3 rashers fat bacon, diced
2 sprigs of parsley
2 sprigs of thyme
2 bay leaves, crushed
1 bottle burgundy
1 tablespoon flour and butter mixed together
salt and pepper

Preheat the oven to 180°C/350°F/gas 4.

Soften the mushrooms and shallot in the butter in a small pan. Add the breadcrumbs and the chopped tarragon leaves, reserving the stalks. Season, and stuff the mixture into the cavity of the fish, and secure with tooth picks. In a lightly greased, ovenproof dish arrange the onion, carrots and bacon, and lie the fish on top. Add the tarragon stalks and the rest of the herbs, and pour over the wine. Cover with buttered paper and bake for 35 minutes. Remove the fish to a dish and reduce the sauce over a high heat by boiling. Thicken with little bits of butter and flour, whisking vigorously. Adjust the seasoning and pour the sauce over the fish.

**When I worked for Rebeka Hardy at Danehill there was a trout lake on the property and, with both her husband and son as avid fishermen, I cooked a lot of brown trout. These quenelles are a very good dinner party starter and can even improve rainbow trout.**

275g (10oz) brown trout
275g (10oz) smoked trout
3 egg whites
pinch of mace
300ml (1/2 pint) double cream
salt and pepper

For the sauce:
150ml (5fl oz) dry white wine
5 tablespoons shallot, finely chopped
150ml (5fl oz) pheasant stock
300ml (1/2 pint) whipping cream
4 bunches of watercress
lemon juice to taste
50g (2oz) butter

Put the fish, both sorts, into a food processor and blend until smooth. Add the egg whites, mace and salt and pepper, and blend a bit longer.

With the motor running, pour in the cream and blend for no more than 20 seconds – the mixture must not be too thin. Chill for at least 30 minutes.

For the sauce, simmer the wine and shallot together for 15 minutes or more, until it forms a soft purée and the wine has almost evaporated. Add the stock and cream and boil until it has reduced by one-third and can coat a spoon.

In a separate pan, blanch the watercress for 2–3 minutes (using the stalks), drain and refresh under a cold tap. Squeeze out the excess water and purée in a food processor for 1–2 minutes until it is smooth. Pour in the hot cream and process, adding the lemon juice and butter in small pieces.

Bring a pan of water to the boil and add salt. Make the quenelles of the fish by fully filling 1 dessertspoon with the fish mixture and using the second spoon to shape it, and poach them in the water for 8–10 minutes. Remove them with a slotted spoon and drain on kitchen paper.

Put the quenelles on a warm dish, strain the sauce and reheat it without boiling. Pour over the quenelles and serve at once.

## sea **trout** with cucumbers and cream

In the days of the Regency, salmon and sea trout were still very common but cucumbers less so. Here is a delicate dish which preserves the flavour of the sea trout.

1 onion, thinly sliced
110g (4oz) butter
1.3kg (3lb) middle cut of sea trout
1 sprig of dill
425ml (15fl oz) single cream
150ml (5fl oz) water
25g (1oz) flour
1 cucumber
juice of 1 lemon and rind from half of it
salt and pepper

Preheat the oven to 200°C/400°F/gas 6.

Butter an ovenproof dish and scatter the onion on the bottom of it. Smear the sea trout with half the butter, season well and place on the onion. Chop the dill and add it to the cream, mix in the water and pour it over the fish. Cover with tinfoil and cook for 25 minutes, or until the fish is cooked. Remove the fish to a warm serving dish.

Melt the remaining butter in a small pan and make a roux with the flour. Pour on the liquid from around the fish. Cut the cucumber in strips and add them and the lemon rind to the sauce. Adjust the flavour with lemon juice, season, reheat and pour over the fish.

## sea **trout** with chard and walnuts

This was inspired by the Filippino idea of wrapping fish in cardoon leaves – another good way of cooking it, however not for the delicate flavour of sea trout. I love chard and feel that people are often somewhat scared of it. This is a lovely dish.

450g (1lb) Swiss chard, leaves and stalks separated
110g (4oz) butter
3 shallots, finely chopped
3 anchovy fillets
175g (6oz) broken walnut pieces
juice and rind of 1 lemon
1 sea trout, skin removed
black pepper

Blanch the stalks of the chard in boiling water and refresh under a cold tap. Do the same with the leaves, leaving them flat.

Preheat the oven to 200°C/400°F/gas 6.

In a frying pan melt 75g (3oz) of the butter and fry the shallots. Add the anchovy fillets and allow them to melt. Add the walnuts and toss quickly, then add the lemon juice and rind. Spread half the chard stalks over the base of a lightly greased, ovenproof dish large enough to hold the fish and then lay the flat chard leaves on top. Smear the fish with the remaining butter, and some black pepper on the outside and sprinkle a little in the cavity too. Lay the fish on top of the leaves.

Spoon as much of the walnut and shallot mixture as possible into the cavity of the fish. Fold the chard leaves over the top, place the remaining chard stalks on top, and pour the remaining butter liquid over the top. Cover with tinfoil and cook for about 40 minutes, depending on the size of the fish.

## grilled **zander** with rocket, beetroot and horseradish

**A simple and delicious way of preparing this fish and one to be done at the lakeside.**

2 medium beetroots, cooked
125ml (4fl oz) olive oil
juice of 2 lemons
110g (4oz) horseradish
1 tablespoon cornstarch
1.3 – 1.8kg (3–4lb) zander
rocket
salt and pepper

Peel and thinly slice the beetroots with a cheese slicer. Combine the oil, lemon juice and seasoning, and pour over the sliced beetroots. Marinate them for 1 hour.

Cut three quarters of the horseradish into matchsticks, and toss in the cornstarch. Fry the horseradish sticks until golden brown and salt them lightly.

Grill the fish, skin side down. Heat some of the marinade in a small saucepan. Grate the rest of the horseradish and toss it in with the rocket. Arrange the salad on individual plates, and put the fish on top with the sliced beetroot and horseradish chips and drizzle over the rest of the marinade.

## **zander** fillets with chanterelles

**This is a Swedish recipe, a country where both pike-perch and chanterelles are abound. People think of zander as too bony to eat, but in many parts of Europe it is a much sought after fish, and the flesh is very delicate and repays the effort. At the Weston Park Game Fair I was confronted by a young man with a Midlands accent who declared it his favourite fish, both to catch and eat. I don't know his name but he will know who he is, and I hope he likes these recipes.**

700g (1$^1$/$_2$lb) zander fillets
8 small potatoes, peeled
225g (8oz) chanterelles
$^1$/$_2$ leek, minced
$^1$/$_2$ small onion, minced
4 tablespoons unsalted butter
1 sprig of rosemary
175ml (6fl oz) dry white wine
175ml (6fl oz) fish stock
175ml (6fl oz) whipping cream
coarse salt and white pepper

Trim the fillets and remove the bones with tweezers. Sprinkle with salt and refrigerate. Boil the potatoes until tender. Blanche the chanterelles briefly and drain them; sauté them with the leek and onion in 1 tablespoon of melted butter. Add the rosemary spikes, wine and stock, and simmer for 5–10 minutes. Then stir in the cream and zap up the heat to reduce by a third. Transfer the mixture to a food processor, with 3 tablespoons of butter, and purée until smooth. Season. Crush the potatoes and mix them with the processed sauce. Pack into ring moulds or shape into patties and keep warm. Grill the fish, skin side down, and do not overcook – by the time the skin is crisp the fish will be cooked. Season and serve on the potato mix.

## pike burgers

600g (1¹/₄lb) pike fillets
dash of Tabasco sauce
pinch of paprika
225ml (8fl oz) single cream
3 eggs
50g (2oz) smoked salmon
150g (5oz) spinach leaves, blanched
110g (4oz) chanterelles
salt and pepper

Put the pike fillets in a blender. Add salt and pepper, Tabasco sauce, paprika, the cream and the eggs one at a time, blending as you go. Add the smoked salmon, spinach and chanterelles, and whizz again. Form into patties, chill and then fry in butter on both sides until golden.

## pike pudding with pumpkin

600g (1¹/₄lb) pike, chopped
525g (1lb 3oz) grated pumpkin
3 tablespoons flour
75ml (3fl oz) fish stock
parsley
breadcrumbs
butter
salt and pepper

Preheat the oven to 180°C/350°F/gas 4. Combine the pike, pumpkin, flour, stock and salt and pepper, and pour into a greased dish. Sprinkle with parsley and breadcrumbs and dot with butter. Bake for 50–60 minutes until crisp and browned.

## hecht smetena

Pike is the best of all freshwater fish and one which we totally ignore in the eating stakes. The Hungarians soak the fish overnight and then poach them like salmon, which dissolves the smaller bones. Poach the fish in *court-bouillon* rather than water (ie. fish stock). The Russians have a complicated dish where they remove the meat from the skin and then mix the flesh with butter, anchovies, nutmeg and all spice before returning it to the skin to bake it. Here is a nice Viennese dish.

*250ml (8fl oz) sour cream*
*1.8kg (4lb) pike, cut into 5cm (2in) lengths*
*3 onions, sliced*
*3 sprigs each of parsley, dill and thyme*
*1 bay leaf*
*1 dessertspoon capers*
*salt and pepper*

Preheat the oven to 190°C/375°F/gas 5.

Butter an ovenproof dish and pour in half the sour cream, add the fish and all the other ingredients except the capers to it. Bake in the oven for 15 minutes or until the fish is opaque.

Remove the fish to a warmed serving dish and keep hot. Strain the sauce and thicken it over a high heat. Add the second half of the sour cream together with the capers, reheat and pour over the fish. Serve with boiled potatoes.

## carp stuffed with baked fruit

This is a dish which recurs throughout central Europe and the Levant and is a French-Jewish recipe from the celebrated Mme. Zette Guinadeau. It is very good and different. Get your fishmonger to scale, clean and gut the fish and remove the backbone, but leave the head and tail on.

*1.8kg (4lb) carp*
*2¹/₂ tablespoons cooked rice*
*110g (4oz) blanched almonds (flaked)*
*1 teaspoon powdered ginger*
*1 teaspoon sugar*
*1 teaspoon cinnamon*
*75g (3oz) clarified butter*
*450g (1lb) stoned dates*
*1 onion, chopped*
*50g (2oz) ground almonds*
*salt and pepper*

Soak the carp for 15 minutes in water to remove any muddy flavour, dry well and rub with salt and pepper. Mix the rice and the flaked almonds, and then add half the ginger, sugar, half the cinnamon and 25g (1oz) butter. Stuff the dates with the rice mixture and stuff the fish with the stuffed dates and sew it up.

Preheat the oven to180°C/350°F/gas 4. Place the fish in a buttered ovenproof dish and add 300ml (1/2 pint) of water. Season and add more ginger, the onion and the remaining dates. Dot with the remaining butter and cook for 45 minutes, basting as you go.

Remove the fish and zap up the oven as high as it will go. Sprinkle the fish with ground almonds and the other half of the cinnamon, baste with butter and return to the oven for another 25 minutes. To serve, remove the thread and place on a dish.

# carp with cherries

This delicious recipe comes from Elana Molokhovet's *A Gift for Young Housewives*, a massive work in four volumes destined for the rising Russian middle-class, a sort of Mrs Beeton for Russia; it sank without trace in the Revolution of 1917. The original recipe suggests keeping the carp's blood mixed with vinegar and adding it to the sauce at the roux stage. Get the fishmonger to clean the carp for you.

1.8kg (4lb) carp

2 bottles beer

1 Hamburg parsley root (or bunch of flat leafed parsley)

1 head of celery, chopped

1 leek, choped

2 onions, chopped

5–6 allspice berries

3–4 black peppercorns

2–3 cloves

2–3 bay leaves

1 crust bread

1/4 glass vinegar

zest of 1 lemon

1–2 tablespoons butter

1 tablespoon flour

1/2 glass red wine

5–6 sugar lumps

110g (4oz) raisins

juice of 1 lemon

15 marinated cherries

lemon slices from 1 lemon

Cut off the carp's head. Bring the beer to the boil and add the parsley root, celery, leek, onion, allspice, black peppercorns, cloves and bay leaves, bread, vinegar and lemon and boil for 30 minutes. Place the fish and its head in another pan and strain into it the boiled beer. Cook over a high flame for 20 minutes.

Make a roux with the butter and flour, cook for 2 minutes and then dilute the roux with some of the broth in which the fish is cooking. Add the wine, sugar, raisins, lemon juice and cherries. Bring to the boil several times, but do not allow to reduce too much. Arrange the carp on a dish strewn with lemon slices and raisins. Pour over the sauce and serve.

## carp à la juive

This is one of the great dishes of European Jewish Cuisine and there are endless variations on the theme. In Russia in the nineteenth century they adopted the French style and added white wine, in Poland they didn't. Some cook the carp whole, some slice it – here is one for you to try. The European Jews make endless varieties of pickled cucumbers, I remember as a child going with my father into the cool dark shops his patients ran in the East End of London to taste them, but new green remain my favourite.

*1.5kg (3lb 5oz) carp*
*2 medium onions, finely sliced*
*300ml (1/2 pint) water*
*600ml (1 pint) white wine*
*peel of 2 lemons*
*juice of 1 lemon*
*2 bay leaves*
*1 sprig of thyme*
*small bunch of parsley*
*salt and pepper*

Clean the carp, leaving the head on. Lay the onions in an ovenproof dish. Place the fish on top of these and pour on the water and wine and add all the other ingredients. Bring to the boil, skimming as you go, cover and simmer very gently until the fish is tender – about 1 1/2 hours. Lift the fish carefully to a dish, strain the stock, and pour it over the fish. Chill, and a delicious jelly will form from the stock. Serve with sliced, new, green, pickled cucumbers.

composite dishes
sauces & stocks

# apician pancakes

I think it was Evelyn Waugh who said he never remembers the original dish but leftovers are lovely. This dish comes from the Roman cook Apicius and, I suspect, is the first recipe for lasagne, but it is made with pancakes. It is a curious dish, but very good for using up leftover game of any description. I usually make extra pancakes when I'm cooking, and freeze them for next time.

For the pancakes:
3 eggs
225g (1/2lb) flour
pinch of salt
50ml (2fl oz) milk
50ml (2fl oz) water

Make a batter by putting all the ingredients in a blender and whizzing for a minute or so. Let the batter stand for 1 hour in the fridge and make six pancakes using a little lard to grease a good frying pan and cook over a high heat.

700g (11/2lb) cooked game or salmon
3 eggs
2 tablespoons olive oil
1/2 teaspoon celery or lovage seeds (or use cumin)
600ml (1 pint) stock
1/2 glass white wine
1/2 glass sweet sherry
flour
1/2 teaspoon ground pepper
110g (4oz) pinenuts or flaked almonds
butter

Mix the meat or fish with the eggs, oil, celery seeds, stock and alcohol and a little flour.

Butter a casserole dish and put a layer of the meat mixture on the bottom; sprinkle with pepper and nuts. Place a pancake on top, repeat the layering, finishing with a pancake layer.

Preheat the oven to 190°C/375°F/gas 5. Pierce a hole in the last pancake to let the steam out. Dot the top pancake with a little butter and bake, uncovered, for 40 minutes, or until heated through. Sprinkle with pepper and serve with a salad.

## stalker's pie

If lamb is shepherd's and beef is cottage, venison must equal stalker's. Shepherd's pie was a traditional use of the joint on Tuesday and the invention of the metal grinder in Victorian times made the dish more popular. My sister Heather first added port or whisky to the white sauce with which she bound her version, and a great improvement it is.

2–3 large potatoes

butter

25g (1oz) flour

25g (1oz) butter

300ml (1/2 pint) milk

1 glass port or whisky

2 onions, chopped

700g (11/2lb) cooked venison, ground or finely chopped

handful of parsley, chopped

salt and pepper

Preheat the oven to 200°C/400°F/gas 6. Boil the potatoes, allow to steam until the steam has evaporated and then mash with a little butter and salt and pepper. Make a roux in a large pan with the butter and flour and cook for 2 minutes. Season it and add enough milk to make a very thick, smooth sauce; add port or whisky and more milk if necessary. In another pan fry the onion in a little butter until it is golden. Add the meat and parsley and cook, stirring well, for a few more minutes. Stir in the sauce. Transfer to a lightly greased ovenproof dish and put the mashed potato on top. Criss-cross the potato with a fork and brush with melted butter. Cook for 30 minutes in the oven until piping hot and nicely browned.

## yorkshire christmas pie

I am always being asked for this recipe. Historically some of these pies were made to huge dimensions, and indeed one sent in 1832 to Lord Sheffield, the Lord Chancellor, broke the wagon with its weight! Make it with whatever birds you choose, I have started with a pigeon, building up to a goose. I usually make mine with puff pastry, but here is the original.

1 pigeon

1 partridge

1 pheasant

1 goose

900g (2lb) forcemeat (veal or pork)

850ml (11/2 pints) hot water

900g (2lb) hot water crust or puff pastry

salt and pepper

1 teaspoon nutmeg

Bone all the birds. Line a pie mould with the pastry and place a layer of forcemeat in it. Stuff the smallest bird with forcemeat and stuff the birds into each other according to size, seasoning as you go. Lay the birds in the pie, and fill in the spaces around it with breasts of pigeon, boned hare or whatever you have, then pack tight with the rest of the forcemeat. Pour in as much clarified butter as it will take, about 110–175g (4–6oz). Place on a pastry lid and brush with egg. Ornament it for fun. Preheat the oven to 170°C/325°F/gas 3. Cover with buttered paper and bake for 4 hours. When you serve it break the crust in front of your guests and cut into thin slices. The pastry is not meant to be eaten.

Spain abounds with paella type rice dishes made with whatever the local ingredients are. It is also a great country for game. My mother and I once visited a place called Puebla Sanabria, north-west of Salamanca surrounded by a valley of hills with a lake in the midst of the dry land and a castle my mother yearned to buy. I always meant to go back but today looking at maps I see a motorway runs through it, so perhaps I'll just keep it in my head. It was a great region for game and there we had a paella made entirely from game. This is great fun for a party and a great user of the rather more battered contents of your game larder.

5 tablespoons olive oil

1.8kg (4lb) mixed game: pheasant strips, partridge legs, rabbit pieces, roe deer chunks for example

75g (3oz) game sausage

110g (4oz) raw ham or bacon

any available livers of game birds, any venison kidneys

3 cloves garlic, chopped

500g (18oz) paella (or risotto) rice, well rinsed

150g (5oz) frozen peas

1/2 tablespoon paprika

pinch of cayenne

3 tablespoons sieved tomatoes or small tin tomato purée

1 small sachet of saffron threads

1.2 litres (2 pints) game stock

200ml (7fl oz) white wine

2 red peppers, grilled and skinned (or a small can)

salt and pepper

Heat the oil in a paella pan or a large flat pan and fry all the meats until they colour, finishing with the ham and then the offal. Then add the garlic, and continue cooking for a minute or two.

Add the rice, peas, paprika, cayenne, tomato, salt and pepper and stir well. Soften the saffron in a little stock and add to the rice. Add half the stock and the wine. When the liquid is absorbed, add more. Cook for about 30 minutes or transfer the pan to the oven and cook at 180°C/350°F/gas 4. Decorate the top with red pepper strips and any green herb that you have handy.

# siberian **shangii**

This is a splendid way of using up leftover meat or fish and gives quite a smart look to an ordinary supper of leftovers. The most famous Russian pie made with yeasted dough is *Koulbiaca* but that is of course because La Carème, returning from the court of the Czar, established it as Parisian Haute Cuisine. Properly made, it is a very complicated dish but this is its simpler country cousin. Remember that Siberia was not always a place you sent your criminals to but a source of much game and wildfowl.

This dish can be made in any size you choose – individual ones are good for parties – but I find this size does more for appearance and succulence. The original recipe called for a few chips of ice to supply moisture but I have used butter or stock. The French have a variant on this theme made with 450g (1lb) baked potato, 150g (5oz) flour, a little olive oil and 1 egg made into a dough, filled with your stuffing and baked as below or fried in smaller cakes.

For the dough:

400g (14oz) plain flour

10g ($^1/_2$oz) yeast

200ml (7fl oz) warm water or milk

1 tablespoon sugar

2 eggs, well beaten

$^1/_2$ teaspoon salt

3 tablespoons butter, softened

For the filling:

450g (1lb) cooked fish or meat

1 medium onion, finely sliced and fried

1–2 tablespoons butter or jellied stock

pinch of whatever herbs go with the filling

salt and pepper

Sieve the flour into a bowl and make a well in it. Gently crumble in the yeast with the liquid, mixing in gently. Cover and leave to ferment for 15 minutes in a warm place. Add the rest of the ingredients and knead well. Divide in two, cover again and leave to rest and rise until it has doubled – about 20 minutes. Knock back and roll out until it is 1cm ($^1/_2$in) thick. Put half of the dough on a greased baking sheet and sprinkle with flour. Place the filling on it and cover with the other half of the dough. Seal the edges carefully. Leave for 30 minutes – the dough will continue to rise – then bake at 220°C/425°F/gas 7 for 40–50 minutes until golden.

You could try pheasant with coriander, or venison with cumin, or salmon with coconut and red peppers. Have fun with it!

## sauce for **pigeon** or **duck**

**This is a variant on a Roman sauce; the original had mint and lovage seed but I like it better without them. This sauce can be served with pigeon or wild duck.**

*1 tablespoon olive oil*

*1 small onion, chopped*

*110g (4oz) stoned dates*

*1 egg yolk*

*1 tablespoon white wine*

*1 tablespoon vinegar*

*1 tablespoon honey*

*1 teaspoon anchovy essence*

*salt and pepper*

Heat the oil in a pan and fry the onion until it colours. Transfer it to a food processor and add all the other ingredients. Blend well, return to the pan and heat through.

## good **gravy**

**This is how I make gravy and it is much enjoyed. The secret to good gravy is good stock, never mind the vegetable water or the stock cube, half a pint of good stock makes all the difference.**

Remove whatever bird or beast you have roasted and pour off any excess fat – keep this for future cooking. Scatter enough plain flour to take up the pan juices, and stir in well with a wooden spoon, making sure no lumps remain. Scrap up any bits that have stuck to the bottom of the pan. When it is smooth, add a certain amount of stock and mix as it heats up, to absorb the flour. Add the rest of the stock allowing to cook gently. Season, add a couple of glasses of red wine and cook some more, then half a glass of orange juice or a little redcurrant jelly. When your sauce tastes right, thin with a little vegetable water or allow to cook to thicken – you can play about with it for some time. Make sure your sauce boat is scalding hot before you pour in the gravy. An Argyle is good for removing fat or if it is greasy when made, ignite some brandy and pour into the sauce to burn off excess fat.

## onion **sauce** vivien

**This is so called because my friend Vivien Cassell and I concocted it in her kitchen. It is lighter than the usual and very delicious.**

*25g (1oz) butter*

*4 onions, cut in half and sliced*

*25g (1oz) flour*

*1 bottle light lager*

*milk*

*salt and pepper*

*1 tablespoon crème fraîche*

Melt some butter in a pan and sauté the onions until pale gold. In another pan make a roux with flour and butter and add the lager a little at a time to make a sauce. Add enough milk to make the right consistency – about 2 tablespoons. Add the onions, season and stir in the crème fraîche.

## plum **sauce**

**This is a good sauce for duck, goose or most game and will keep well in the fridge. You can use preserved plums.**

*1 onion, chopped*

*1/2 teaspoon fennel seeds*

*225g (1/2lb) plums or damsons*

*2 tablespoons honey or mead*

*600ml (1 pint) game stock*

*1 glass red wine*

*1 tablespoon olive oil or butter*

*1/2 teaspoon ground pepper*

In a blender grind together the pepper, onion and fennel seeds. Add the chopped damsons, the honey (or mead) and blend quickly. Add the rest of the ingredients and whizz a bit. Transfer to a saucepan and simmer very gently for 30 minutes.

## bread sauce

This use of stale bread in making a sauce is truly medieval. I love bread sauce, hot with white game, cold in sandwiches. There are many ways to make it – some like the onion cut up, some like it cooked whole and then mashed up before serving – I make mine in a double boiler. You can make it in advance, freeze it, or keep it in the warming drawer but this is what I do.

For about 600ml (1 pint) enough for 4:
*1 onion, liberally stuck with cloves*
*1 loaf white bread (crust removed and cut into cubes)*
*600ml (1 pint) full fat milk*
*good pinch of ground mace or freshly grated nutmeg*
*1 bay leaf*
*150ml (5fl oz) double cream*
*salt and pepper*

Put the onion in a pan and arrange the bread around it, pour on the milk and season with salt and pepper, nutmeg and bay leaf. Bring to the boil and reduce to a very low heat on a heatproof mat if possible. Simmer gently, partly covered for 2–3 hours, adding more milk if needed. The thickness of the sauce is your choice. Just before serving, discard the bay leaf, add the cream, stir it in and heat through.

## green sauce

This is the traditional medieval sauce to be served with fish and game. It is sharp and if you find it too much add a finely mashed yolk of a hard-boiled egg and a little olive oil. It is, I suppose, the precursor of mint sauce and probably came back from the Crusades. Use what herbs you have but let mint and parsley dominate.

*12 sprigs of fresh herbs*
*50g (2oz) fresh fine white breadcrumbs*
*2 tablespoons cider vinegar*
*1 clove garlic (or if available tops of wild garlic, finely chopped)*
*salt and pepper*

Finely chop the herbs. Sprinkle the breadcrumbs with the vinegar and leave for 10 minutes. Crush the garlic in a mortar, add the herbs, breadcrumbs, salt and pepper and pound well. Add enough vinegar to bring to the consistency of thin bread sauce.

## rowan jelly

*1.8kg (4lb) almost ripe rowan berries*

*1.2 litres (2 pints) water*

*450g (1lb) preserving or caster sugar to 600ml (1 pint) juice*

Strip the berries from the stalks. Put into a pan with the water, bring to the boil and simmer for 15 minutes (do not exceed this time as the juice becomes bitter). Strain the fruit through a jelly bag, and be careful not to squeeze or poke the bag or the jelly will be cloudy. Measure the juice, return to a clean preserving pan and add the correct amount of sugar. Stir over a low heat until the sugar is dissolved. Boil rapidly, stirring as you go and skimming when necessary. Test for setting on a cold plate. Pour into heated jars, cover with waxed paper and allow to set. Screw on the lid.

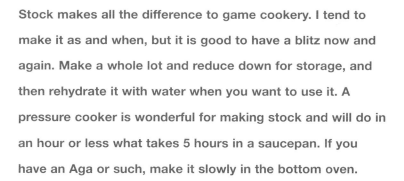

## game stock

**Stock makes all the difference to game cookery. I tend to make it as and when, but it is good to have a blitz now and again. Make a whole lot and reduce down for storage, and then rehydrate it with water when you want to use it. A pressure cooker is wonderful for making stock and will do in an hour or less what takes 5 hours in a saucepan. If you have an Aga or such, make it slowly in the bottom oven.**

*900g (2lb) game meat*

*900g (2lb) game trimmings*

*3.6 litres (6 pints) water*

*110g (4oz) onions, chopped and browned*

*110g (4oz) carrots*

*2 leeks, sliced*

*2 sticks celery*

*1 faggot of herbs*

*9 peppercorns*

*3 cloves*

Put the meat and trimmings in the cold water, bring to the boil and simmer for 1 hour. Then add the rest of the ingredients and simmer for 4 hours, skimming as you go. Strain, allow it to go cold and remove the excess fat. Return to the pan and reduce by two thirds. Freeze in cubes in ice-trays, turn out the cubes into a bag, label and use as needed, adding water as needed.

## game **chips**

Some people serve crisps with game – tut tut. Game chips are easy to make and even the best of potato crisps don't measure up. If you must, use Tyrells which are made by a diversifying Herefordshire farmer and are quite the best. For perfect game chips you must use old potatoes, preferably bought from a farm shop so they haven't been irradiated and chilled like the supermarket variety, and when you have sliced them very thinly using a mandolin or a food processor or a very sharp knife you must wash them well in running cold water to remove the starch. Dry them very thoroughly on kitchen paper or a tea towel.

Heat your oil, vegetable not olive, in a deep fat fryer until it is very hot and plunge in your chips. I cook mine twice. If you cook them until they just start to change colour then drain them on newspaper or kitchen towel; if you're fussy you can keep them on the paper until the last minute and then return them to the oil to finish off. This saves time at the end as first time round you can only cook them in small batches or they will stick. You can be fancy and do this with parsnip chips or beetroot but don't cook them with the potatoes.

## potato **olad**

This is a Russian dish from Belarus and a good way of using up leftovers. You can mix and match your ingredients until your heart's content and it makes a great supper dish; the Russians eat it with soured cream. You can add yeast and a beaten egg to make more of a cake at a ratio of 500g (18oz) potatoes to 75g (3oz) flour, with 1 egg and 25g (1oz) yeast mixed with 50ml (2fl oz) warm water.

For the pancake:
*4 large potatoes*
*2 tablespoons flour*
*110g (4oz) butter*
*salt and pepper*

Grate the potatoes, squeeze dry in a cloth and season. Mix in the flour using your hands. Heat the butter in a heavy frying pan and put half the potato mix in and form a flattened cake. Fry for a few minutes and then place a dollop of filling on top. Cover with the rest of the grated potato and when the underside is crisp and well set flip over and cook until the bottom side is done. Alternatively you can put it under the grill to brown the top, but brush with oil or melted butter so that it doesn't burn.

### Suggested fillings

Cooked pheasant with soft cheese and capers
Cooked venison with cranberries
Duck with marmalade sharpened with lemon juice
Salmon with blue cheese or macerated fruit (the sort you get given
   or win in a raffle like peaches in brandy or some such)

# stuffed **onions**

This is a perfect way to use up leftover game. Edward VII's favourite breakfast was onions stuffed with kidneys, cream and brandy – delicious but perhaps not for breakfast. Stuffed onions make a great supper dish and you can stuff them in advance and stick them in the oven while having your bath. The onions can either be parboiled and then roasted, or raw and then braised.

*4 large onions*

*50g (2oz) butter*

*25g (1oz) bacon, finely chopped*

*25g (1oz) fresh white breadcrumbs*

*2 tablespoons chopped herbs (whatever goes with you filling plus parsley for colouring)*

*225g (8oz) of game, (see right for suggested fillings)*

*salt and pepper*

Carefully peel your onion and if parboiling do so in boiling water for 10 minutes and allow to cool until you can handle it. Cut off the root end to make a platform then cut a lid about 1cm (¹/₂in) from the top and carefully cut out the insides leaving a 1cm (¹/₂in) wall.

Preheat the oven to 190°C/375°F/ gas 5. Heat the butter in a frying pan, chop the removed onion innards and cook in the butter until golden. Add the bacon, breadcrumbs and the remaining ingredients and fry for a bit longer. Spoon into the onions and replace the lids. Put into an oven dish and paint the onions with olive oil to prevent them drying or pour over 150ml (5fl oz) of stock. Cook in the oven for 40 minutes, and half way through cover with some tinfoil.

**Suggested fillings 50g (2oz) per onion**

Venison kidneys with cream, brandy and mushroom

Pheasant with herbs, cream cheese, sherry, cayenne and chilli

Pheasant with wild mushrooms

Duck with bottled cherries or damsons

Duck with green peas and mint

Venison with squares of beetroot (parboiled).

The options are endless!

## beetroot pancakes

These eighteenth century pancakes make an attractive
accompaniment to game and can be eaten hot or cold
which make them a nice addition to a buffet table.

*175g (6oz) beetroot, cooked and peeled*

*2 tablespoons brandy*

*2 tablespoons double cream*

*4 egg yolks*

*2 tablespoons plain flour*

*2 teaspoons caster sugar*

*1 teaspoon nutmeg, grated*

*clarified butter*

Put all the ingredients except the butter in a food processor and
mash well together to create a pancake mixture. Heat a little butter
in a small frying pan. Make pancakes with the mixture but be
careful as they burn quite easily. Turn them after a minute or two –
they cook quite quickly.

## gratin with leeks

This is another good leftover dish but to give it a bit of zip
make your cheese sauce with half Stilton or another blue
cheese and add a few capers and cayenne pepper. Use any
leftover game you have, either singly or mixed for extra
curiosity!

*450g (1lb) potatoes, thinly sliced and washed to remove starch*
*1 dessertspoon capers*
*450g (1lb) cooked game, sliced*
*leeks or heads of chicory, sliced into 5cm (2in) pieces and*
  *blanched*
*600ml (1 pint) cheese sauce, made with a good Cheddar*
*salt, pepper and cayenne*

Preheat the oven to 190°C/375°F/gas 5. Butter an ovenproof dish
and line it with a layer of potatoes. Sprinkle with capers and
season. Put on your slices of game and your leeks or chicory, add
another layer of potatoes and pour over the sauce. Scatter some
grated cheese on top, dot with butter and bake in the oven for
about 45 minutes.

# meat suppliers

**Aberdeenshire**

Forbes Raeburn & Sons, 7 Bogie Street, Huntly, AB54 8DX.
01466 792818.
*Honey-cooked ham on the bone, pork and venison sausage, prize-winning black pudding, certified Angus beef*

H. M. Sheridan, 11 Bridge Street, Ballater, AB35 5QP  01339 755218

**Bedfordshire**

L R. Clayton Ltd., Family Butcher, 19 Market Square, Potton, SG19 2NP.
01767 260351.
*Brawn chitterling, faggots, home-made sausages and home-cooked hams.*

T. Harper & Son Ltd., Bell Farm, Studham, Nr Dunstable, LU6 2QG.
01582 872001.
*Award-winning pies (beef and red wine); make own bacon and sausages, including some gluten-free.*

**Buckinghamshire**

J. H. Clark & Sons, 4 High Street, Princes Risborough, HP27 0AX.
01844 344025.
*Traditional family butchers of Scotch Premier beef, pork and lamb, wild venison from Balmoral;; wine licence, moniac wines.*

G. Martin Butchers (formerly Goddens), 46 High Street, Chesham, HP5 1EP.
01494 773580.
*Sausages, rabbit pie, cold and hot game pies.*

Richardson's Fine Food Ltd, 7 Packhorse Road, Gerrards Cross, SL9 7QA.
01753 886636.
*Large selection of wet fish, excellent delicatessen and cheese counter. Hosts the National Barbeque Championship.*

**Cambridgeshire**

Barker Bros, 43 High Street, Great Shelford, CB2 5EH.  01223 843292.
*More than 30 different sorts of sausages; own hams and bacon, full selection of game in season, cheeses, pickeles; all meat hung in the side.*

**Carmarthenshire**

Eynon's of St Clears, Deganwy, Pentre Road, St Clears, SA33 4LR.
01994 230226.
*Welsh specialists, saltmarsh-reared Welsh lamb from Portmeirion (late May to September), free-range pork from Surrey, Welsh Black beef.*

**Cheshire**

Steve Brooks, Quality Cuts Ltd., 25 High Street, Sandbach, CW11 1AH.
01270 766657. www.qualitycuts.co.uk
*Excellent shop with fine selection of meat, cooked goods, sausages, faggots.*

R. F. Burrows & Sons, Old Post Office, Bunbury, Nr Taporley, CW6 9QR.
01829 260342.
*Slaughter own meat, buy beasts from local farms, make own sausages and black pudding.*

R. Minshall & Son, 42 Church Street, Weaverham, Northwich, CW8 3NJ.
01606 852199.
*10–15 varieties of sausages at a time, including venison, pork and black pudding, pork, apple and cheese.*

**Co. Durham**

Dirk Pittaway, 2–4 Borough Road, Darlington, DL1 1SD. 01325 466804.
*Rear own Angus-cross beef, hang own texel lamb for 1 month, make own sausages, cooked meat, pease pudding, Severy ducks, black pudding.*

**Cornwall**

Norman Brooks, 16 Duke Street, Padstow, PL28 8AB.  01841 532351.
*Locally sourced meat,. His woodland sausage is sent for by customers in London.*

**Cumbria**

Cranstons Ltd., 12 Stramongate, Kendal, LA9 4BN.  01539 735207.
Front Street, Brampton, Penrith, CA8 1NG.  01697 72362.
*Seven shops, run by two experienced butchers. Direct farm sourcing, local produce, local labelling, great Cumberland sausage.*

Peter Gott, Sillfield Farm, Barrow in Furness, LA8 0HZ.  01229 830956.
*Raises wild boar and is a traditional cheese-maker. His bacon is second to none and his Dunmow Flitch brings tears to my eyes.*

Higginsons, Keswick House, Main Street, Grange-over-Sands, LA11 6AB.
01539 534367.
*Local meat, award-winning dry-cured bacon and ham, Cumberland sausages, saltmarsh lamb from Morecambe Bay.*

Holker Hall Food Hall, Cark-in-Cartmel, Grange-over-Sands, LAQQ 7PL.

G. A. Steadman, 2 Finkle Street, Sedbergh, LA10 5BZ. 01539 620431.
Aberdeen Angus, Kendal Fell lamb from a 20-mile radius, Garsdale pork, own bacon, hams, pancetta, air-dried ham. Also bakery for pies, fresh or frozen ready-meals.

**Derbyshire**

Andrew Armstrong Butcher, The Square, Bakewell, DE45 1BT.  01629 812165.
*Won 1998 best East Midlands shop awards for pork pies and black puddings.*

Owen Taylor & Sons Ltd., 27 Main Road, Leabrooks, Alfreton, DE55 1LA.
01773 603351.
*79 years in restaurant and hotel trade. Meat hung for 3 weeks: beef, pork, lamb, veal, game, Derbyshire poultry.*

## Devon

Hayman's, 6 Church Street, Sidmouth, EX10 8LY. 01395 512887.
*Founded by the great-grandfather of the current owners. All meat locally sourced. Scotch eggs sell 50 a week in midwinter. Make their own brawn, pickle tongues, brisket, cure own bacon and gammon.*

Lloyd Maunder Ltd.
7 The Strand, Dawlish, EX7 9PS. 01626 863150.
46 Fore Street, St Marychurch, Torquay, TQ1 4LX. 01803 327108.
17 Bank Street, Teignmouth, TQ14 8AW. 01626 774510.
2 Exeter Road, Exmouth, EX8 1PL. 01395 272286.
31a Fore Street, Kingsbridge, TQ7 1PG. 01548 856400.
5 Bampton Street, Tiverton, Devon, EX16 6AA. 01884 252525.
16 Bolton Street, Brixham, TQ5 9DG. 01803 852706.
*Long-established group of Devon Butchers specialising in West Country meat and a wide range of specialist products; lots of barbecue specialities in summer. On request.*

Palmers of Tavistock, 50 Brook Street, Taverstock, PL19 0BJ. 01822 612000.
*140-year-old business. All meat sourced within Devon and Cornwall. Replacing rusk with traditional breadcrumbs. Hogs pudding, cook own ox tongue, make own haggis.*

## East Sussex

Lew Howard, 66 Springett Avenue, Ringmer, BN8 5QX. 01273 812309.
*Family butcher for 40 years. All local meat, eg. Southdown lamb, Sussex (and Scottish) beef; supply sausages exclusively for Harrods; specialise in hand-made sausages of free-range meat.*

## Essex

Allen & Son, St Botolph's Street, Colchester, CO2 7DU. 01206 573443.
*Traditional third-generation butchers. All meat locally sourced. Beef hung for 3–4 weeks. Local game in season. See themselves as butchers, not cooks, although they do make sausages and pies.*

Buntings, 89 High Street, Maldon, CM9 5EP. 01621 853271.
*Company with 120 years' experience. Traceability of stock, beef form Orkney.*

Hepburns of Mountnessing, 269 Roman Road, Mountnessing, Brentwood, CM15 0UH. 01277 353289.
*Sells immaculate local meat and is a model of Q Guild imagination, inventiveness and education.*

R. H. Simons & Son, Cage End, Hatfield Broad, CM22 7HL. 01279 718271.
*I remember this shop when I was a little girl and they make wonderful sausages. They still have very good meat.*

## Glasgow

Andrew Gillespie Butchers, 1601 Great Western Road, Anniesland Cro, G13 1LP. 0141 9592015.
*100 years of local business. Stock sausages, steak pies, black-faced lamb, Aberdeen Angus, pork from Ayrshire.*

## Gloucestershire

W. J. Castle, The Green, Northleach, Cheltenham, GL54 3EX. 01451 860243.
*Sister shop to Jesse Smith of Cirencester. Local Hereford beef, Buccleugh beef, 10 varieties of sausage, local lambs, Gloucester Old Spot, pies cooked, meat, olives*

Robin Jenkins Family Butchers, 160 Bath Road, Cheltenham, GL53 7NF. 01242 514801.
*Home-made sausages, home-cured bacon, barbecue specialist, local venison, pheasants and pigeons, meat from Forest of Dean, Hereford beef, Welsh lamb.*

Jesse Smith, Long Street, Tetbury, GL8 8AA. 01666 502730.
14 Blackjack Street, Cirencester, GL7 1LD. 01285 653387.
*As seen on 'Two Fat Ladies'. Splendid traditional butchers with Highgrove beef, smashing faggots, Old Spot pork and lots of lovely made-up goods.*

## Greater Manchester

Lords of Middleton, 18 Old Hall Street, Middleton, M24 1AN. 0161 6434160. www.lordsofmiddleton.co.uk.
*Founded 1893. Traditional Scots pie, beef well hung; family butcher whose customers travel to shop with them.*

## Hampshire

Buckwells of Southsea, 70 Osborne Road, Southsea, PO5 3LU. 02392 827053.

R. F. Hadlow Butchers, 22 South Street, Titchfield, Fareham, PO14 4DJ. 01329843240.
*Aberdeen beef from Scotland, 100 different patés, own cooked meats, 100 international cheese, own faggots, haggis, bake own French bread.*

Manydown Farm Shop, Scrapps Hill Farm, Worting, Basingstoke, RG23 8PU. 01256 460068.
*All own beef, lamb and free range chickens, pork from plantation pigs, pies and sausages.*

Ron Reeve, 38 Drift Road, Clanfield, Wate, Portsmouth, PO8 0JL. 02392 593633.
*Game, wide range of pies, venison, wild rabbits, lamb, sausages include liver and bacon. Scottish meat, free-range pork from plantation pigs.*

## Hertfordshire

Eastwoods of Berkhampsted, 15 Gravel Path, Berkhamsted, HP4 2EF. 01442 865012.
*Serious providers of organic meat: Highgrove beef and poultry. Won team award in All Britain Barbecue competition 2002 with a Levatine Lamburger.*

Hamblings Butchers, 2 Moneyhill Parade, Uxbridge Road, Rickmansworth, WD3 2BQ. 01923 772557.
*Traditional family butcher proud of knowledge and service. Hang beef for 3 weeks.*

Keith Waterton Butchers, 5 Dolphin Square, Tring, HP23 5BN. 01442 827575.
*Scotch and local meat; sausages – country pork is their bestseller, made to a recipe Mr Waterton grew up with.*

## Highland
Ian Wynne & Son, 5 Airds Crossing, High Street, Fort William, PH33 6EU. 01397 702666.
*Very proud of his haggis and black pudding. Local meat used where possible: game, local wild venison.*

## Humberside
Brian Fields Butchers, 7 Hull Road, Anlaby, Hull, HU10 6SP. 01482 657497.
*Orkney beef, 10 different sausages, local pork, fancy products, individual beef Wellngtons.*

## Kent
C. J. Barkaway, 6 West Street, Faversham, ME13 7JF. 01795 532026.

Dennis of Bexley, 1&2 Bourne Parade, Bourne Road, Bexley, DA5 1LQ. 01322 522126.
*Overall Team Award in British Barbecue with Devils Fingers. Pies: caters weddings and occasions.*

## Kincardineshire
Charles McHardy, 11 Market Square, Stonehaven, AB39 2BT. 01569 762693.
*Judged top shop in Great Britain in 1997 and top Scottish shop four times. All meat sourced from local farms, game in season. Ready meals, eg. steak with haggis and whisky in puff pastry.*

## Lanarkshire
D. W. Ferguson, 3 Buchanan Street, Airdrie, ML6 6BG. 01236 763333.
*Beef from Forfar, Lanark lamb, dry-cured bacon and gammon from female pigs; 25 different cooked meats, barbecue range; instore bakery, 40 pastry products; large range dishes for Slimming World.*

## Lancashire
Brendan Anderton (Butchers), 19&21 Derby Road, Longridge, Preston, PR3 3JT. 01772 783321.
*Family firm. All local meat cut to customers' specification; sausages, black pudding, MacSween's haggis, wild boar, guinea fowl, veal, venison, Herdwick lamb from fells.*

S. Huyton & Son, 73/75 Town Green, Aughton, Nr Ormskirk, L39 6SE. 01695 423308.

R. & M. Scott, The Market House, High Street, Garstang, PR3 1HY. 01995 602135.

## Leicestershire
David R Clarke & Son, 29 Main Street, Quenilborough, LE7 3DB. 0116 260 6383.

Northfield Farm, Whissendine Lane, Cold Overton, Nr Oakham, LE15 7QF
Tel: 01664 474 271  Fax: 01664 474 669     www.northfieldfarm.com
*Provide rare and traditional British breeds of beef, pork and lamb, home-cured bacon and hams, and game. Also a wide selection of cheese, condiments, cordials and wines. Finalists in the Great Taste Awards for the last several years.*

## Lincolnshire
George Adams Retail Butchers, 25-6 The Crescent, Spalding, PE11 1AG. 01775 725956.
*Well-known established pork farmers who use all their own meat. Wondeful hand-raised pork pies, haslet and faggots, excellent hams.*

F. C. Phipps, Osborne House, Mareham-Le-Fen, Boston, PE22 7RW.
*Won Britain's Best Butcher and is accredited for Rare Breeds Trust. Has own abbatoir. Specialises in Lincolnshire stuffed chine, haslet, kassler, local cure in beer, juniper berries and black treacle.*

## London
Borough Market, Southwark Street, London, EC1 1TJ. 020 7407 1002. Food market, Friday 12am-6pm, Saturday 9am-4pm.

Frank Godfrey Ltd., 7 Highbury Park, Highbury, N5 1QJ.  020 7226 2425.
*Traditional English butcher, passed down craft to family; maturation, home-made English hams.*

Kent & Sons, 59 St John's Wood High Street, NW8 7NL.

C. Lidgate Butcher, 110 Holland Park Avenue, W11 4UA.  020 7221 5878.
*Packed full of meat from all the best sources: Shetland and saltmarsh lamb, Highgrove beef and many specially prepared dishes. If the independent butcher's shop has a saviour, David Lidgate is it.*

Randalls Butchers, 113 Wandsworth Bridge Road, Fulham, SW6 2TE. 020 7736 3426.
*Gordon Ramsey described them as the best butchers in London. All beef is Scottish except when from Highgrove.*

H. G. Walter, 51 Palliser Road, Barons Court, W14 9EB.  0207 385 6466.
*Won best small shop in Great Britain. Free range and organic produce; Buccleugh beef, plantation pigs, 20 different sausages, marinades, cheeses from small producers; cooked meats.*

## Lothian
George Bower, 75 Raeburn Place, Stockbridge, Edinburgh, EH4 1JG. 0131 332 3469.
*Best game butcher anywhere in Scotland, beautifully hung beef and fat pork.*

John Livingstone & Sons, 3 Court Street, Haddington, EH41 3JD. 01501 740343.
*All Scottish meat, venison, cattle sourced from one farm. Big bakery side producing bread, pies, rolls.*

C. D. Peat & Sons, 3 Court Street, Haddington, EH41 3JD.  01620 823192.
*My own butcher, so very high standards. All meat locally sourced. Linda Dick chickens, excellent sausages, game in season, wild rabbit, local venison.*

John Saunderson, 40 Leven Street, Edinburgh, EH3 9LJ.

## Merseyside
Brian Harris, 43 Oxton Road, Birkenhead, CH41 2QQ.  0151 652 5867.

## Middlesex
Daines & Gray, 31 High Street, Shepperton, TW17 9AB.  01932 226313.
*Sausages, game, Scottish and Oxfordshire beef, free-range pork, barbecue products, crowns and rack roasts, Brtish farm standard, reputation for free-range turkeys.*

## Monmouthshire
Hancocks of Monmouth, 34 Monnow Street, Monmouth, NP25 3EN. 01600 712015.
*Awards for sausages, South Wales Butcher of Year 1999. Dry-cured bacon, all local meat from a 20 mile radius. Welsh lamb, hand-raised pork, pies.*

Vin Sullivan, 114 Frogmore Street, Abergavenny, Gwent, NP7 5AE. 01873 856989.

## Norfolk
J. & D. Papworth Farms, 34a Market Place, Swaffham, PE37 7QH. 01760 724753.
16 Millers Walk, Fakenham, NR21 9AP.  01328 855039.
46 Station Road, Sheringham, NR26 8RG.  01263 823189.
*Own home-reared beef, pork, lamb from our farms, slaughtered in own abbatoir, so complete traceability of source.*

## North Yorkshire
J. B. Cockburn & Sons, 12 Market Place, Bedale, North Yorkshire, DL8 1EQ. 01677 422126.
*All local; extensive game; has own farm breeding pedigree Highland cattle; pies, award-winning sausages and burgers, well-hung sirloin, Swaledale lamb, rare breeds, organic.*

Highside Butchers, Main Street, Kirkby Malzear, Nr Ripon, HG4 3RS. 01765 658423.
*Small family business. Local meat, local cheese, pies, boneless stuffed chicken, flavoured lamb joints, meatballs in tomato sauce and lasagne.*

A. P. Jackson Butchers, 10 High Street, Ruswarp, Whitby, YO21 1NH. 01947 820085.
*Pork pies, locally sourced meat, own farm for beef where possible, dry-cured bacon, 20–30 types of sausages, including continental.*

E. B. Nicholson & Son, Market Place, Helmsley, YO6 5BL.  01439 770249.
*All beef and lamb local and mostly from a farm 2 miles away; ready meals, pies, cure own bacon, delicatessen.*

J. Thompson, 125 High Street, Northallerton, DL7 8PQ.  01609 773336.
*Established 1890. All English beef, pick cattle live from local farms, favour Hereford Angus cross, hang beef for 1 month; outside catering for barbecues, own bake house, own pies and sausages.*

## Northamptonshire
Saul's of Spratton, 27 Brixworth Road, Spratton, Nothampton, NN6 8HH. 01604 847214.
*Small butchers and farmer. Influenced by year spent year in Germany doing deli studies. Everything home-made; awards for black pudding; locally sourced meat; pig roasts.*

## Nottinghamshire
Clive Lancaster, 1 Eaton Place, Market Square, Bingham, NG13 88D. 01949 875010.

Marshall Retailing, The Butchers Shop, Farnsfield, Newark, NG22 8EF. 01623 882251.
*Meat either sourced locally or from Derbyshire. Suckling pigs, pork, beef and lamb, open pie, Lincolnshire poultry, Lancaster sausages, curry, cajun; customer requests.*

## Oxfordshire
W. J. Castle, 111 High Street, Burford, OX8 4RG.  01993 822113.
*Local lamb, Hereford and Buccleugh beef, duck breasts in sauce, sausages (8 flavours at time), Old Spot pork, Wiltshire cured bacon, home-made pies, cheese, patés, French salamis.*

M. Newitt & Sons, 10 High Street, Thame, 0X9 2BZ.  01844 212103.
*Voted Britain's best butcher. Pork from Southwold, Orkney beef and lamb. Raymond Blanc once ordered 25 partridges at 4.30pm on Christmas Eve and got them!*

Patrick Strainge (Butchers), Bridge Street, Bampton, Witney, OX18 2HA. 01993 850350.
*Farmer's son so most meat his own or from friends; hangs beef 2–3 weeks; faggots; makes own pastry for his pies.*

## Perth and Kinross
D. G. Lindsay Butcher, 15 North Methven Street, Perth, PH1 5PN. 01738 621496.
*Family butcher since 1871. All meat boned on premises in front of customers; local meat, steak pies. I can recommend their pork and chive sausages.*

## Powys
J. D. Powell, 16 High Street, Builth, Wells, LD2 3DN. 01982 553681.
*Beef and lamb from local farms, beef hung 2–3 weeks, lamb from daughter, pigs from Herefordshire, ready-meals all cooked by Mrs Powell.*

## Ross-shire
Kenneth Morrison, Strath, Gairloch, IV21 2BX. 01445 712485.
*Family business. Black and white pudding, all local beef, lamb, pork, wild venison, game birds, free-range turkeys.*

## Roxburghshire

Denholm Meat Suppliers, Main Street, Deholm, Hawick, TD9 8NU.
01450 870451.
*Johnny's butcher. Excellent pork, locally sourced meat, delicious sausages and haggis.*

## Shropshire

A. H. Griffiths, 22 High Street, Lentwedine, Craven Arms, Shropshire, SY7 0LB.
01547 540231.
*Father started own abbatoir 60 years ago; all animals from local farms; Hereford, Angus and Welsh black beef, Christmas poultry, game, including squirrel, in season.*

## Somerset

Barrett Bros, 25 Market Street, Crewkerne, TA18 7JU.  01460 72900.
*Family butchers. Traditional stance, cure own bacon, own sausages, cook own hams, hang beef for 2–3 weeks, all British beef, lamb, pork, large selection of cheeses.*

Bonners Butchers, 37 Silver Street, Ilminster, TA19 0DW.  01460 552465.
*Delicatessen; source meat within a 15-mile radius, free-range bacon, cooked meats, only heifer meat and the mother has to be English.*

Jon Thorner's Ltd., Bridge Farm shop, Pylle, Shepton Mallet, BA4 6TA.
01749 830138.
*Traditional butcher. All meat sourced locally; rare breeds meat.*

## South Yorkshire

Eatons, 8 Market Place, Tickhill, Doncaster, DN11 9HT.  01302 742360.
*All local meat, own pork pies and sausages, family beef hung for a minumum of 2 weeks, English hams, cure dry-salted bacon.*

## Staffordshire

Boxley's of Wombourne, Windmill Bank, Wombourne, WV5 9JD.
01902 892359.
*The man who gave the pork and leek sausage to the nation winning the first Sunday Times sausage contest in the 1980's, also the inventor of the pork and tomato sausage. Local meat..*

Bradshaw Bros Ltd., 76 High Street, Chase Terrace, Burntwood, WS7 8LR.
01543 279437
*Fourth-generation business. Farm, abbatoir, food hall, vegetables, delicatessen, restaurant. All meat from local farmers, game in season, pigs, some rare breeds.*

Plant & Wilton, 14-16 High Street, Newcastle-under-Lyme, ST5 1RA.
01782 610130.
*Cook and cut everything, all local meat, pies, sausages, no preservatives, Andrews sausage; hang beef for 4 weeks, free-range pork in carcase, all British products, game in season.*

## Suffolk

Andrew's Quality Burchers, 74 High Street, Hadleigh, Ipswich, IP7 5EF.
01473 827720.

Barwells of Bury St Edmunds, 39 Abbeygate Street, Bury St Edmunds, IP33 1LW.  01284 754084.
*Sister shop to Harpers in Bedfordshire; Meat mostly from Cumbria; game in season, free-range venison from Denholm, local rabbits and pheasants (boned, rolled and stuffed); hand-crafted pies, cold game pie, chicken and ham, 150-year-old sausage recipe.*

E. W. Revett & Son, 81 High Street, Wickham Mark, Woodbridge, IP13 0RA.
01728 746263.
*Delicatessen, bakery, off-licence selling quality wines; very famous pork sausage selling 2–3 000 lb per week. All local meat and poultry, beef hung for a minimum of 2 weeks, game in season.*

## Surrey

George Arthur (Butchers) Ltd., 70 Guildford Road, Lightwater, GU18 5SD.
01276 472191. www.georgearthur.com
*36 varieties of sausage, crocodile, kangaroo, ostrich; have made own pies for 50 years.*

R. A. Bevan & Sons, 136 Richmond Road, Kingston-upon-Thames, KT2 5EZ.
020 8546 0783.
*All free-range meat, Orkney beef and lamb, plantation pigs, cheese; smoke own bacon, cure own gammon, cooked meats.*

Kenneth J. Eve, High Class Butcher, 9 Corner House, Epsom Road, Ewell, KT17 1NX.  020 8393 3043.
*Orkney gold beef; create innovative dishes, eg. Leeky Lamb (eye of fillet wrapped in minced best end and wrapped in leek leaves ready to cook).*

V. A. Gibson Butchers, 301 Lower Addiscombe Road, Addiscombe, Croydon. CR0 6RF.  020 8654 5147.
*Traditional butchers, 10 ypes of sausage, Orkney beef and lamb, Suffolk pork.*

C. H. Wakeling Ltd., 41 Farncombe Street, Godalming, GU8 5RD.
01483 417557. www.wakelings.co.uk
*Local farmers providing Angus beef, plantation and rare-breed pigs. Small local slaughterhouse, hang beef for minimum of 2 weeks, Christmas beef 1 month.*

## Tyne & Wear

R. Brown Family Butchers, 237 Chillingham Road, Heaton, Newcastle upon Tyne, NE6 5LJ.  0191 265 9115. www.northerncounties.co.uk
*Mostly Northumbrian beef and lamb, all meat northern-bred and raised; 15 types of sausage, venison, bratwurst.*

G Haswell, 1&2 Frances Street, new Silksworth, Sunderland, SR3 1EN.
0191 521 0240.
*Est. 1836. Most meat sourced from own farm at Durham, local poultry, turkeys from Peter Smith at Penrith, home-produced sausages; beef hung for a minumum of 2 weeks.*

Charles Nicholson & Son, 140 Park View, Whitley Bay, NE26 3QN.
0191 252 5250.
*Third generation. Sources live direct from Northumberland farms; all pies in-house with own shortcrust pastry, cure own bacon.*

George Payne Butchers, 27 Princes Road, Brunton Park, Newcastle upon Tyne, NE3 5TT. 0191 236 2992.
*Rare breeds, local lamb and Black-face hill sheep, Saddleback, Middle White pigs, British poultry from small producers, own bacon and sausages, Berkshire where possible.*

## Warwickshire

Alf Jones Butchers, 35 Clemens Street, Leamington Spa, CV31 2DP. 01926 45049.
*All British meat, game in season, venison sausages from wild venison, beef hung for at least 3 weeks, spring lamb, wet-cured, dry-cured bacon from English pigs, own sausages.*

## West Midlands

Poxons Butchers, 96 Windmill Lane, Castlecroft, Wolverhampton, WV3 8HG. 01902 761693.
*Buccleugh Scottish beef, local lamb and pork, own sausage (pork, onion and mustard) and pies (own water crust).*

P. Richards, 64 High Street, Albrighton, Nr Wolverhampton, WV7 3JA. 01902 372878.
*Quality meat, bake bread and cakes, make own pork pies, buy Scottish beef, English lamb, pigs from Much Wenlock, dry cure own bacon, jams and preserves; delicatessen counter.*

Robinson's of Tettenhall, 18 High Street, Tettenhall, Woverhampton, WV6 8QT. 01902 751692. www.cookingbutcher.com
*Est. 1905. Aberdeen Angus beef, beef hung for 16–21 days, Shropshire lamb and pork, home-made sausages, black pudding; delicatessen section; small restaurant.*

## West Sussex

L. M. Clapham, 3 Elm Grove, Horsham, RH13 4HX. 01403 252822.
*All meat sourced from Scotland and hung for 3 weeks; cook tongues and hams and roast meats, total traceability. Customers can see preparation room. Free-range local poultry.*

West Yorkshire
Addy Butchers, Flowery Fields, Holmfirth, HD7 1RT. 01484 682897.
*Small country butchers. Meat from local farmers, hang beef for 2–3 weeks; dry-cured bacon and pies.*

Lishmans of Ilkley, 25 Leeds Road, Ilkley, LS29 8DP. 01943 609436.
*National championship sausage makers 1999 and 2001. Pork saddlebacks reared on open farm in Dales (perfect crackling every time), dry cured bacon. All local Yorkshire lamb and beef.*

George Middlemiss & Sons, 3 Market Street, Otley, LS21 3AF. 01943 462611. www.dalesnet.co.uk
*Est 1889. All live meat killed locally, 50% straight from their own farm, game in season, own baking, pies, pig chaps, sausages, black pudding, tripe.*

C. & G. Starkey, 8 Wolsey Parade. Sherburn-in-Elmet, Leeds, LS25 6BQ. 01977 682696. www.c-gstarkey.co.uk.

*Traditional family farmer-butchers. Hang meat for 2–3 weeks; game, wild boar, corn-fed chickens, own pies, pork, chaps to order, potted meat.*

Wilsons, 38 Austhorpe Road, Crossgates, Leeds, LS15 8DX. 01132 645448.
*Family business. Own sausages, Yorkshire pork pie champions. Locally sourced meat from family-run abbatoir, beef hung for 2 weeks, poultry from family firm.*

## Wiltshire

K. & E. J. Crump & Son, 120 High Street, Wootton-Bassett, Swindon, SN4 7AU. 01793 853284.
*Fourth-generation family business. All British meat, Scotch Premier, lamb and pork from Cheltenham, beef hung for 2 weeks, hams, barbecue goods; awards for pies.*

Michael Hart Traditional Butcher, 99 High Street, Cricklade, Swindon, SN6 6AA. 01793 750213.
*Traditional butchers, hang beef for 3–4 weeks, Scottish beef, Welsh lamb, local pork. Sell 1000 pies a week, champion sausage maker, proud of Cricklade pork sausage.*

## Worcestershire

Chekcetts of Ombersley, Old Worcester Road, Ombersley, Droitwich, WR9 0EW. 01905 620284.
*Locally sourced meat, generally heifers, hung for 2–3 weeks, pig roasts; sign in shop saying where local meat from each week; free-range chickens, pies, barbecue products.*

## Wrexham

J. T. Vernon Ltd. Fresh Food Hall, The Cross, Holt, Wrexham, LL13 9YG. 01829 270247.
*Apart from the butchery shop they run a food hall with a wide range of delicatessen products.*

# cooking glossary

**Argyle** A specially designed gravy boat, the idea of John, 4th Duke of Argyll, which allows the gravy to sink to the bottom and the fat to be poured off before serving it.

**Bain marie** Can be any deep container, half-filled with hot water, in which delicate foods are cooked in their moulds or terrines. The bain marie is put into a low or moderate oven. The food is protected from direct heat by the gentle, steamy atmosphere, without the risk of curdling. The term bain marie is also used for a similar container which holds several pans to keep soups, vegetables or stews warm during restaurant service.

**Barding** Wrapping meat, game or poultry which is low in fat with thin slices of bacon or pork fat to prevent it from drying out while roasting.

**Barding fat** Ask the butcher to give you this.

**Basting** Spooning roasting juices during cooking over meat to moisten and add flavour.

**Beurre manie** Paste mixture of flour and butter which is used to thicken sauces and stews.

**Bouquet garni** A small bunch of fresh herbs used to flavour stews, casseroles, stocks or soups, usually consisting of parsley stalks, a sprig of thyme, perhaps a bay leaf and an outside stalk of celery. Remove before serving.

**Bursa test** The Bursa is a blind vent above the anus, the purpose of which is still really unknown; it closes completely when the bird reaches sexual maturity, so a toothpick inserted will tell all – it will go up 1cm (1/2in) in a young bird.

**Carving other game birds** Grouse, snipe, woodcock, teal, golden eye, partridges, quail, pigeon etc. are always served whole, unless cooked as a salmis or casserole. To take the meat of any of these delicious little birds, start with the legs towards you and your fork firmly fixed to the left of the breast bone. Begin just above the wing, working your way upwards towards the dividing breast bone. Once one side is clean of breast meat, turn and repeat on the other side. Cut or tear of the legs and wings, and eat them in the time honoured way – with your fingers.

**Caul fat** Lacy membrane that surrounds the organs in the abdominal cavity of the pig. It melts away during cooking and imparts richness to the ingredients.

**Clarified butter** Butter cleared of impurities and water by melting slowly. Remove the salty skin with a spoon. The clear butter is the clarified butter; discard the liquid at the base.

**Coarse fish** Freshwater fish other than members of the salmon family.

**Coffyn** Simply means a box in Medieval English; in culinary terms it refers to a thick pastry box, with or without a lid, in which things were cooked and served direct to the table.

**Confit** Meat, especially goose and duck, preserved the French way, in fat – delicious!

**Crop** Pouch in the oesophogus where undigested food is stored in a bird. It needs to be removed when cleaning and gutting the brid.

**Cutting a bird in quarters** Pull the leg away from body. With a sharp knife cut through the skin joining the leg to the body, pull the leg away further and cut through more skin to free the leg. Bend the leg outwards and back forcing the bone to come out of its socket close to the body. Cut through the flesh between the end of the thigh bone and the carcase to remove the leg. Split the carcase along the breastbone, cut through the ribs on each side to take away the fleshy portion of the breast.

**Cutting a hare/rabbit in quarters** Use a sharp knife to sever the fore end just below the shoulder blade. Then divide the saddle by cutting down the centre of the back bone.

**Cutting a bird in two** Use a sharp knife to cut right through the flesh and bone, just on one side of the breastbone open out the bird and cut through the other side immediately next to the backbone. Then pull the backbone away from the half to which it remains attached.

**Darne** The cut at the thickest part behind the head of a fish.

**De-glaze** Diluting pan juices by adding wine, cream or stock to make gravy, scraping all the bits for flavour.

**Drawing** To clean out the intestines from poultry.

**Dressing** To pluck, draw and truss poultry or game.

**Drumstick** The tibia of a bird.

**Dusting** Sprinkling lightly with flour, sugar, spice or seasoning.

**Faggot of herbs** A bundle of herbs.

**Fillet of rabbit** The section along the backbone below the shoulders.

**Freezing** All game freezes very well. Bag whole birds separately or cut the game into pieces; remove from the bone or mince. Remember to label what you freeze or you get interesting mixtures. I reduce my game stock down as much as possible and freeze in ice cube trays, then pop out the cubes and bag them so that I can just take out one or two as I need them. Do remember to use your frozen game throughout the year, shooting wives are for ever sorting out the bottom of the freezer in September to make room for the new season's crop, and like all things that freeze they are better used within 6 months.

**Flank**  Side of an animal from the ribs to the thigh.

**Forcemeat**  Meat (usually pork or veal or game) chopped finely and heavily seasoned. It can be used as a stuffing or made into balls.

**Game fish**  Freshwater fish of the salmon family with the exception of grayling.

**Game trimmings**  Accompaniment for the roast game birds: game chips, bread sauce, gravy and redcurrant jelly. It can also refer to the wings, liver, cleaned gizzard, heart. neck etc. of birds that make a tasty stock.

**Giblets**  Edible internal organs of poultry and game including the liver, heart, gizzard, neck, pinions, and often in days gone by the feet and cockscomb.

**Gizzard**  The stomach of birds in which the food is ground.

**Glaze**  A glossy finish applied to food by brushing with milk, beaten egg, sugar, syrup or jelly after cooking.

**Gnocchi**  Small dumplings made from semolina, potatoes or choux pastry.

**Gutting**  To remove the inards from a fish, poultry or game and clean thoroughly ready for cooking.

**Hanging**  Wild game is often dry and tough. By hanging it after shooting to remove blood, the meat is tenderised. The longer the hanging time the more gamey the flavour, and the greater the change in the molecular structure of the meat. Older game tends to need longer hanging than young animals. To describe game as high implies a very strong gamey flavour.

**How Long to Cook Game**  It is traditional to eat most game rare, the exceptions to this is pheasant or partridge, and even they should be slightly underdone or they will dry out. Some people like grouse very blue, (personally I prefer mine rare – still red but not bloody,) others prefer them more cooked but they should always be slightly red. Where not otherwise indicated the cooking times in the recipes are for medium rare and if two sets of time are given the shortest is for rare and the longest for as long as is acceptable without drying the meat out.

Venison, when roast, should be pink like lamb as it will become too dry if cooked any longer.

Fish should always be slightly underdone, Remember there is nothing you can catch from undercooking game or fish, and pheasant, unlike chicken, is not subject to salmonella when undercooked.

**Joint**  To divide meat into individual pieces, separating it at the joints.

**Jugged**  Meat dishes stewed in a covered pot.

**Lard**  Natural or refined pork fat.

**Larding**  Threading strips of fat through lean meat using a specially designed needle. This stops the meat from drying out when roasting.

**Lardons**  Small pieces of thick cut bacon, sold ready-chopped. As an alternative to lardons, thick rashers of bacon can be cut lengthwise into strips and then into small dice.

**Marinade**  Blend of oil, wine or vinegar, herbs and spices. Used to make the meat more tender to add flavour.

**Mead**  An alcoholic drink made by fermenting honey and ater, often flavoured with spice.

**Offal**  Edible internal organs of meat, poultry and game.

**Paella**  A traditional Spanish recipe. Dish of saffron rice, chicken or shellfish, named after the traditional pan in which it is cooked.

**Parson's Nose**  The piece of fatty flesh at the tail end of the bird.

**Paunching**  To remove the guts of an animal, the paunch being the prominent portion of the abdomen.

**Pinion**  The wing, and in particular, the last joint of the wing of the bird, or it can be used to describe the outermost flight feather on the wing.

**Pluck**  To remove the feathers from a dead bird.

**Polenta**  Corn meal, made from maize dried and ground.

**Primary feathers**  The longest of the flight feathers on the wing, and furthest away from the body.

**Raised Pie**  Usually made with hot water crust, and containing meat and stock which forms a jelly.

**Ratatouille**  Mediterranean stew of aubergines, onions, peppers and tomatoes cooked in olive oil.

**Reducing**  Concentrating a liquid by boiling and evaporating excess liquid.

**Roux**  A basic liaison of equal parts butter and flour which is used as a thickening agent.

**Quenelles**  Usually poached, these are forcemeat dumplings often made of fish, and occasionally chicken and veal.

**Saddle**  Butcher's cut inluding a part of the backbone with the ribs.

**Salamander**  A hot metal plate for browning meat.

**Salmi**  A ragoûût of previously cooked game or other meats.

**Seasoned flour**  Flour seasoned with salt and pepper.

**Sewing up**  Use a needle with some strong thread and sew up any meat. Remove thread before servng.

**Singe**  To quickly flame duck or geese to remove all traces of feathers and down after plucking. A taper is very useful for doing this.

**Sippet**  Morsel of bread, often eaten with soup.

**Skirt**  Midriff of meat.

**Smoking**  Curing meat or fish by exposing it to warm or cold wood smoke over a period of time.

**Skinning game birds**  To save plucking, you can skin your birds; this is really only successful with pheasant as duck and goose skin is arguably the nicest bit. Remember to remove the leg sinews from an unplucked bird. If you are using any of the casserole recipes for pheasant just skin them. There is an interesting way to remove the breast from a whole pheasant: lay the bird on its back on the floor, put your feet on either side of the bird firmly on each wing, grasp the legs and pull upwards and your pheasant will come in half leaving the breast to be cut off the wings. If you pull the sinews before starting this then you can just skin the legs as well and devil them or make confit with them.

**Skinning, jointing and paunching hares and rabbits**  You can paunch them after they are skinned. Sever all 4 legs at the first joint, then cut through the skin of the hind legs half way between the leg joint and the tail. Peel the skin from the hind legs. Tie them together and hang over a bowl with a little vinegar beneath to catch the blood. Pull the skin over the body and forelegs. I remove the head but you can skin it and keep it on. Cut it up the middle, but don't cut into the gall bladder. Tip the blood from the rib cage into the bowl. Paunch it by discarding the guts, keeping the liver. Rinse in cold water and dry with kitchen roll. Remove the blue membrane.

**Spatchcock**  With a sharp knife cut lengthways down the middle of the bird and spread the two halves out flat.

**Spur**  Claw-like projection at the back of a bird's leg.

**Suet**  Fat around beef or lamb kidneys.

**Supreme**  The breast from poultry or game – that is, including some of the wing by cutting it off at the first joint.

**Tendons**  Bands of fibrous tissue, attaching muscles to the bone; in game birds they can be annoying and are best removed to make the leg meat totally edible. Put the foot of the bird over a suitable hook and pull gently down, twisting as you pull. The tendons should come out and remain with the foot.

**Trivet**  A metal plate placed in a pressure-cooker to raise the food to be cooked off the bottom of the vessel.

**Trussing**  Tying a bird or joint of meat in a neat shape with skewers and string before cooking. Butchers should do this for you.

## Useful website addresses

**www.basc.org.uk**  British Association of Shooting and Conservation
**www.bssc.org.uk**  British Shooting Sports Council
**www.bds.org.uk**  The British Deer Society
**www.cla.org.uk** Country Land and Business Association
**www.countryside-alliance.org.uk**  Countryside Alliance
**www.countrysideireland.com**  Countryside Ireland
**www.face-europe.org**  Federation of Fieldsports Association of European Union
**www.fga.net.au**  Australia Field and Game
**www.gametoeat.co.uk**  Campaign for eating game
**www.gct.org.uk** Game Conservancy Trust
**www.igfa.org** International Game Fish Association
**www.nationalgamekeepers.org.uk** The National Gamekeepers' Association
**www.salmon-trout.org**  Salmon and Trout Association
**www.trcp.org** Theodore Roosevelt Conservation Partnership
**www.wingshooters.co.za**  South African Wingshooters Association
**www.wwt.org.uk**  Wildfowl and Wetlands Trust

# game calendar

| | | |
|---|---|---|
| **Pheasant** | *2-3 servings* | October 1st to February 1st |
| **Partridge** | *1 serving* | September 1st to February 1st |
| **Quail** | *1 serving* | September 1st to January 10th |
| **Grouse** | *1 serving* | August 12th to December 10th |
| **Wood Pigeon** | *1 serving* | No close season |
| **Woodcock** | *1 serving* | October 1st to January 31st<br>(Scotland – September 1st to January 31st) |
| **Snipe** | *1 serving* | August 12th to January 31st |
| **Duck** | | |
| Mallard | *2 servings* | September 1st to January 31st<br>(below high water mark to Feb 20th) |
| Smaller ducks<br>eg. teal, widgeon | *1 serving* | |
| **Geese** | *6 servings* | as for duck |
| **Rabbits** | *2–3 servings* | no close season |
| **Hares** | *4-6 servings* | no close season, but may not be offered for sale from March – July |

| | England | Scotland |
|---|---|---|
| **Red Deer** | | |
| **Stag** | August 1st to April 30th | July 1st to October 20th |
| **Hind** | November 1st to February 28th | October 21st to February 15th |
| **Roe Deer** | | |
| **Buck** | April 1st to October 31st | April 1st to October 20th |
| **Doe** | November 1st to February 28th | October 21st to March 31st |
| **Fallow Deer** | | |
| **Buck** | August 1st to April 30th | August 1st to April 30th |
| **Doe** | November 1s to February 28th | October 21st to February 15th |

**Muntjac** and **Chinese Water Deer** have no close season.

# index

# picture acknowledgements